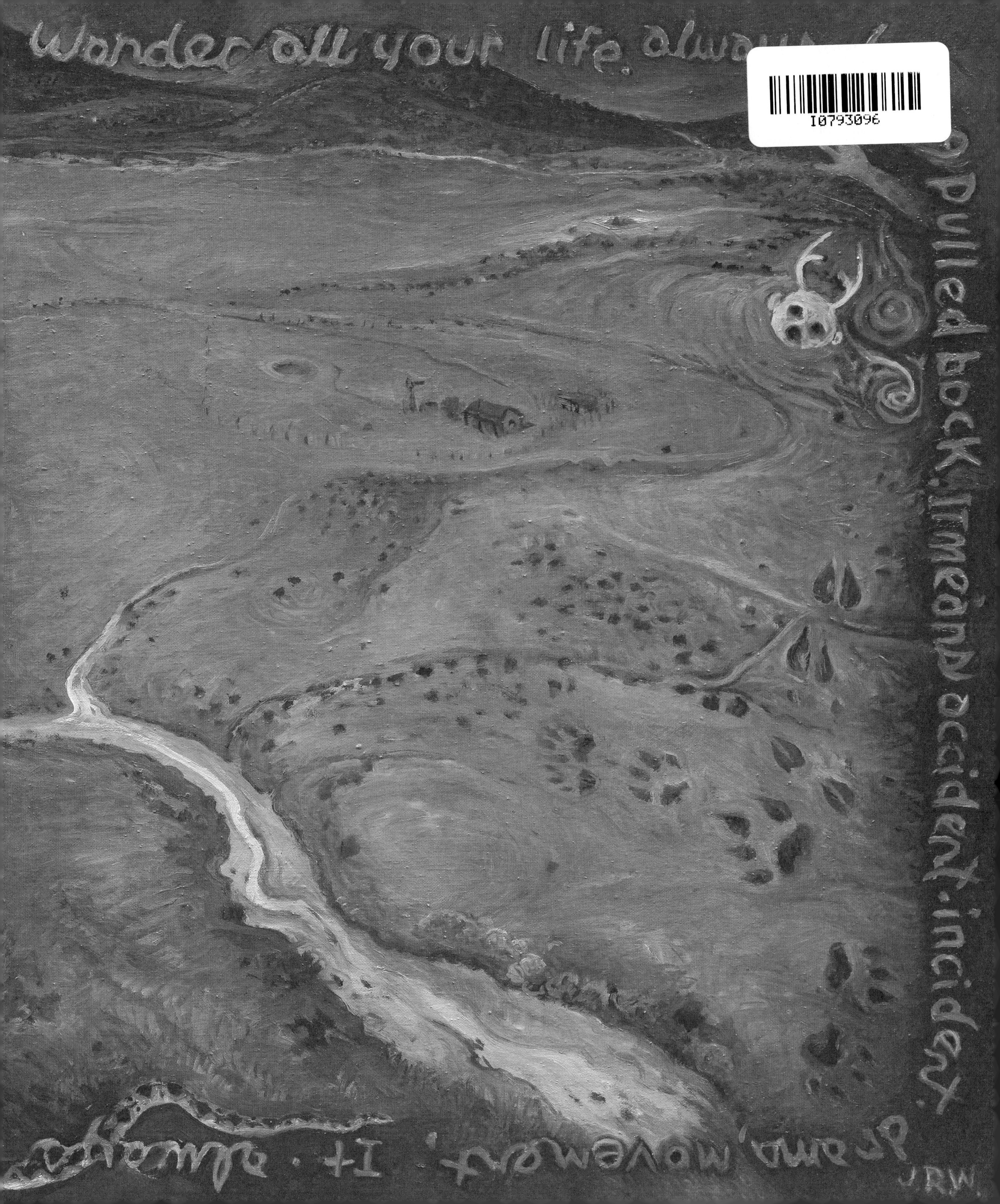
Wander all your life, always
J.R.W.

Jerry West

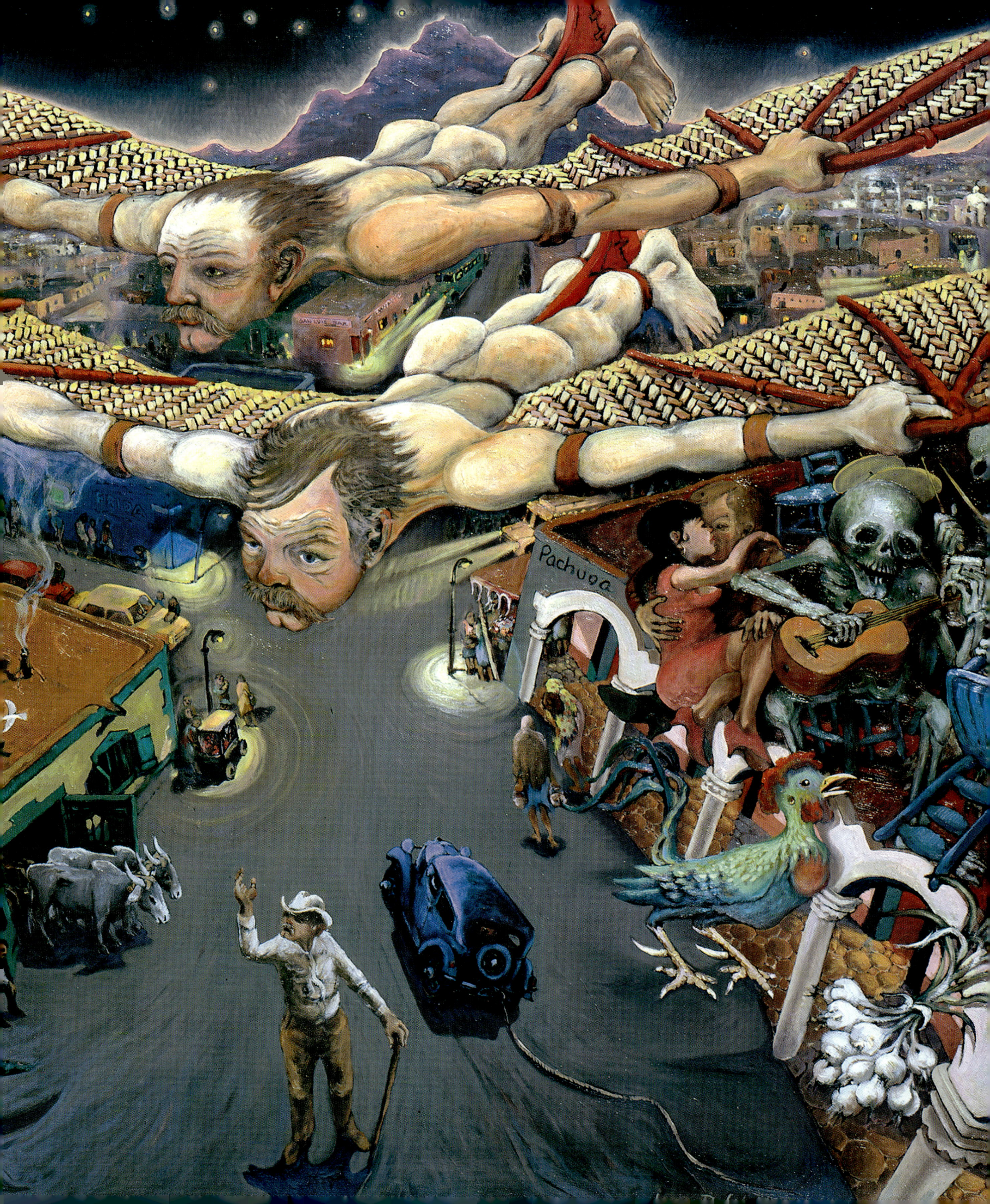
FRIDA
Pachuca

Jerry West

the alchemy of memory

A Selective Retrospective
by Jerry R. West

With essays by Rebecca Solnit
and MaLin Wilson-Powell

Foreword by Joseph Traugott

Museum of New Mexico Press

Santa Fe

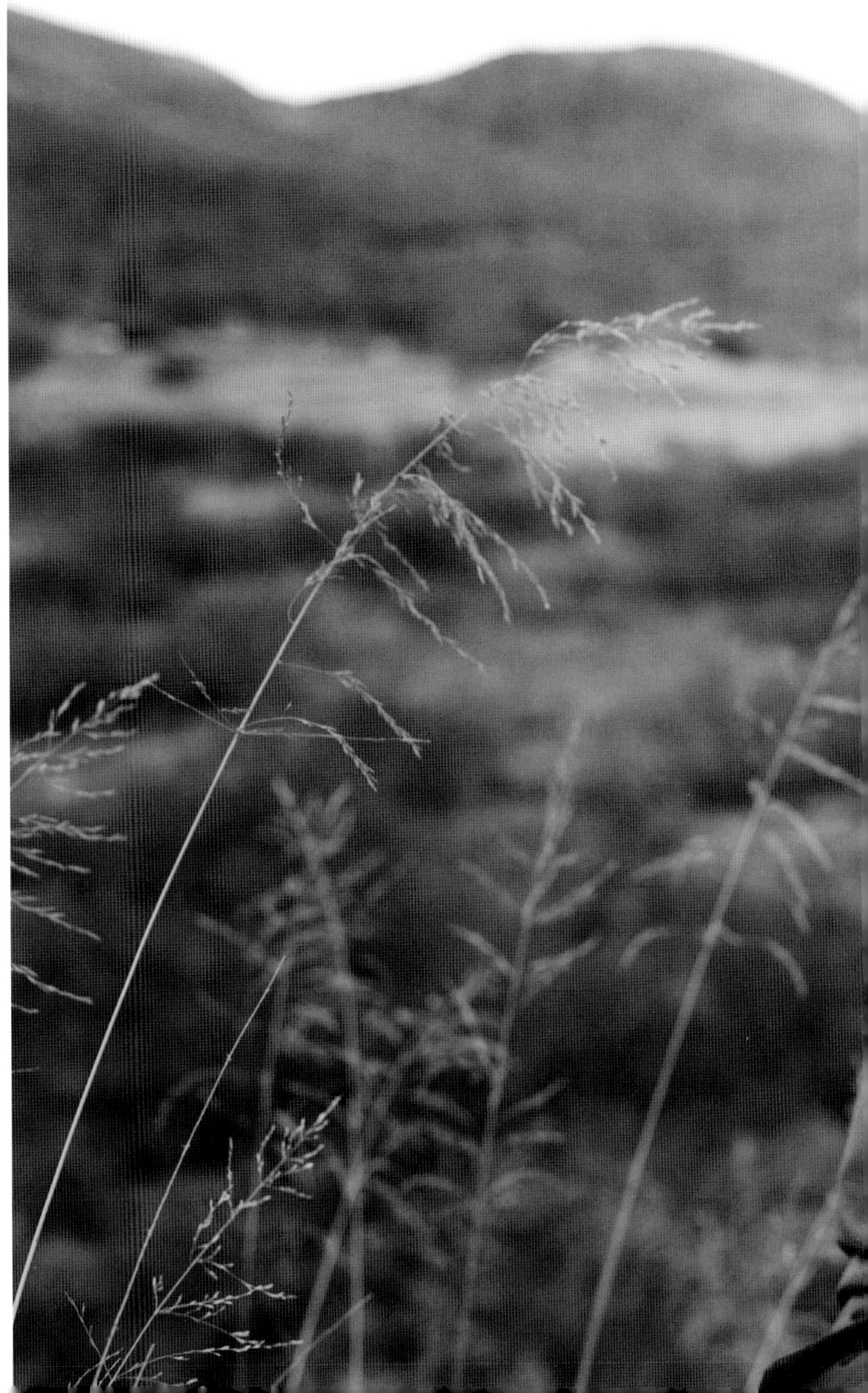

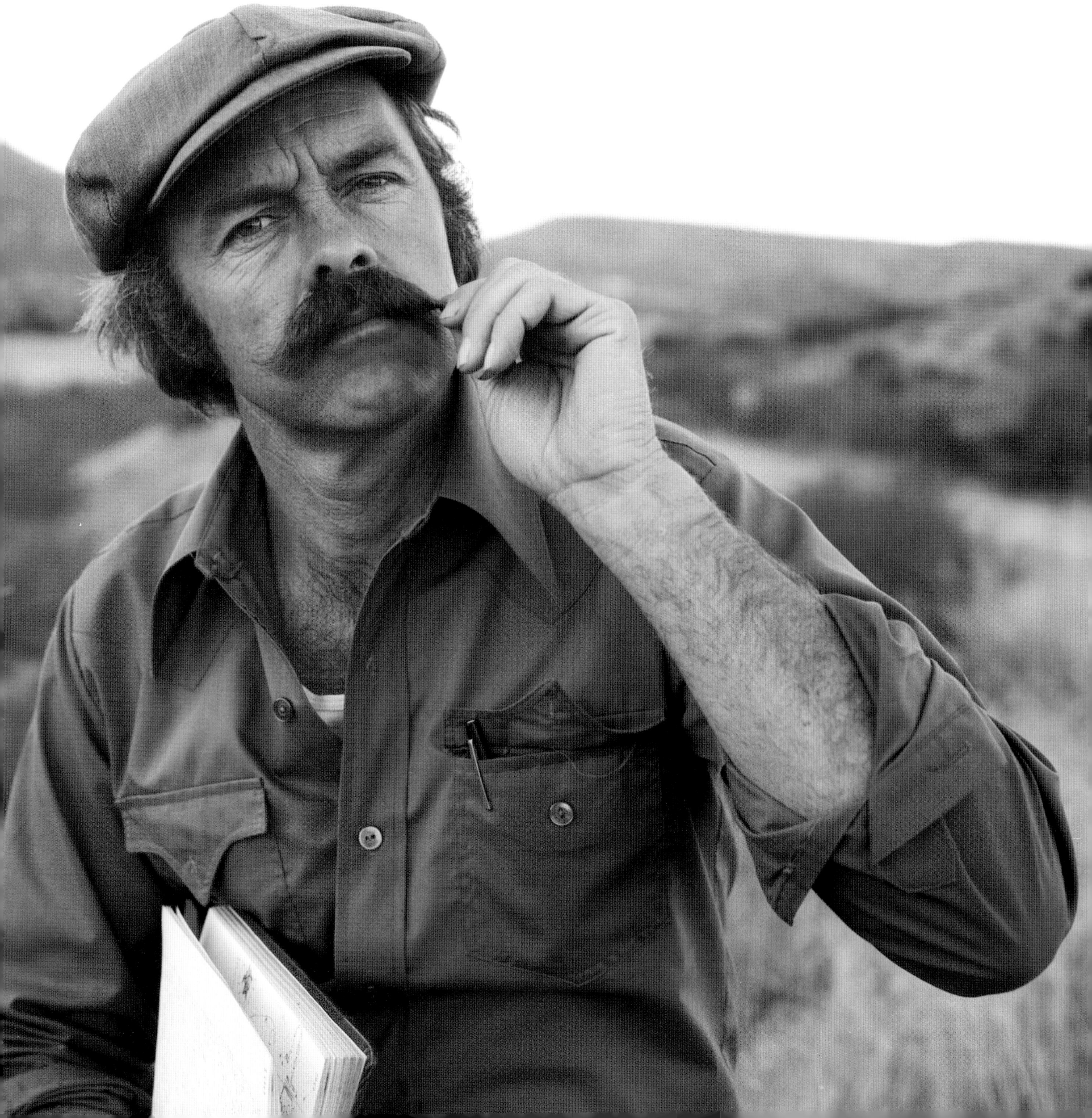

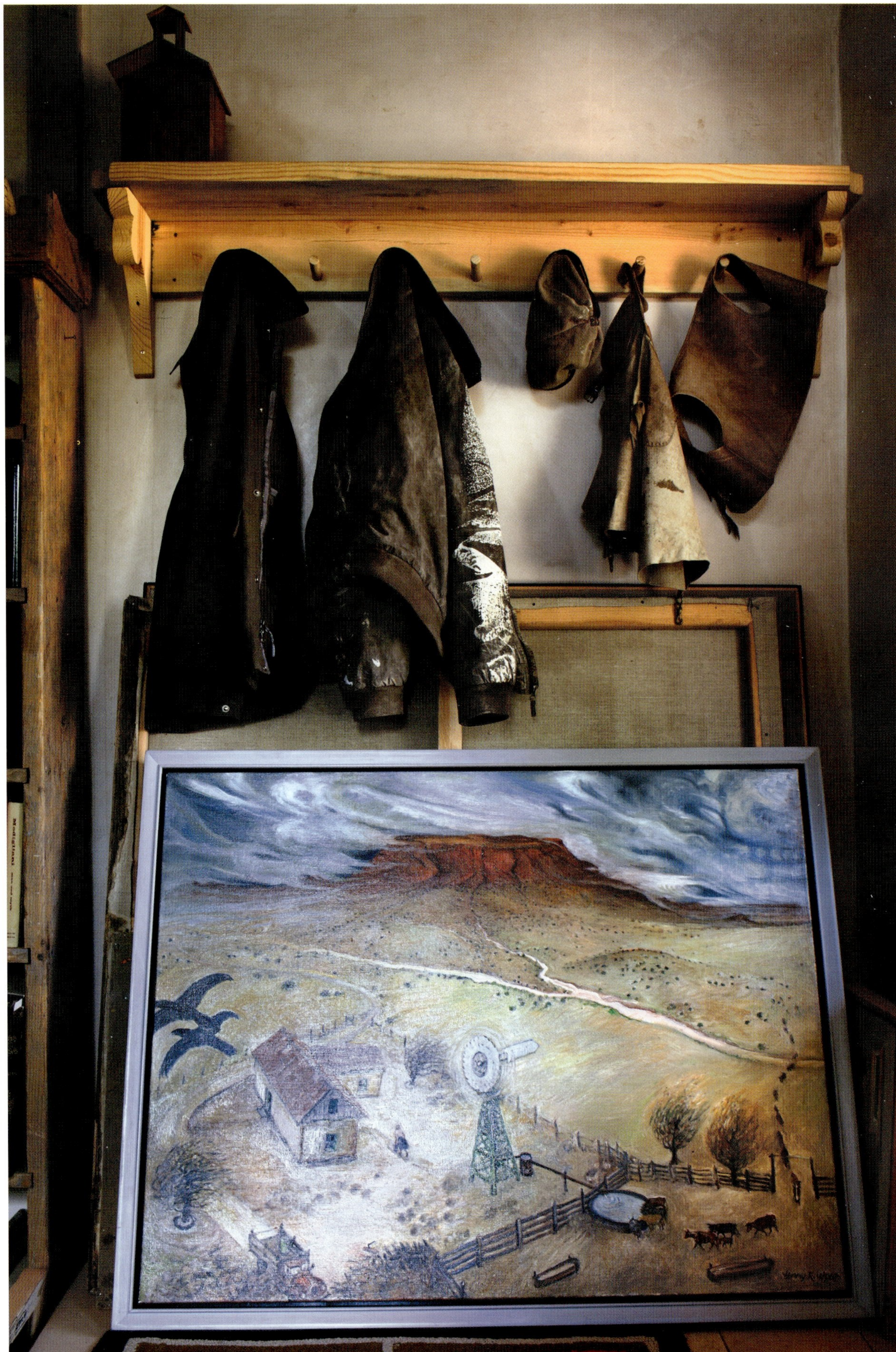

Contents

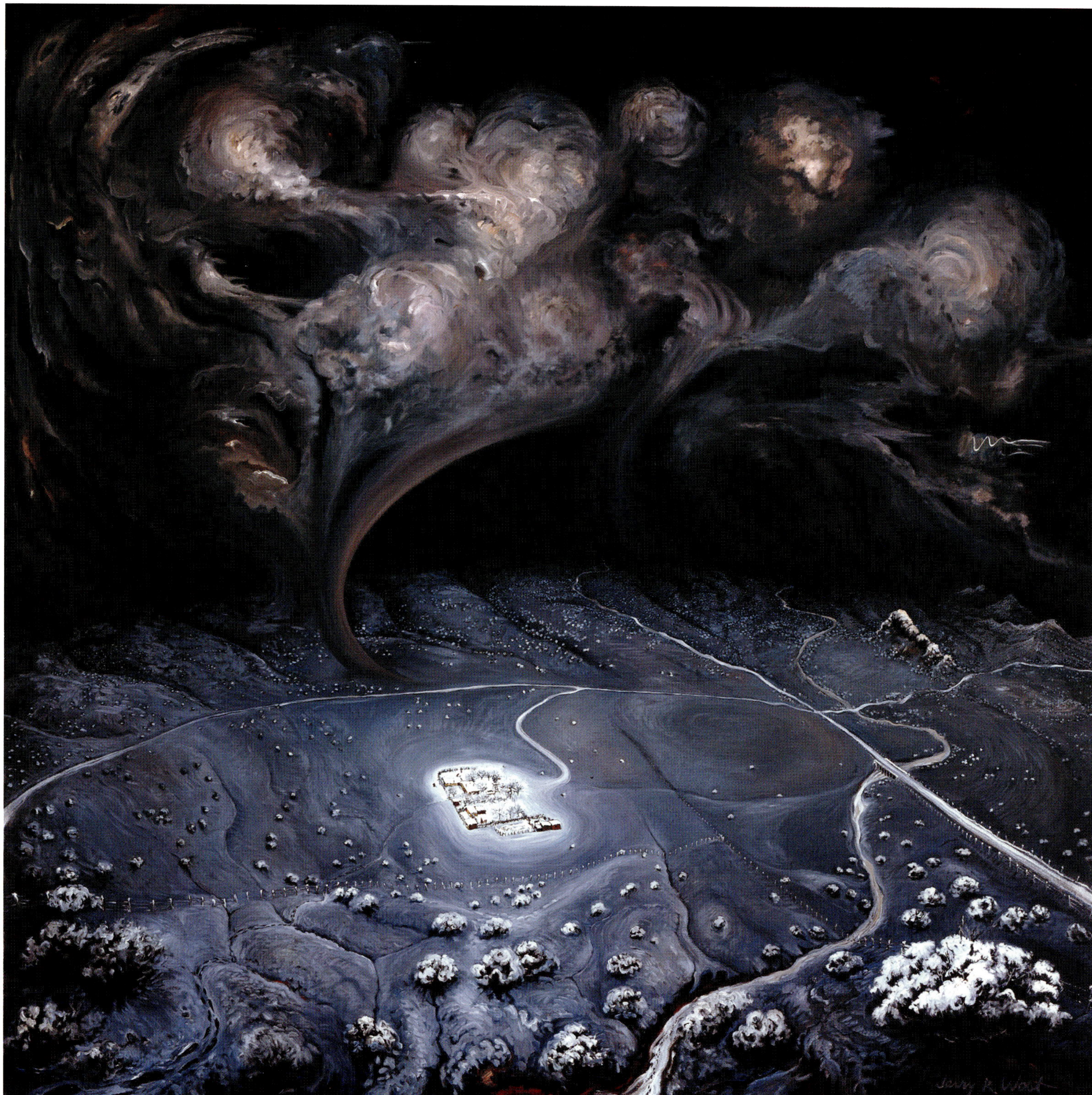

Prairie Homestead with Approaching Cosmic Storm, 1986
Oil on linen, 54 × 54 in.
Collection of New Mexico Museum of Art

Foreword

Joseph Traugott

Jerry West is an artist whose work has captured, with grace and understanding, the contradictions of modern life, along with the evolution of New Mexico art. His visual narratives personify the radical changes that occurred in New Mexico art between the Great Depression and the Great Recession. As a consummate storyteller, a simple cup of coffee will send him off on an unbroken series of reveries that comment on the changes he has experienced.

West's father, Hal, was also an artist, but neither ranching nor selling woodcuts of cowboy scenes was always successful. The economic hardships caused by the Great Depression complicated West's childhood on a New Mexico ranch. He valued the freedom of open spaces but not the ranch's isolation at a time when most youngsters need to interact with peers.

Prairie Homestead with Approaching Cosmic Storm, 1986 offers West's insights into the tension between freedom and the loneliness of ranch life. The scene suggests a winter night with the family home providing a warm refuge against the cold, but vast spaces surrounding the homestead serve as a sign of the isolation of ranch life. The oncoming tempest implies that it's time to leave, for the artist to find his own way.

West presents another view of the tension between freedom and loneliness in his remembrance of the Japanese American detention camp in downtown Santa Fe during World War II. West's father and uncle worked as guards at the camp, and Jerry often visited them at work. More than sixty years later his memories of this period materialized as *A Westward Glance, a Place Called the "Jap Camp," a Strange Story* (page 10), a work incorporating figures representing his father and uncle. West asks viewers to reconsider attitudes previously accepted without question about the war, internment, and the nature of his father's job. The painting expresses a sardonic reassessment of this period with metaphorical connotations for today by suggesting what attitudes currently accepted will be subject to review in the future.

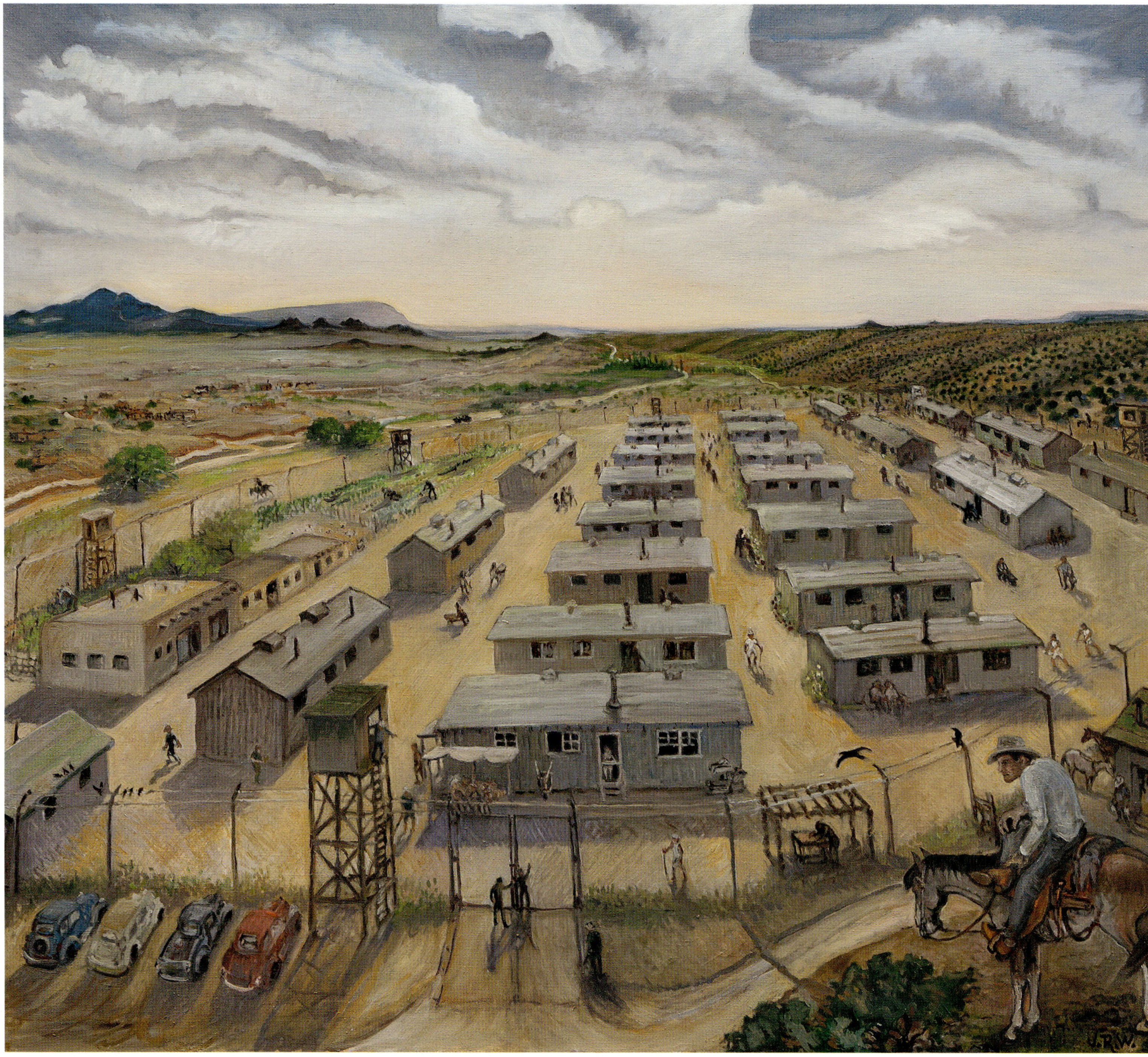

During the second half of the twentieth century, New Mexico art experienced cathartic changes. Touristic genre scenes associated with the Taos and Santa Fe art fraternities gave way to abstraction, nonobjectivity, and minimalism. West's modernist images challenged local audiences accustomed to nostalgic genre scenes.

By including an eclectic mix of twisted perspectives, flattened forms, and contradictory content, West's paintings epitomize the changing character of New Mexico art, retelling local anecdotes in a modern manner without nostalgia or repeating worn-out southwestern formulas.

Jerry West addresses provocative American themes allegorically, from an idiosyncratic perspective: West as America.

A Westward Glance, a Place Called the "Jap Camp," a Strange Story, 2009
Oil on linen, 48 × 48 in.
Collection of New Mexico Museum of Art

From the few times that our dad drove us down to the dusty, dirt Alameda Street in the late 1930s, I can remember seeing row after row of wooden pitched-roof barracks and a few old corrals and barns that were the main camp for the Civilian Conservation Corps. Hal, in those years, was an artist working with the WPA. After December 7, 1941, Hal went directly to work for the Justice Department at the newly created Japanese Internment Camp on the grounds of the CCC. About 4,500 men were detained there over the years. Some of them were held for over six months after the ending of World War II. I painted this painting of the Japanese Internment Camp based partly on the sketches by my father Hal along with my memories of those childhood years.

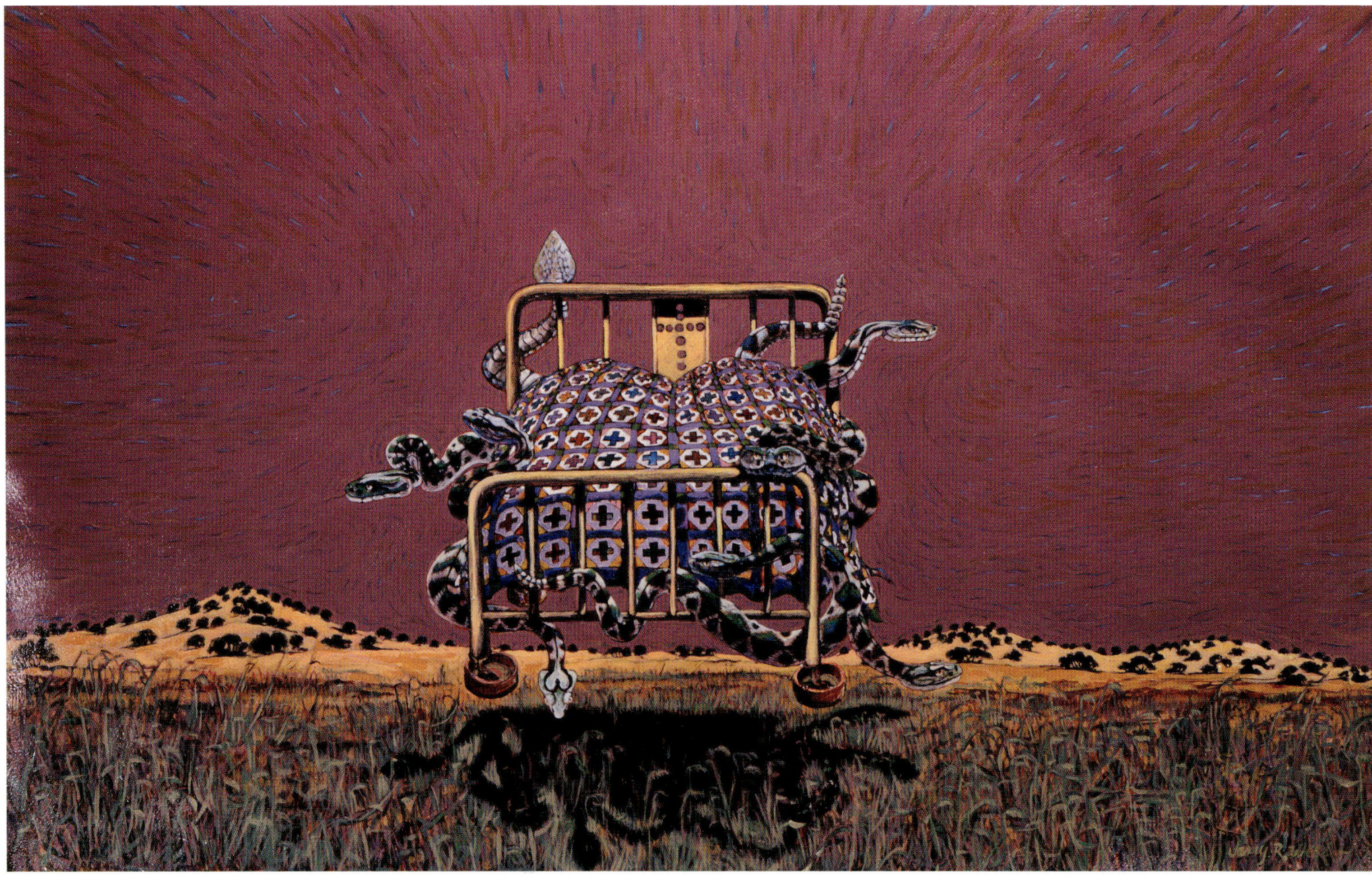

A Prairie Dream, 1981
Acrylic on paper, 36 × 24 in.
Collection of Ray Graham

Jerry West: The Vernacular Sublime

MaLin Wilson-Powell

Jerry West was born in 1933 and raised in a New Mexico that had not yet entered the twentieth century, a leap forward that only occurred because of World War II. West remembers the smell of ink his father Hal West used to make prints in their little adobe home. The artist's birthright not only included a printmaker and painter's tool chest but, more importantly, an overriding respect for American regionalist painting, especially Thomas Hart Benton's dramatic, swirling compositions and Ben Shahn's social realism. West grew up when the Santa Fe arts colony was still producing late nineteenth-century-style paintings that romanticized cowboys and Indians and equated the majesty of the Sangre de Cristo Mountains with Manifest Destiny. The more modern Santa Fe artists were exporting abstract renditions of skies and landscapes that glorified the purity, spirituality, and redemptive qualities of the desert. West knew better. His upbringing had been one of barely subsistence, and his New Mexico was scrubby flatlands and plateaus, prickly plants and animals, and artifacts from tribes decimated by drought. He knew firsthand the endless cycle of labor he had in common with his Pueblo and Hispanic neighbors.

Steeped in the clichés of New Mexico, West steered clear of prevailing Christian, utopian, and formalist tropes, and, after decades of searching, finally let his dreams be his guide. By reconciling his connection to the high desert and the vast internal space of his psyche, he tapped into an unbound, generative source of imagery. In 1982, at the age of forty-nine, West exhibited his dream-inspired surrealist paintings for the first time. This breakout "Prairie Night" installation followed five years in his studio painting canvasses that uncovered demons from his familial past. He found snakes in his bed, and he painted them. In *A Prairie Dream*, 1981, eight diamondback rattlesnakes raise their venomous heads and rattle their tails as they uncoil from beneath a homemade quilt patterned with crosses. The bed floats with its feet stuck into tin cans that are ineffectual protections—like the field of crosses on the quilt—for the dreamer. It is aloft in a cloudless sky the color of a bruise and casts a disturbing shadow suggestive of a drooling, hungry beast on the run. West hung his dream paintings in a gallery painted night-sky blue with rabbit tracks crossing the floor, handprints climbing the walls and traversing the ceiling, and the words of W. B. Yeats written on the walls:

> *Now that my ladder's gone, I must lie down where all ladders start*
> *In the foul rag and bone shop of the heart.*

The gallery was scented by bundles of sage, chamisa, and saltbush, and accompanying the exhibit was a murmuring soundtrack of laughter, silverware clattering, people singing, water running, dogs barking, cattle lowing, and birds cawing, all recurring elements in West's theater of the night.

The artist's southwestern variant on surrealism is rooted in a lifetime of affection, however fraught and complicated, for family and friends, with the caveat that everyone he meets is a potential friend. Born during the Great Depression, West is the third of five children. He credits his conviviality to his parents' example, especially their respectful one-on-one encounters with a wide variety of people. Hal West came from poor white southern roots and grew up with Indian kids and black kids. Jerry remembers how easily his father made friends with interesting people, how open and honest his relationships were, and how he often brought people home. His mother, Mildred Olive West, a midwestern teacher who was the daughter of a preacher-turned-professor would welcome them all—vagabonds, bankers, cowboys, intellectuals, bartenders, city slickers—to sit down for dinner with the children (after their chores), along with whomever the Dust Bowl blew onto their property.

West's youth was itinerant, marked by a succession of moves from Canyon Road to an area at the southern edge of Santa Fe to the remote Puyé Cliffs. By the time Jerry was twelve, Hal was earning a steady paycheck working at a World War II German prisoner-of-war camp in Texas that enabled the family to buy a 240-acre homestead, an isolated, hardpan place on the high plains eighteen windswept miles of hungry cattle and sagebrush from Santa Fe's plaza. Remarkably, three generations of the extended West family still live in adobe houses made from this prairie dirt, surrounded now by Santa Fe bedroom communities.

The West siblings started their days before sunup hauling water, milking the cow, tending chickens and rabbits, every day, whether it was windy, hot, and gritty or bone-chilling cold and snowing, accompanied by the ever-present creaking of the windmill. All entertainment was homemade. They listened to adults tell stories, sing songs, make music. Their mother prized education, and the children walked a long way to and from a school bus that was a long ride on dirt roads to their Santa Fe schools. West liked school, and he was well liked. As a kid in Santa Fe he made a little money selling the *Saturday Evening Post* on the plaza, then as he grew bigger, stronger, smarter, he found work digging, hauling, plastering, roofing, painting—and always building. Throughout high school, West was the strong back and helpful hands for his first important art teacher, the Cinco Pintores cubist painter Josef Bakos.

Drawing was as bred in the bone as his easy-going friendships. Prior to teaching himself painting, the line was his primary artistic concern. The lines of West's drawing and printmaking are like nests and establish the underlying structure for his narrative paintings and murals. As early as third grade, his teacher asked him to draw on the blackboard and then preserved his drawings for months; and in junior high and high school he drew programs for dances and events. Prophetically, in light of his theatrical surrealist tableaux, he also joined the Puppet Club. In high school, West was given an award for his prints by Elmer "Skinny" Schooley, an influential and much-loved professor of art at New Mexico Highlands University in Las Vegas. After high school, a Ford Foundation scholarship made it possible for West to follow his older sister Sarah to Colorado State University, where his maternal uncle taught zoology. After obtaining a master's degree in biological sciences in 1958 from the University of New Mexico, he married and eventually returned to Santa Fe with his young family and settled into working as a high school teacher. Holidays and summers he worked construction.

During this interlude, the necessity to make art never diminished for West. His sketchbook was always at hand, and he was part of a life-drawing group that met evenings in the basement of the New Mexico Museum of Art (then the Museum of Fine Arts), which included Ford Ruthling and Bob Ewing. Beginning in 1964, he attended three summer art intensives at Highlands, where Schooley became a close friend and important mentor, finally convincing West to return to art school full time in 1969. In Las Vegas, he spent half the day in the printmaking workshop, the other half painting. Printmaking was a language that came naturally to West, who sought to emulate Rembrandt's velvety blacks and delicate nuances of light and dark as well as Goya's dramatic tension and subversive subjects. Schooley was a devoted modernist painter and vociferously objected to the storytelling in West's paintings. Genuinely perplexed, the student asked the teacher why narrative prints were acceptable and narrative paintings were not.

With the benefit of hindsight, West's journey to the psychological Prairie Night paintings looks like an improbable odyssey littered with obstacles. And what at first seems so personal—the artist's self-conscious historicizing and reworking of his childhood—also feels universal. His courage is contagious and inclusive. West's transition from high school teacher to artist coincided with a free-wheeling, tumultuous period. He was bolstered by an open, generous, polymorphous moment in American culture. In the university milieu of Las Vegas, casual beat-culture bonhomie flowed through the studio space he shared in a derelict storefront on the plaza. All through the days and nights, jazz records spun on the turntable, emitting the sophisticated insouciance of Dave Brubeck's improvisations. There were lively communal meals. Woven through the bohemian freedoms was the serious business of politics: Hispanic classmates and friends organized successful resistance to Anglo-American takeover of land and influence.

Beginning in the mid-1970s, for six years West split his time between New York City and Santa Fe. Dressed in a gambler's short-brim Stetson, he walked the streets of Manhattan from Harlem to Battery Park, disarming strangers with his affability. He also took his first vacation ever and his first trip abroad—to Greece. Distance clarified what West had left behind, and he began dreaming of the prairie. Whenever he was back home in Santa Fe, he met with a Jungian analyst. Through his explorations of new terrain—external and internal—he began to reconstitute meaning for himself, learning to slip into the stream of lingering psychological conflicts, finding the depth and strength of his roots by uprooting himself. During all of his future travels—to Italy, France,

England, the Caribbean, Mexico, India, and Indonesia—his nights were as vividly active as his days, with New Mexico dreamscapes populated by family, friends, ravens, mongrels, horses, cattle, snakes.

In Manhattan, West made his first dream-inspired images—small circular black-and-white etchings floating within, and poking into, fields of color. He printed at Bob Blackburn's cooperative Printmaking Workshop, a thoroughly democratic studio, where he met feminist artists, black artists, and artists from all over the world. He talked to everyone, and his amiable invitation to sit down for meals together took some of the chill out of the workshop. Conversations, friendly differences of opinion, and laughter tumbled onto the table; everything was up for discussion. Concerns revolved around a much broader stream of artistic production than prevailing, institutionally touted and approved practices, and far beyond the narrow confines of mainstream minimalism or pop art.

The emergence of West's Prairie Night paintings coincided with neoexpressionism's reassertion of narrative and figurative painting during the late-1970s through the mid-1980s. Overtly inspired by German expressionism, neoexpressionism was an international aesthetic style, a return to objects that were mythic, emotional, sensuous, and erotic, often with the use of a vivid palette. West tends toward strong, saturated colors that pump up the visual vibration of side-by-side complementary colors, red next to the same value of green and orange next to blue. Like West, the neoexpressionists were skeptical about the cool formal effects of modernity and unashamed of emotionalism and poignancy. Cultural anthropologist Francesco Pellizi described neoexpressionist and post-neoexpressionist paintings as "swarming collisions on canvas." Cross-pollination of painters and musicians, video artists and writers was a hallmark of the era, as were the legacies of romanticism, fantasy, magic realism, visionary art, and, of course, surrealism.

West's work has much in common with the autobiographical, performative approach of first-generation women surrealists Lenora Carrington, Leonor Fini, Frida Kahlo, and Dorothea Tanning. While these artists explored adult psychology, West uses adult psychology to explore the traumas and joys of his childhood, a direction employed by such contemporary artists as Amy Adler and Julie Heffernan. Although the surfaces and strokes of his paintings are decidedly muscular, even rough, scenarios are often tender carriers of a child's vulnerability before the cultural hardening of gender roles. In *Living on the Edge*, 2002 (plate 34), a little boy dwarfed by an immense land and skyscape flies a teensy white kite before an advancing storm. The perspective is vertiginous. A snug adobe ranch house sits atop a mesa on a thin veneer of sun-struck green vegetation. Outside is a battered flatbed pickup, laundry flapping in the breeze, a windmill, a low-flying raven, and the child. A huge section of the mesa has caved off, with the barbed wire and fence posts dangling in empty space. Falling into the abyss is a step away, hyper-vigilance a necessity.

West arrived at this moment in the American art world, when figuration and narrative made a resurgence, with his New Mexico roots intact. Historically insulated by remoteness, New Mexico's cultural complexity is international, embedded with mix-and-match legacies spanning three continents and, at least, five centuries (predating the founding of the United States by three hundred years), and includes diverse preconquest indigenous tribes in combination with pre-enlightenment Spanish Catholicism, Arabic, and Mexican influences.

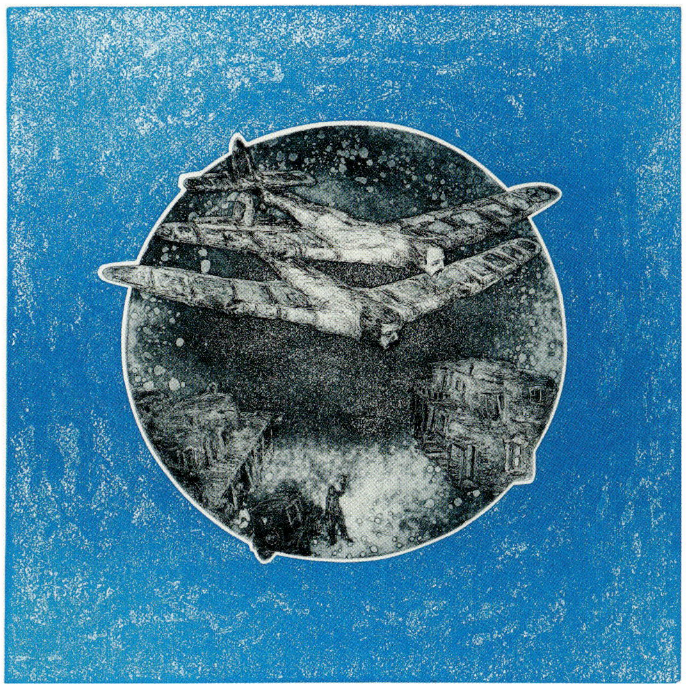

Flight over Juárez, Dream Series, 1975
Etching, 13 in. dia.
Edition of 10

With his Prairie Night paintings, West tapped into a mother lode of themes and methods. He read Gabriel Garcia Marquez's *One Hundred Years of Solitude*, which he found a resounding validation of his journey into the subconscious. West saw Marquez's mixture of magic, fantasy, and dreams—unfolding through difficult yet loving family entanglements and framed with historical accuracy—as a literary equivalent of how he wished to present the complexities of his own personal history. However littered with explosive material, these were rich veins to mine.

In the Southwest, the grandeur of the vast sky is an essential fact. Westerners grow up moving and standing on the earth in the sky. A bird's-eye view is a natural perspective for an artist raised on the prairie, as natural as archetypal dreams of flying. Among West's first dream images—all nightscapes—is an etching of himself and his younger brother Archie soaring naked through the starry night, wings outstretched in pure, joyous release. This image was revisited later in the painting *Flight over Juárez*, 1981 (plate 20). West's three-plate etchings perfectly amplify the eeriness and sketchiness of experiences in the dark of night, when sharply focused vision is impossible. The succession of 1980s paintings also evokes night's unfathomability, in, for example, the memory of a December night when World War II bombers flew low "like demons" over the family homestead (plate 5). In the high desert night sky, stars appear to wheel in the firmament, and West's painted skies clearly pay homage to Vincent Van Gogh's swirling skies from a similarly arid clime in the south of France.

The New Mexico sky is also a year-round magnificent, psychedelic light show, and West favors the light of the magic hour, or golden hour—the time just after sunrise and before sunset—when both the rods and cones of the eye respond to peak illumination of reds *and* blues. It is a perfect time to silhouette one of the artist's favorite portrait subjects, big, old gnarly trees, which he paints as venerable survivors and living treasures, pulsing with moody presence.

By the late 1980s, conflagration became a recurring theme for West, who says, "I grew up in the armpit of Los Alamos." His skies roil with hybrids of unfurling, atomic-blast mushroom clouds and the towering, billowing thunderheads of summer. In *Storm Cellar, Nuclear Family*, 1989 (plate 23), he conflates his parents' progressively toxic and combustible relationship—buried for decades in survival mode—with New Mexico's atomic history. He also repeatedly revisits the theme of the ever-present dangers of fire for solitary homesteads that can rage uncontrollably. The luminist, symbolist flames in Charles Burchfield's hallucinatory nightscapes inspired and affirmed West's own fire compositions, as did Burchfield's use of repetitive wavy lines to render rays of light and heat as well as sound waves of raucous night creatures. Like Burchfield and other early modernists, West deploys ways of melding internal emotional conditions with external, phenomenal conditions.

The importance of feminism to West's generation of artists, and to West in particular, cannot be overstated. Raised by strong pioneer women, the demand for agency and equality by 1970s feminists was obvious and fundamental to him. *Prairie Matriarch with Rooster*, 1988 (plate 23) presents his mother's strength and upright rigor, and *The Latest in Tea Shops*, 1981 (plate 9), a canvas bursting with spring, is a testament to his beloved Aunt Etna's irrepressible intellectual curiosity and buoyancy. The artist married three independent-minded women, each with her own career, each capable and creative, and each to whom he feels grateful for being a major part of his life. While many feminist artists are as courageously and brutally honest in their self-exposure as West, it is difficult to name other male artists who are as audaciously self-deprecating and humble.

Not all of West's visionary images are apocalyptic—growling with World War II military aircraft, threatening storms, and atomic fallout. Through the decades of developing his individual style of magical surrealism, West's terrors have been drained. With persistence and unflinching honesty, he has heeded the therapeutic dictum: whatever you resist will persist. Life may be precarious and provisional, circumstances extreme, but it is also precious. His swelling delight in simple pleasures is palpable, whether waking to a blanket of fresh snow, glimpsing a pregnant nanny goat in a neighboring field, crunching over the desert crust in comfortable work boots, or seeing a herd of cows lounging on a startling green field through the aperture of a gray concrete underpass. His imagery became more celebratory through working on public mural commissions, initially for his 1989 Santa Fe City Hall mural *Recuerdos y Sueños de Santa Fé* (plate 88).

Taking his lead from Mexican muralists Diego Rivera and David Siqueiros, West's historical reprise of the City Different, his community of eighty years, surges with annual fiesta crowds. The mural valorizes democracy and the citizens of this small cosmopolis mingling and brushing against one another in the public sphere.

In 2012, West participated in the Roswell Museum and Art Center's year-long program as their New Mexico centennial artist. He seized the opportunity to be honored as an *eminence gris*, with no time to lose, and produced a huge body of ambitious work. In

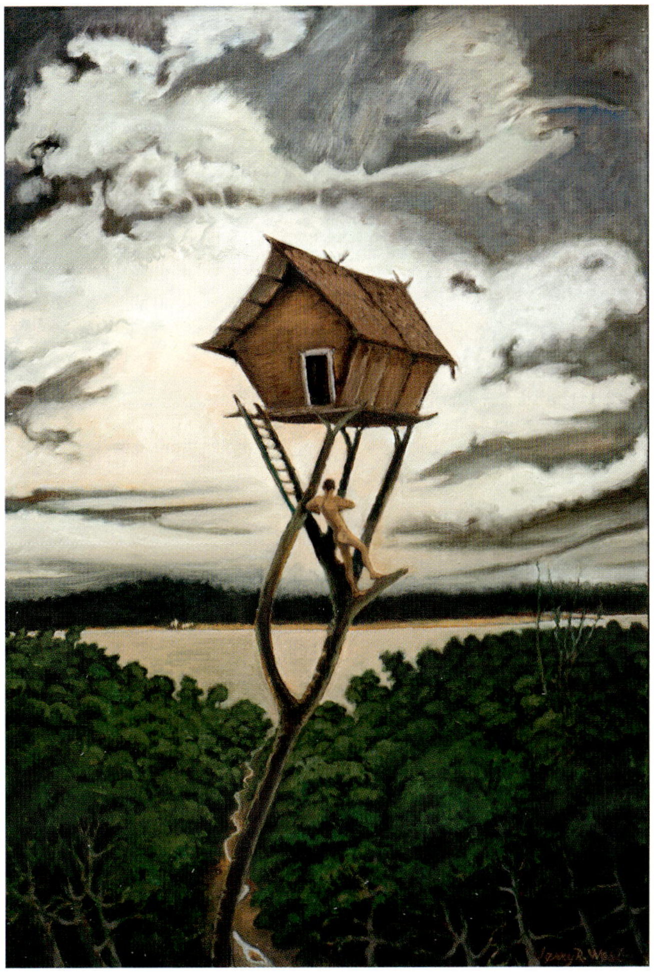 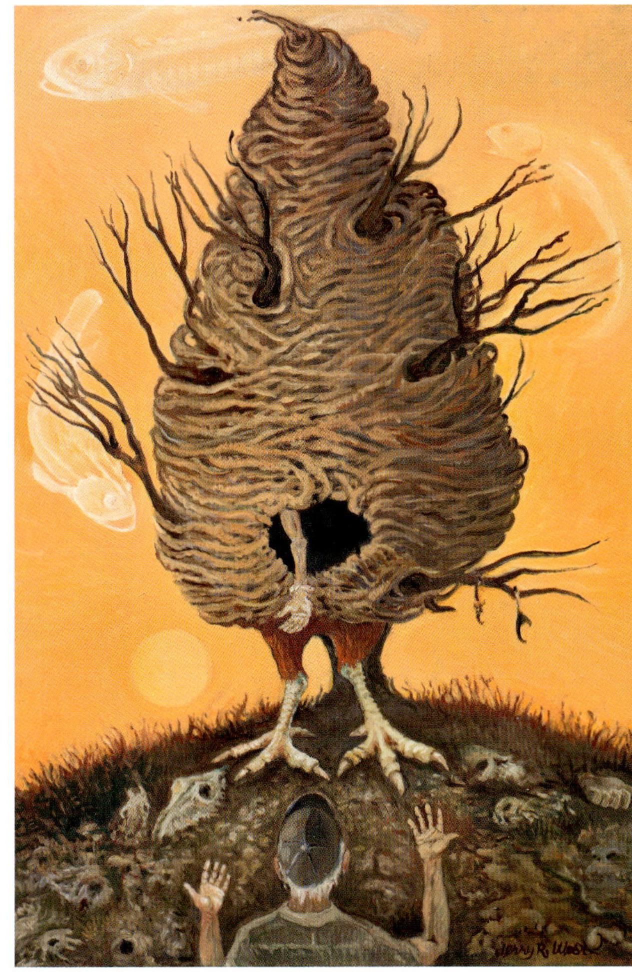

the Roswell canvasses, he not only reprises and restages earlier themes, including *Cosmic Storm Approaching Roswell* (plate 72) on a grander scale but introduces a number of childhood narratives for the first time, as in *The Lookout* with its serene melancholy and *An Older Artist Confronts an Even Older Curandera* with its mood of equanimity.

Forty years ago West was unwilling to join the modernist lineage of reductive and conceptual impulses, and he initiated his journey to self-invention, standing well outside the canon of approved art. Today, the art world has become more diverse but not necessarily more generous. West continues to present his art with courtesy, respect, and earnestness, eschewing the posture of authority and maintaining his position as a supplicant, a searcher asking questions. He offers the sublime in the vernacular and dignifies the quality of attention that shines on familiar and intimate relationships. His work is a testament to the tumult of ongoing human endeavor, and the power and appetite for paintings that tell stories. Maverick American artists like Jerry West are the artists who have populated their storytelling images with Ur-American characters, keeping alternative and embodied histories alive. As always, no one can know what art will be valued in the future, but smart money is on the mavericks.

The Lookout, 2012
Oil on linen, 24 × 30 in.
Collection of Marcy Heller and Brian McPartlon

An Older Artist Confronts an Even Older Curandera, 2012
Oil on linen, 24 × 30 in.
Collection of Ronald and Gretchen Phillips

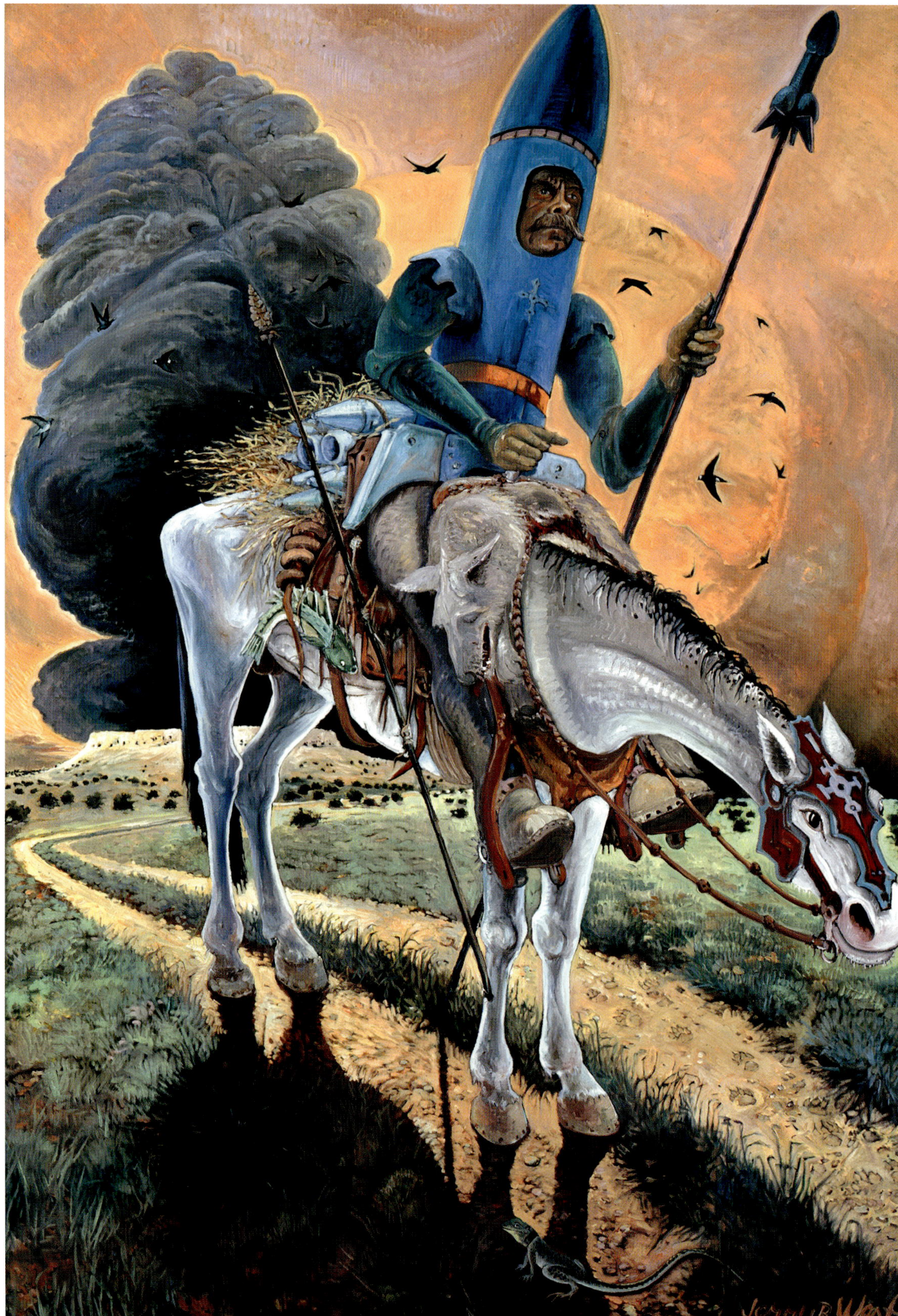

Return of the Nuclear Warrior, 1988
Oil on linen, 52 × 86 in.

A Bird in the Hand (and Seventeen More in a Ponderosa Pine)

Rebecca Solnit

Early on in my long friendship with Jerry West, when I was young and soaking up ideas about how to live from everyone around me, he told me that sometimes you could find Native American beads on anthills, because the beads were the size and shape of the gravel the ants preferred to place around the entries to their interior world. This comes to mind again when I see his painting of red ants grown gigantic, crawling from the foreground over the body of a man splayed across the road (plate 25). The ants, the man, who looks very much like Jerry, and the landscape—that recurrent, magnetic, exquisite, arid place in which much of his life has unfolded, about eighteen miles south of downtown Santa Fe—are all familiar; their conjunction here a little less so. I looked at anthills for perhaps a decade hoping to see a bead, enjoying the scrambling busyness of the insects and remembering that Native people might have walked across the very places I examined. I never found a bead, but I found many things besides, thanks to his reminder to look.

Listening to Jerry, I learned what a storyteller is, one who observes, who remembers, who has the confidence to take the time it takes to let a story unfold like a song, like a banquet, someone who is not in a hurry and can convince listeners that they, too, have all the time in the world or at least the time the tale takes to unfold. When a story is told right, time stands still, reaches back, holds us in its embrace. The storyteller is confident in his gift and the listeners that it *is* a gift, and they come together under the spell of the story, deeply present in the telling and deeply elsewhere in what is told. A stoyteller is an enchanter.

I remember a story, about a time when Jerry's mother, Mildred West, was still living in the house with the porch and the cottonwoods in which Jerry's son and his family now live. It was about how, when Mildred was very old, a suitor from the ancient past who carried a torch for her that was still smoldering reappeared. He gave her a long Bel Air sedan in which she rode up and down the back roads with her grandchildren, affirmed, by old suitors, by the summer breeze, by the grandchildren, by the coming together of all those things.

As I write, I imagine that Mildred's car could also be a painting, recall the beautiful photographic and video portraits of Mildred from behind, braiding her long white hair that seemed to drift and shift like the vaporous water in a tall waterfall, by Meridel Rubenstein (Jerry's fellow artist and great encourager and for twenty-something years his wife, still his friend). I write after looking at scores of images of Jerry's prints and paintings, at landscapes, at skies, at fliers, at coyotes, ravens, horses, dogs, at scenes of violence and redemption and mystery, at endless encounters between beings who might love each other or not and understand each other imperfectly.

Once Jerry recommended I stop at a particular diner—in Tehachapi, I think—on the long drive home from Santa Fe to San Francisco. I did; I mentioned the next time that the food wasn't that great, and he gently let me know that that wasn't the point. It was about the way the waitresses radiated humanity and the customers blossomed under their attention. It was about those subtle little openings in which people connect. I also went to Earl's, the big diner in Gallup, every time I passed through on Highway 40 because of his recommendation and learned that all the Navajo women and children approaching the tables to sell jewelry were to be greeted as gift-givers for their presence, rather than ducked out of fear of obligation.

If there were a secret underlying principle to Jerry's work, I'd be transgressive and try to interpret his life, too, because they seem all of a piece: the building and making art, the raising of kids and caring for hordes of others, the great storytelling and the gift for drawing out everyone's story, the unhurried sense of time in which all this transpires and the deep sense of place. There are intersections between the meaning of generous and generative, and this is borne out in the generation of houses, children, art, stories, friendships, conversations. I think about the man; I look at the eight books of paintings privately produced, recall hours poring over paintings and prints in his studio a few months before, and wonder at the abundance. Twenty years or more ago he told our friend Catherine Harris, while she was helping him build a wall, that he and his construction co-workers used to, when young, write the names of girls they liked in the scratch plaster—the underlayer that would later be smoothed with a finish coat. They were casting spells, doing work that would provide no pay or return, only a tenderness inside the walls and an expressiveness in the hearts of young men. I see images of workmen writing what will never be read when I recall this story.

If enough time is spent looking at Jerry's work, everything—stories, phrases, metaphors—starts to metamorphose into images, as though his paintings teach us to see the world more vividly. His eyes are particular eyes; his paintings let us see through them a little. This might be partly because he has lived most of his life in the world of tangible things—houses, building materials and tools, trucks, trees, animals, children, the New Mexico earth and the illimitable ever-changing New Mexico sky—rather than indoors in the sensorily starved world of information and images. There is a camel or two from a trip to India in these paintings, but mostly they depict the familiar creatures and places from many decades of living in one place, the cast of characters of a labyrinthine story on the prairie south of town.

I think of him as a bridge between that old self-reliant prairie world of homesteaders and horse breakers, of people who didn't expect anything much to be comfortable and easy and mostly didn't go far from home, and the new internationalism of big ideas, many cultures, fast, disembodied information and news, of access to remote things at the cost of less intimacy with local things and maybe displacement altogether. Thinking that makes me see Jerry himself arched over one of the little arroyos in his neighborhood, in the colors of his own paintings, in the landscape of his own life, a body bridging the difference, and I realize how soaked I can get in this river of images, so that even my own thoughts become images in his vein.

I remember a vast triptych of his depicting Reagan-era advisor Oliver North as a fallen, broken statue, the head roped up and being lifted by an unseen crane, in a rough, rocky landscape of ruins and of ravens, the paint itself scumbled into roughness, leading to a stormy sky that is beautiful anyway despite his or our failings. It is a piece that recalls the great painter Anselm Kiefer, whose work has tried to reckon with German history. But like those of Kiefer, Jerry's paintings that interrogate national policy aren't propaganda, aren't uncomplicated, aren't only politics.

Or, rather, in them politics is not a realm apart but the large-scale version of the machinery that shapes how we live, believe, treat each other, what we make and destroy. What happens publicly can also feed nightmares, dig deep into the psyche, shape a life. Our collective nightmares often arise from the sins of the powerful and from our acquiescence to them. Presiding figures govern households or nations; their illnesses, weaknesses, and blind spots matter in both. The wars abroad and at home and within are all wars, and we all have to choose how to participate or at least position ourselves in each.

In *Return of the Nuclear Warrior* (page 20), a man comes riding down the road on an old and weary horse with jutting hipbones and sagging neck. The rider, a frowning man with Jerry's big gray moustache, wears blue armor that is a missile casing. He carries a spear that has a cock and balls at the end and is the same blue as the armor. In the distance a mushroom cloud looks like an egg-domed hornet's nest. The painting was done in the era of the nuclear freeze movement and the era of fear that the way the Soviet Union and the United States played nuclear chicken with each other might kill millions of human beings and devastate expanses of the Northern Hemisphere. We can think of this knight as a soldier in the global conflict or an emblem of it.

Or we can go deeper, thirty-five miles northeast by road from Santa Fe (far less as the crow flies—and crows and ravens often fly in Jerry's paintings) to Los Alamos National Laboratory, the site where the world's first atom bombs were designed and built. After all, there does seem to be a volcanic caldera in the background that approximates the Jemez caldera on whose rim Los Alamos sits. In many places in the West, nuclear war was a local enterprise, too: uranium was mined or parts were manufactured, weapons tested or waste dumped. In New Mexico all four of these happened, and some of them are still happening. "All politics is local," said one of the great political leaders of the 1970s and 1980s, Tip O'Neill. Though often considered an international issue, nuclear weapons are very local to northern New Mexico.

There are other forces at work in the painting *Nuclear Warrior.* Jonathan Schell's 1982 book about the peril of nuclear weapons and war, *The Fate of the Earth,* impacted Meridel and Jerry, as it did millions who became antinuclear activists; in their case, she told me, it influenced their decision to get married, to embrace a possible future in the face of no future. In the late 1980s, Meridel worked on a vast collaborative project about the birth of the bomb in Los Alamos called *Critical Mass*. In that series and others from the era, she often used Jerry as a photographic model, turning the tables on male photographers whose wives posed for them, often nude. Jerry was not only one who looked but one who was looked at, the spouse of an artist and an artist's model, perhaps a radical role for a man of his generation.

Return of the Nuclear Warrior speaks of all these relationships as well as to this army veteran's questioning of the old roles handed down to men—that ludicrous armor, that phallus on the tip of the lance, as if for raping without even touching. Not only is all politics local, but feminism declared that the personal is political: this painting is about the relationship between our largest and most intimate troubles. It is, of course, with that skinny nag and the inevitable lance, also a nuclear cowboy version of Don Quixote. It is a political painting, but every painting here is concerned with these issues of who we are and how we are to take care of the world and relate to its creatures. These tangles we might call politics at a distance but love and its opposites up close.

These are also paintings governed by dreams, paintings formulated in the night as well as the day. It could even be argued that, if politics seeks to protect the space in which its constituencies flourish, there is a dream politics that calls for something more and deeper than the logic of daylight for our imaginations and our lives. And our art. If those who inhabit the world of dreams came to visit the waking world, they would be surprised by its rules: That gravity applies equally to all beings everywhere; that only the living come walking down the road; that things stay the same size and their size is not an indication of their psychic power. These principles would perturb the citizens of the dream world, and they would find our world very confining. In their world, time is a coil of barbed wire; in ours, it has already been strung along the fence posts we call history, and we can only follow the wire forward, though we can look back. Their time, their tangle, goes backward, forward, inward, and the most important things never happen only once, though they may not happen the same way twice.

These paintings are governed, as far as I can tell, by the dream world's rules more than ours. Or they, too, are a bridge, this time between dreamtime and historical time, between the powers of the unconscious and the obligations of the conscious, and of conscience. A horse flies across the sky in the mural Jerry painted for Arturo and Lucy Gonzales's restaurant in Roswell, and a flying woman reaches down to the rider in that turbulent sky (plate 92). In another Roswell painting from a year later, the artist revisits a 1973 dream painting in which his long-dead father, driving "the old Chevy," tows him and his brother Archie so they can fly. This time they are white-haired, older men, while in the earlier version they are brown-haired, in their prime, flying over a Juárez populated by skeletons playing music. The wings, Jerry says, came from the Mexican artist José Guadalupe Posada.

Many of the other paintings don't show fliers but show us the world as it might look to a flying or floating man or a bird. In *Prairie Homestead with Approaching Cosmic Storm* (page 8), that beautiful blue and black night painting, we look down from a great height on the homestead tiny in the landscape. Towns, the Santa Fe Plaza where Jerry once sold the *Saturday Evening* Post, and open country are all shown from far above in paintings where we fly with the artist. In *Prairie Apparition* (plate 11), a gigantic figure with a ram-skull head rides a skeletal horse whose four hooves straddle a broad swathe of that prairie-homestead landscape. Death shows up often in Jerry West's paintings but seems to take no one away: the dead come back anyway to do what they left unfinished, and the animals also have missions to carry out.

The seventeen ravens in the print of the Ponderosa pine could be from nature (plate 82), and the tree is keenly observed, but the two bears in the etching could not, because they're walking upright, carrying an old kerosene lantern between them, and wearing what appear to be bear-claw necklaces. They, too, are of this place, of some dream-wrought mix of the Indian dances and the prairie homesteaders. The stream of bats flying out of a cave in another print (plate 79) was really there in a particular place: Jerry told me how he and Archie as boys out adventuring in the Puyé hills frightened them. They flew out in a great stream like smoke into the sky, which was glorious, but then never came back to their home, which was terrible. The sky into which this long-ago colony of bats flew up is the color of roses, and the trees here and there are delineated lovingly in fine black lines. There are so many beautiful skies in these paintings, dawns and nights and days and storms and clouds in all colors.

In that other world where borders are fluid, where some of us can fly, where animals are always carrying meanings and messages even when they're not lost family members, where we not only can but must return to the oldest places, power is palpable. It is in all these things and most of all in the place itself. These are paintings of people, of animals, of relationships and emotions and encounters and events, but most of all of a place. There is the larger place that is northern New Mexico, and most intensely, most vividly, most lovingly—with that way we love family we didn't choose and can't choose to leave—the vicinity of that old homestead, where Jerry and two of his children, his grandchildren, and his brother Archie live in houses up and down the old road, recently paved, that beautiful place where the expansiveness of the prairie buckles into arroyos and erupts into that jagged little hillock topped by a cross and those dainty conical peaks to the west, that place where the sun early and late in the day gives the round low junipers and pinõns long shadows, where so many nights have come and gone, so many dreams been dreamed. That place.

Many artists chose New Mexico and places within it, but Jerry was given to New Mexico before he was old enough to choose, and it seems as though the place chose him and chose to never let him go. We speak as though people own places, but they own us in other ways that can be more powerful. This three-quarters of a century unfolded in one place is expansive, time to grow acquainted as few will anymore on this earth full of displaced and migrant and restless and indoor people, people who may not fly but whose feet don't quite touch the ground.

Maybe it takes so many decades for things to become this tactile, this tangible, to assume their true nature so fully, to go so deep. Together Jerry West's paintings constitute a bestiary, a regional atlas, a natural history, an autobiography, a dream journal, and maybe an alchemical treatise, all written in images that we can read but only partially, and none reads alike. They are all these things and also a feast, the testament of an artist who knows what he has been given and also how to give.

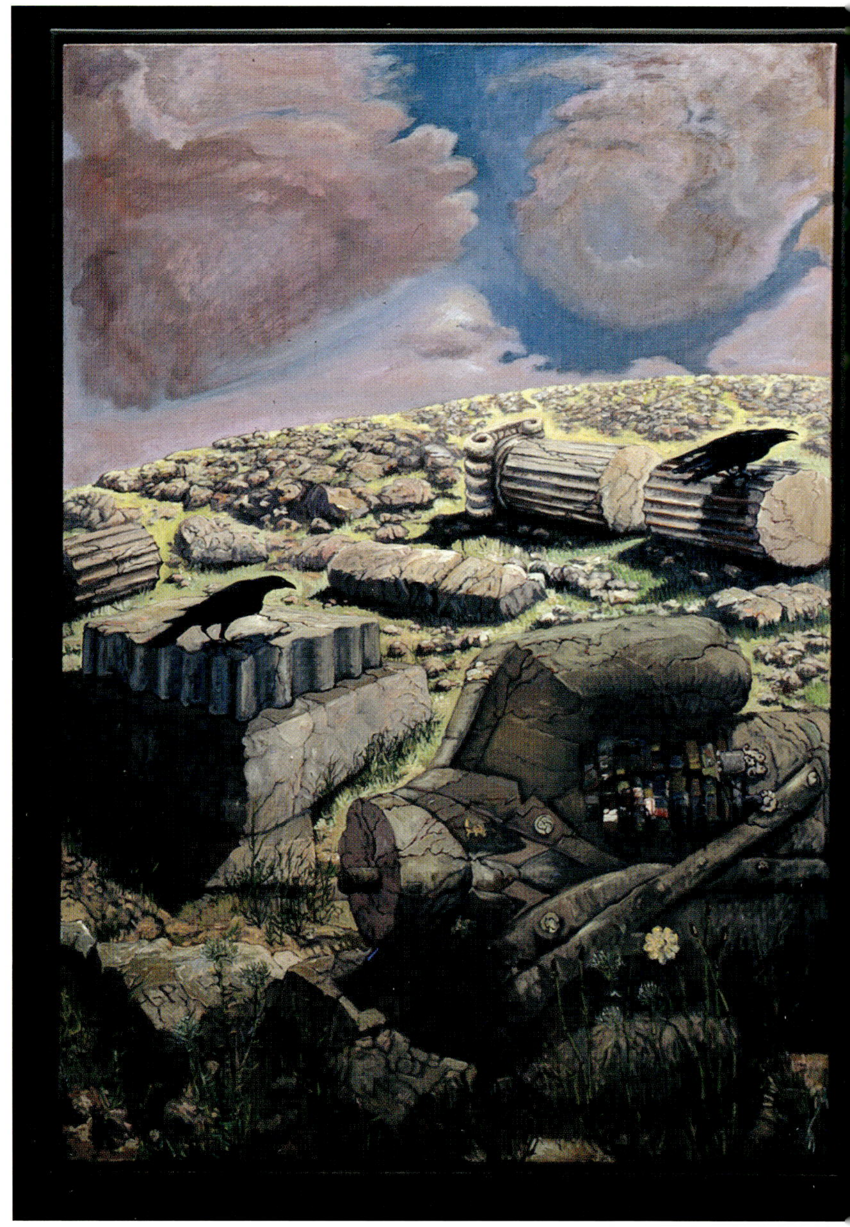

The Residue of Conquest, "Ode" to Ollie North, 1992
Oil on linen, triptych, 174 × 72 in.

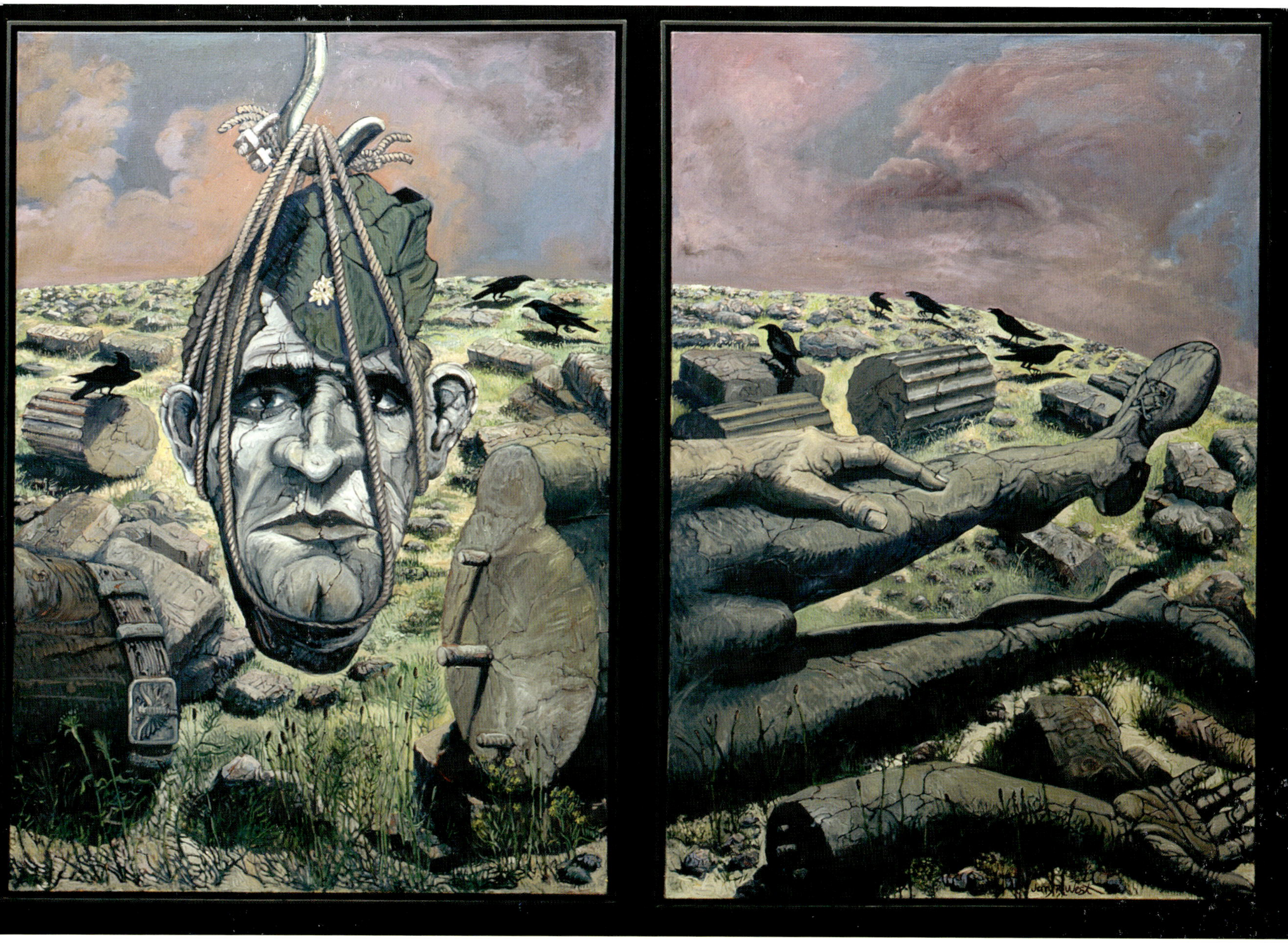

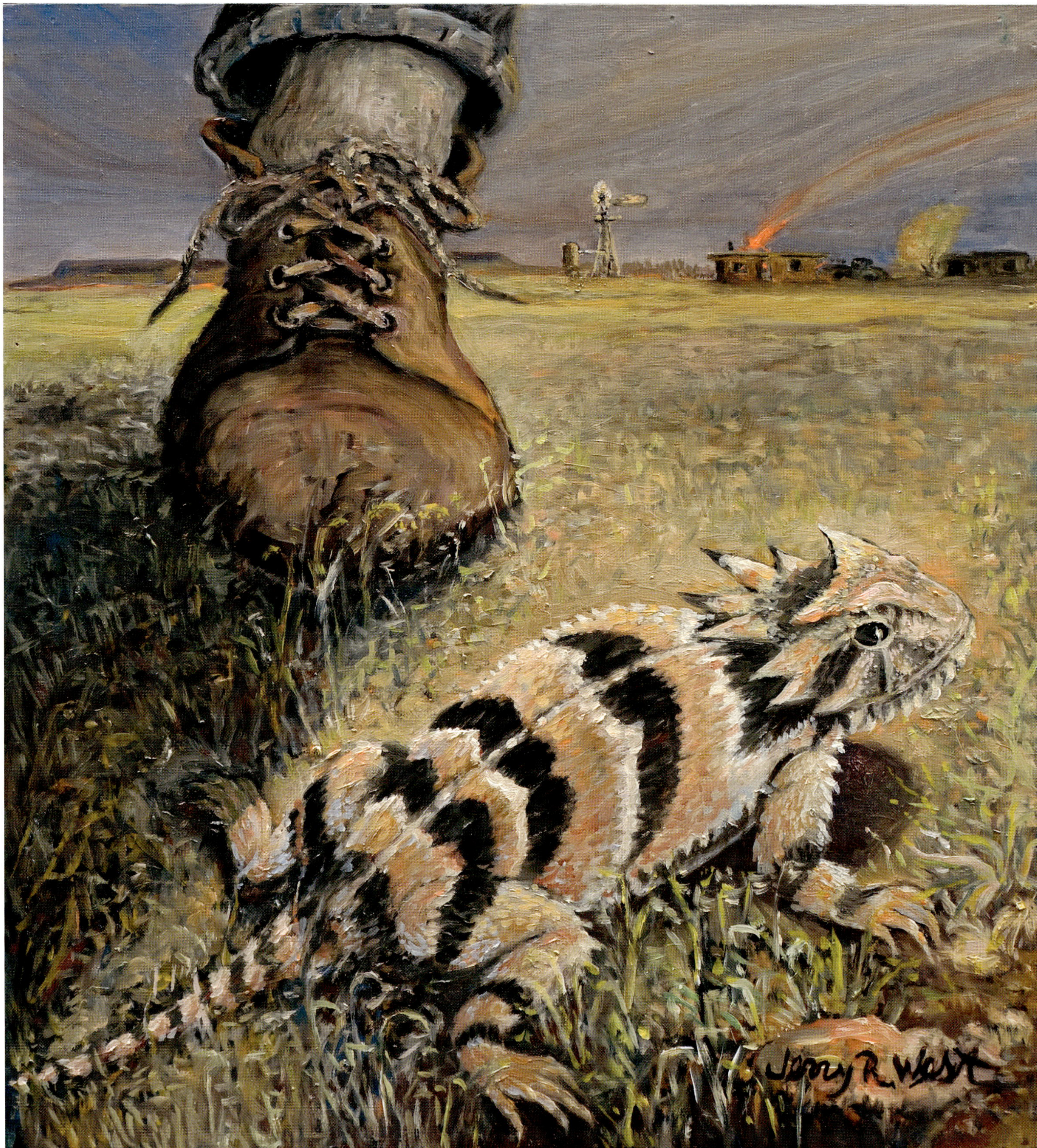

Intricate Shuffle of God's Living Creatures, 2009
Oil on Masonite, 24 x 30 in.
Collection of Robert Nelson

Artist's Statement

Jerry R. West

This book presents paintings, and some prints, primarily from the work I produced since the late 1960s. In many ways, the paintings are as variegated and as disparate as my own life. I bounced continually back and forth between teaching school, raising a family while inventing a neighborhood, designing and constructing custom homes and studios, traveling to interesting places, making drawings and etchings, and always painting. If there is some degree of coherence or unity in the work, it results from my deep connection with and love for the high desert prairie world with its lizards, snakes, nighthawks, and coyotes, along with the humans who coexist in it.

Like all painters, I have had a love affair with paint and the act of painting, and with that, the fascination and romance that accompany our own projections that we place on the lives of painters. Also, like many other painters and artists, I have had inspirational and caring mentors. My own list of painter heroes includes Rembrandt, Van Gogh, Goya, Orozco, and Rivera, with whom I would like to believe I share a social conscience.

My father, Harold E. West, was a printmaker and painter, and he was a major inspiration for my becoming an artist. I grew up in an environment that included his many artist friends and acquaintances. My family welcomed a wide variety of people into our lives, and I have been influenced by that interest in, and respect for, a broad socioeconomic cross-section of humanity. I had no shortage of living heroes.

Among my contemporaries is a long list of poets, writers, and builders who also profoundly influenced me. Of course, my social and artistic points of view are derived from my own personal psychology, which was informed from birth by a colorful and complex family, a childhood in the harsh but beautiful Depression era, a world scarred by World War II, Viet Nam, and the ongoing conflicts of our times. As a child I lived on Canyon Road in Santa Fe, New Mexico, on the prairie south of town, and for a while at Puyé on the Pajarito Plateau, in the neighborhood of Los Alamos, the birthplace of the atomic bomb, and I became an unwitting member of the generation most affected by the psychological fallout of this strange political agenda.

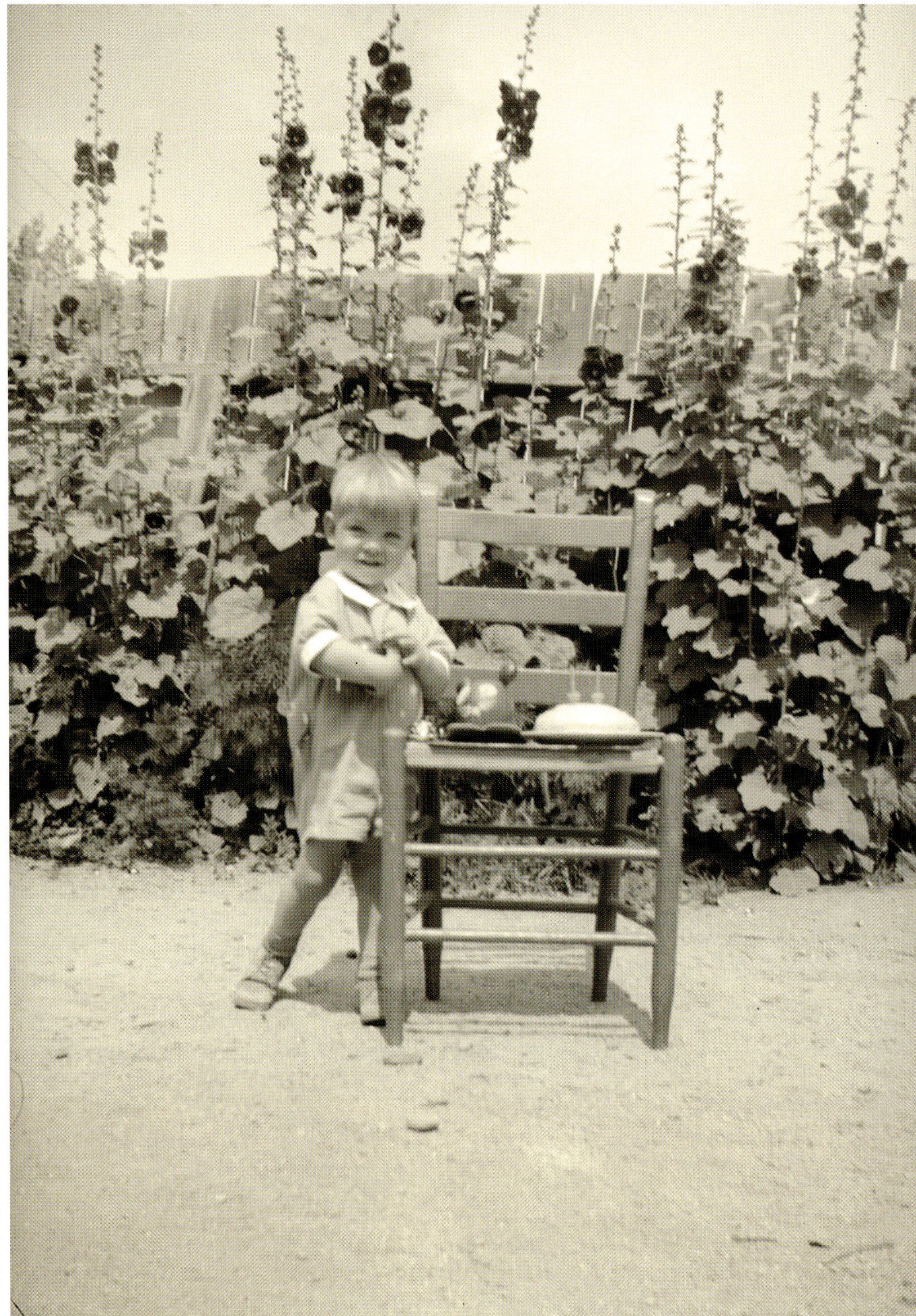

Jerry's second birthday, Canyon Road, 1935,
photograph by Mildred Olive West.

I use direct observation and experience, enhanced by vivid memories and aided by a very active dream world that I readily access. All of this contributes to the process of using metaphor and allegory that speaks to powerful human issues I examine in my work. This complex mix of stimulation has helped me develop meaning in my landscapes, or *dreamscapes*, which challenge viewers but still strive, at the same time, to be beautiful. In creating these images, I hope to encourage people to adopt a more thoughtful and generous relationship with a world that I feel is frightening, mysterious, and magnificent.

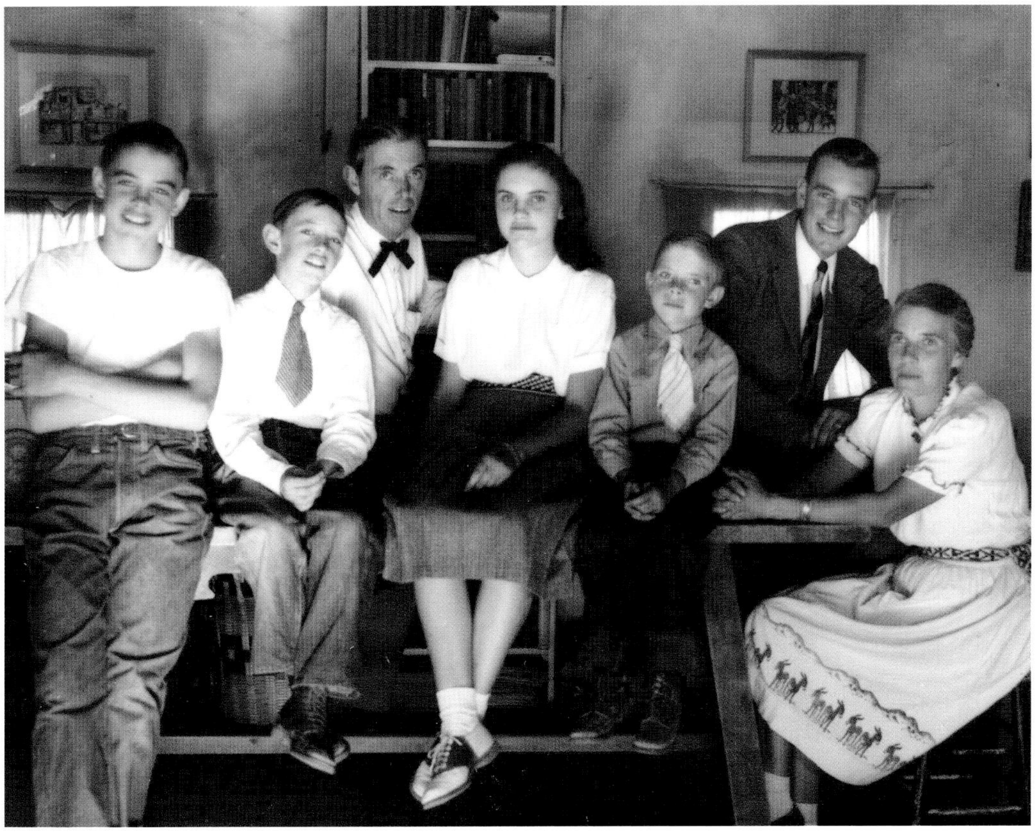

West family at the homestead, late 1940s. From left: Jerry, Archie, Hal, Sarah, Philip, John, and Mildred. Photograph by Tyler Dingee.

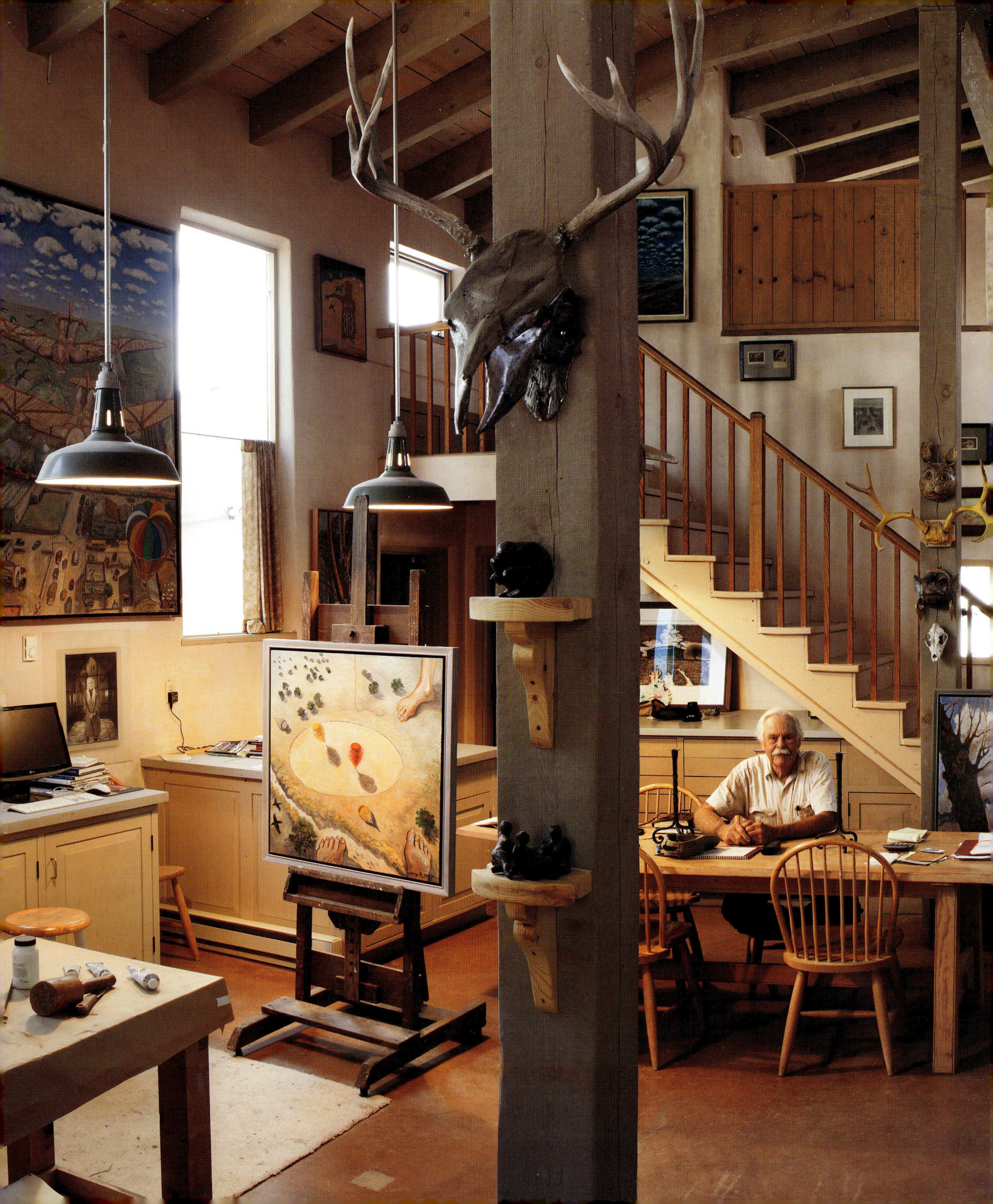

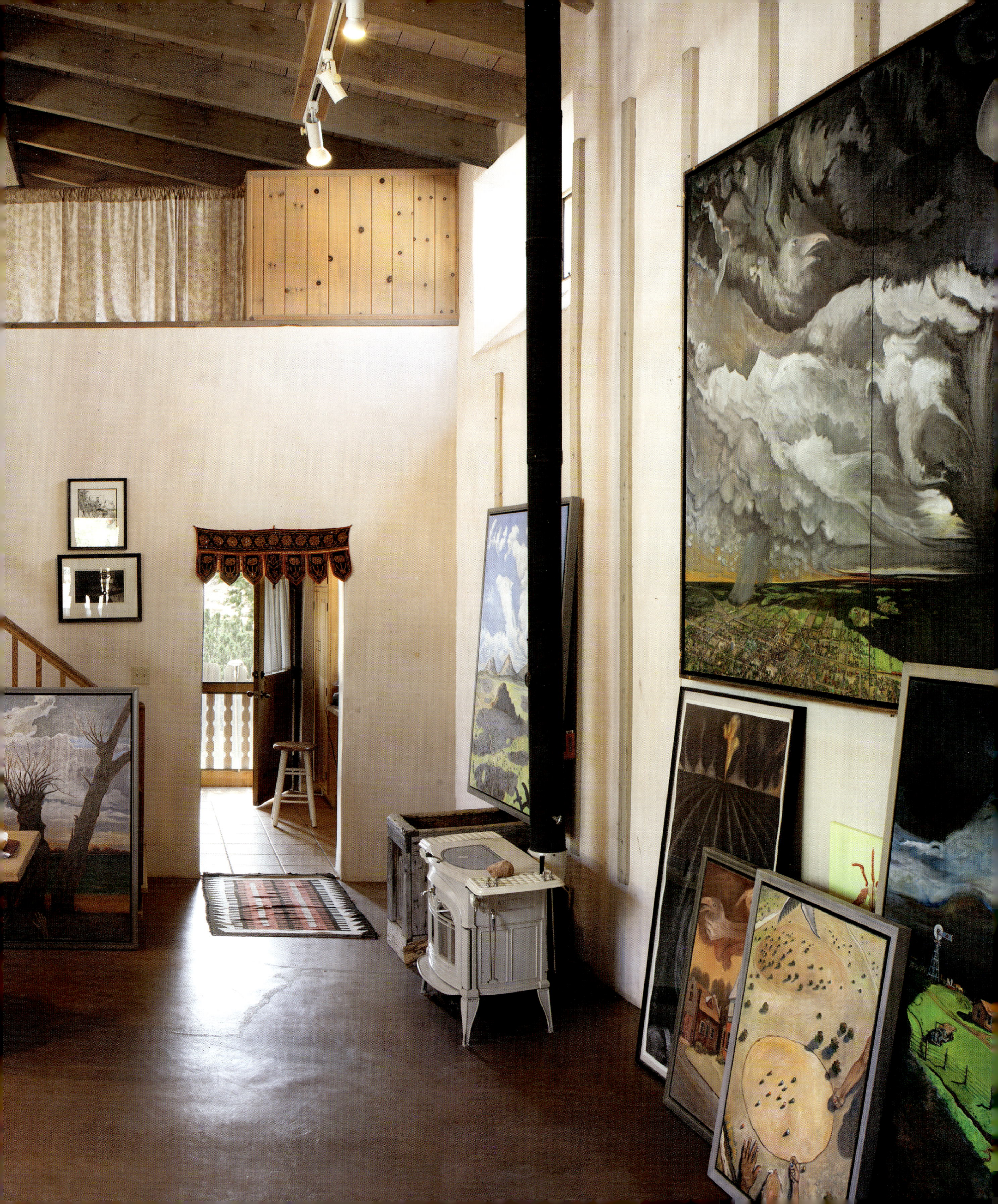

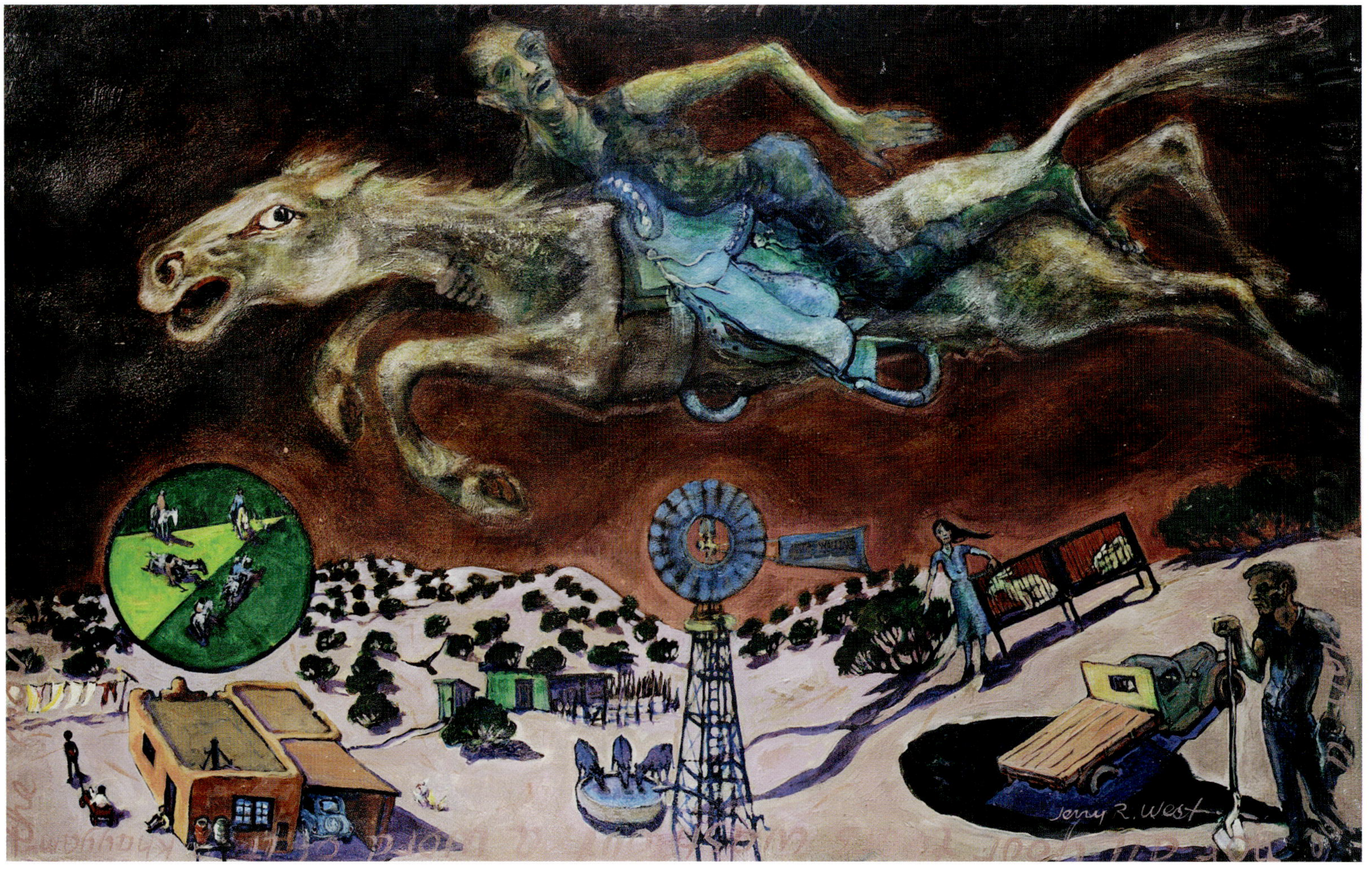

1.
Tumbleweed Goes Mad, 1981
Acrylic on paper, 36 × 24 in.

Tumbleweed goes mad.
Archie stays tight in a blue saddle without a horn.
Lili appears and disappears, Gene gets his old truck stuck
in the only existing water hole.
Mildred scolds.
I see green at the end of a telescope.

—JRW

1. A Praire Night

To be born on the prairie means to wander all your life, always being pulled back. It means accident, incident, drama, movement. It always means dreams. No matter where else, no matter what else or who else, all are inventions, all are departures from the pungent prairie realities, the early heroes, the early places. However, the landscape, the distant and mysterious mesas, continue to shimmer through the inner agonies, the outer violence and betrayals, the constant madness of humankind.

I place these paintings in the beginning not because they are the first and earliest of my work but because they directly represent my personal views, derived from memory and dreams. Many evolutionary experiences led to this body of work: childhood days on Canyon Road; the early prairie years with family; my school years, college years, graduate school studying biology; my marriage to Sharon Joyce and our children—Tamara, Valli, and Joe; time in the military, teaching, and construction work. In the late 1960s I decided to return to graduate school, this time to study art. The death of my father at this time had a powerful impact on me.

It was an exciting and rewarding period of early art making in graduate school, studying with Elmer Schooley. He and I became compadres in the printmaking and etching studio, and I gained respect for his philosophy of contemporary painting. I made many good paintings in graduate school. However, I never felt that what I was doing was really my own work. After graduate school, I painted, made prints in El Paso, and worked in construction. This was a time of personal upheaval that stimulated me to follow my instincts to be a painter. Eventually, I met Elaine Freeman, who encouraged me to go to New York.

During my first visit to Manhattan, I found my way to Bob Blackburn's Printmaking Workshop studio and began a time of making many prints there off and on for three years. I worked side by side with artists from many places in the world. When I traveled I also dreamed. Almost always the dreams were involved with my growing up in a complex, emotionally rich prairie world. It was in Blackburn's studio that I first began to incorporate my dreams into my etchings.

When I returned to New Mexico on a more permanent basis, I began to paint again. I also had many discussions with a Jungian therapist who urged me to consider my dreams as starting points for my paintings. Beginning a new, loving relationship with the photographer Meridel Rubenstein provided a boost to my painting, as she was greatly respectful of my work and also of my family. When she took a position at the University of Colorado in Boulder, I followed and found an upstairs studio on the old Larimer Street in Denver. Over a long winter I made twenty-six acrylic paintings drawn from my sketchbooks in which I had documented my dreams over many years. The paintings represented my deep love for the New Mexico landscape along with a profound caring and respect for my prairie family. Combined, my paintings also revealed a human landscape with complexities of emotions and memory.

I showed the paintings in 1982 at a gallery installation show in Santa Fe, where I painted the gallery walls a deep blue and inscribed them with poetry, included three-dimensional elements such as masks and shrines, and played an audiotape that I'd made of environmental sounds from the prairie world: windmills, birds and animal sounds, disparate voices of family members, chants, and the voices of old Indian friends. I hoped that all this would create a mood for the dream world and give viewers a greater grasp of the underbelly of my prairie world. Creating this group of paintings gave me confidence to continue making images that had deep personal meaning, and this body of work has informed all of my work since. It all began with "A Prairie Night."

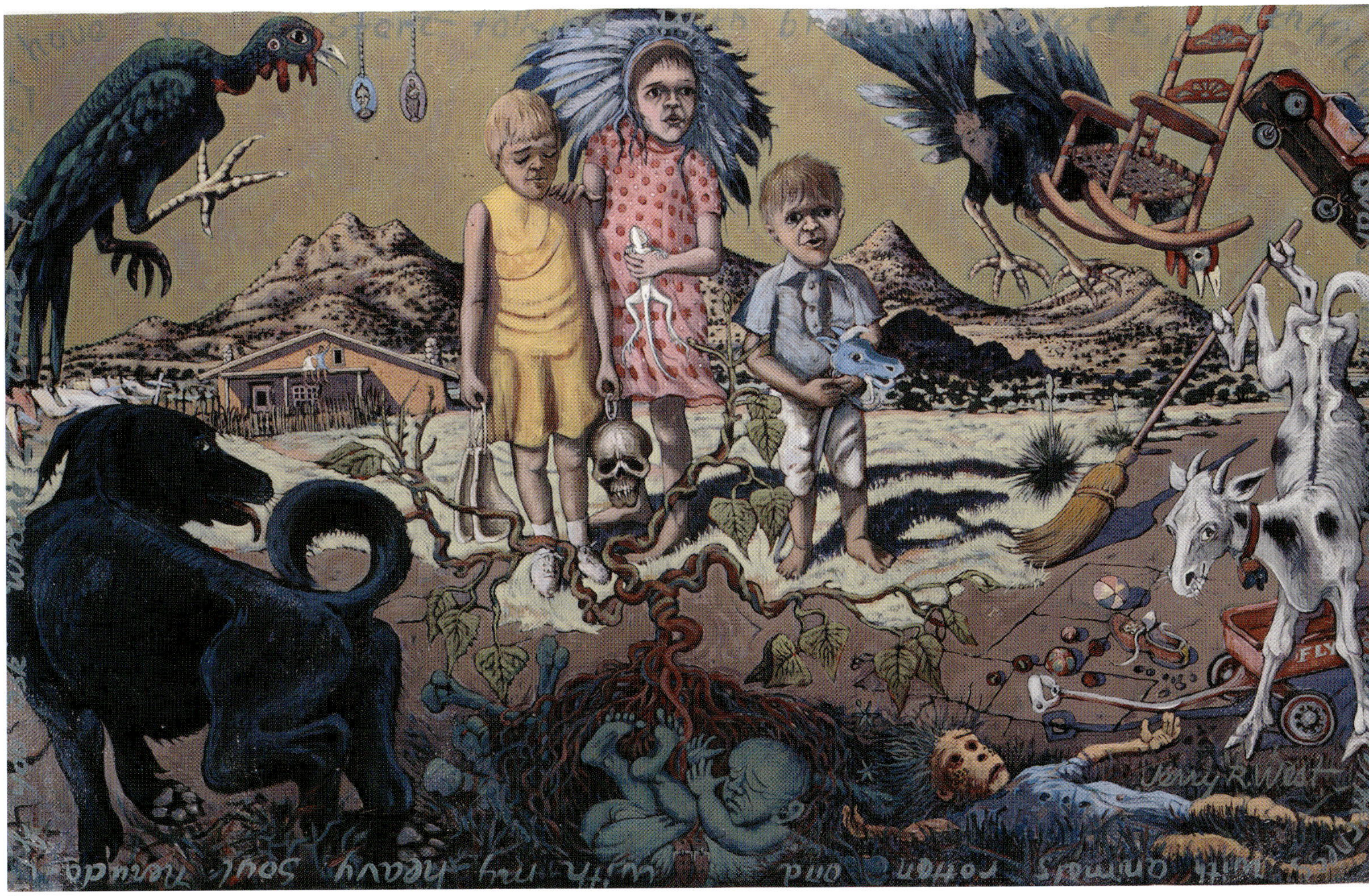

2.
Prairie Children, 1981
Acrylic on paper, 36 × 24 in.
Private collection

If you ask where I come from I have to start talking with broken objects,
With kitchenware that has too much bitterness,
With animals quite often rotten, and with my heavy soul.

—Pablo Neruda

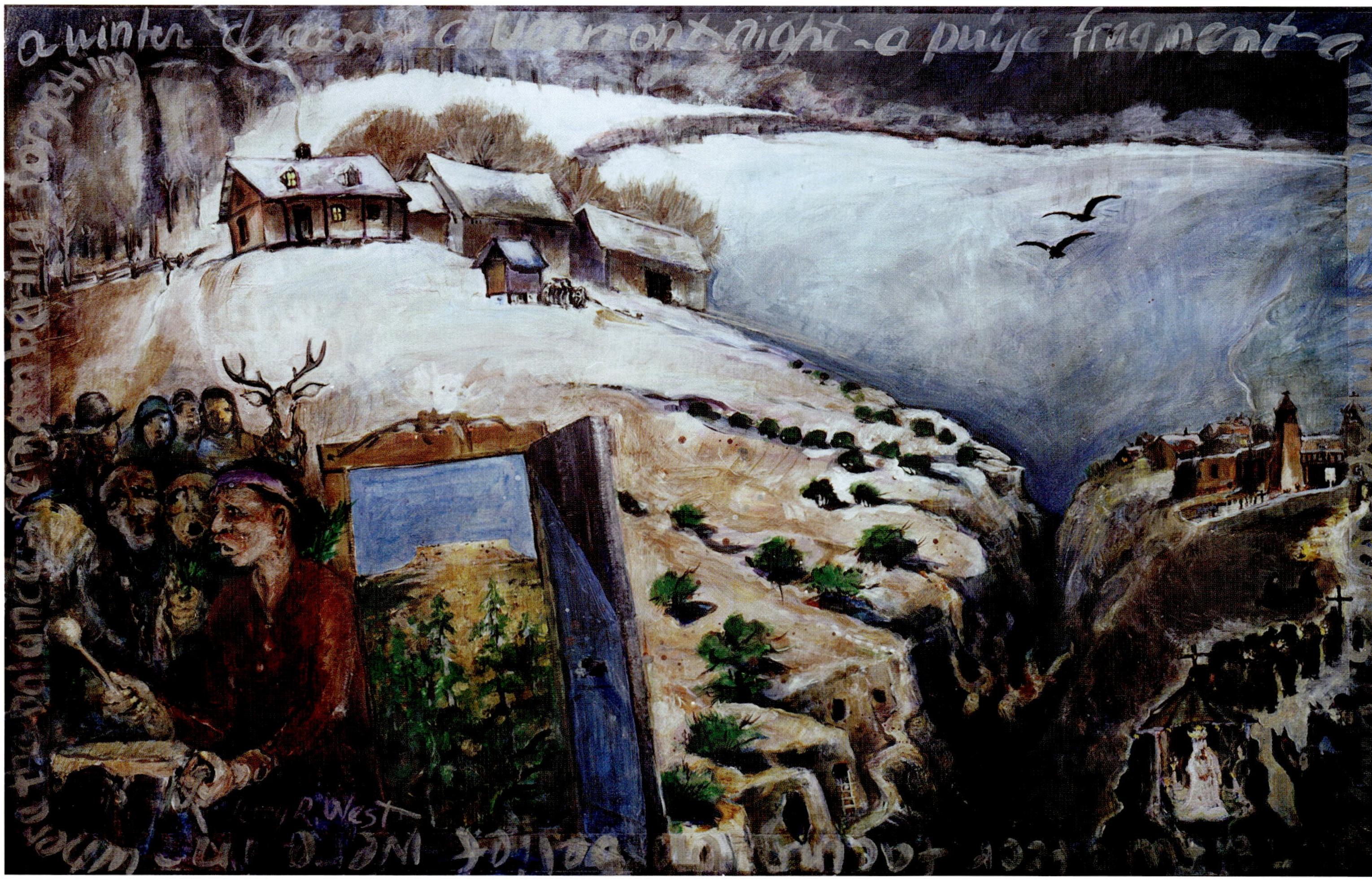

3.
A Winter Dream, A Jonestown Nightmare, 1981
Acrylic on paper, 36 × 24 in.
Collection of Meridel Rubenstein

A winter dream, a Vermont night, a Puyé fragment,
A Truchas glimpse, a Jonestown nightmare.
We fear most the belief system we're in.
And wherein lies the balance between
Remembering and forgetting, the balance between
Using old forms and inventing new?

—JRW

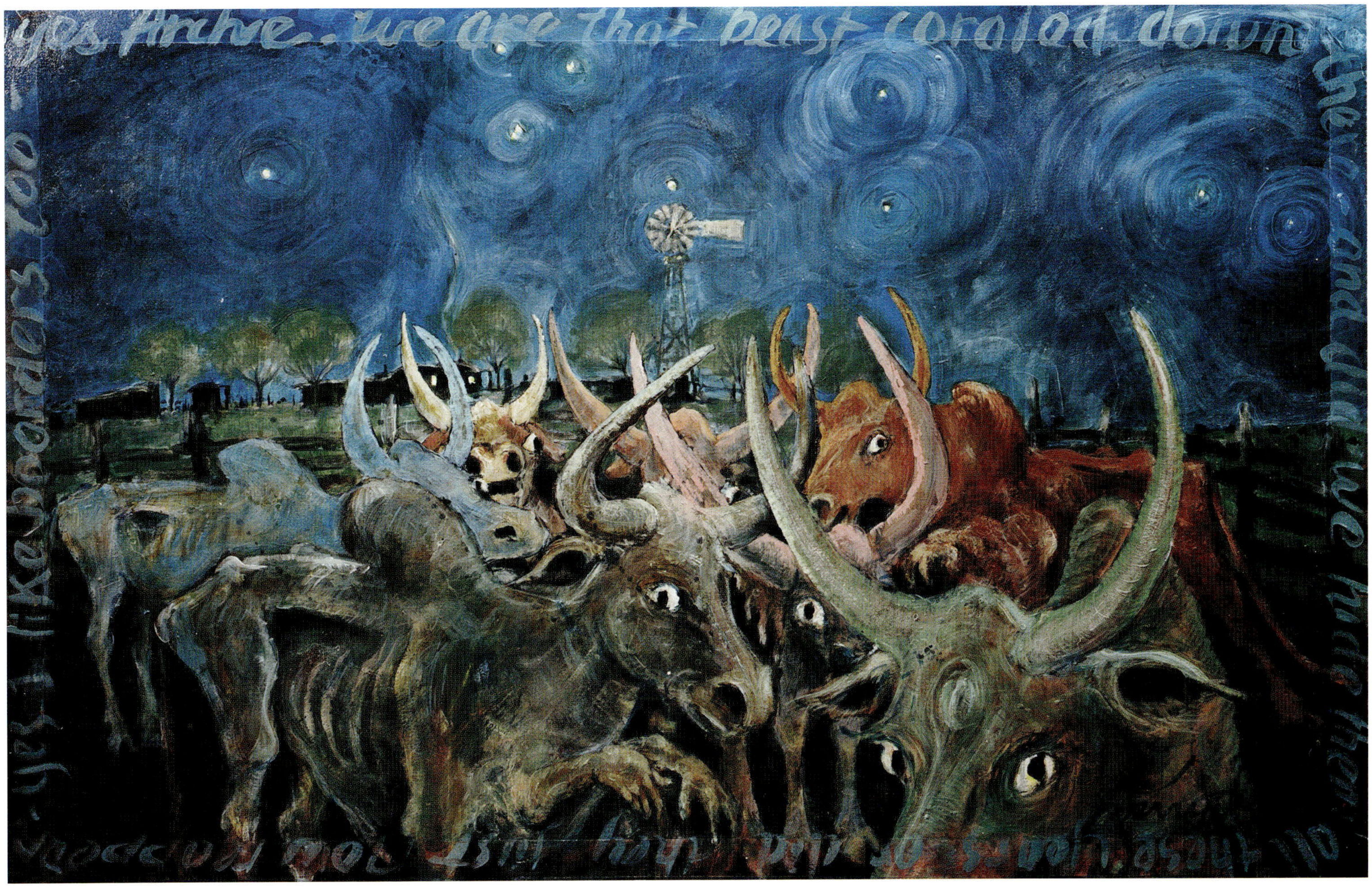

4.
Cows Penned Up Down in the Corral on a Moonlit Night, 1981
Acrylic on paper, 36 × 24 in.
Collection of Gilbenkian Foundation, Lisbon

Yes, Archie, I wonder, are we the beast down in that corral?
My feeling is that for all these years you were hiding them
Somewhere back in the Cerrillos Hills and now you've brought them out. Is that true?
Were they there all this time?
Or did they just now appear?

—JRW

5.
Invasion from Sheepherder Hill, 1981
Acrylic on paper, 36 × 24 in.
Private collection

Sheepherder Hill, Arroyo de Gallina
Visitations to our sacred flats.
A December night—and like dreams
The prairie memories live on to
Nourish our souls.

—JRW

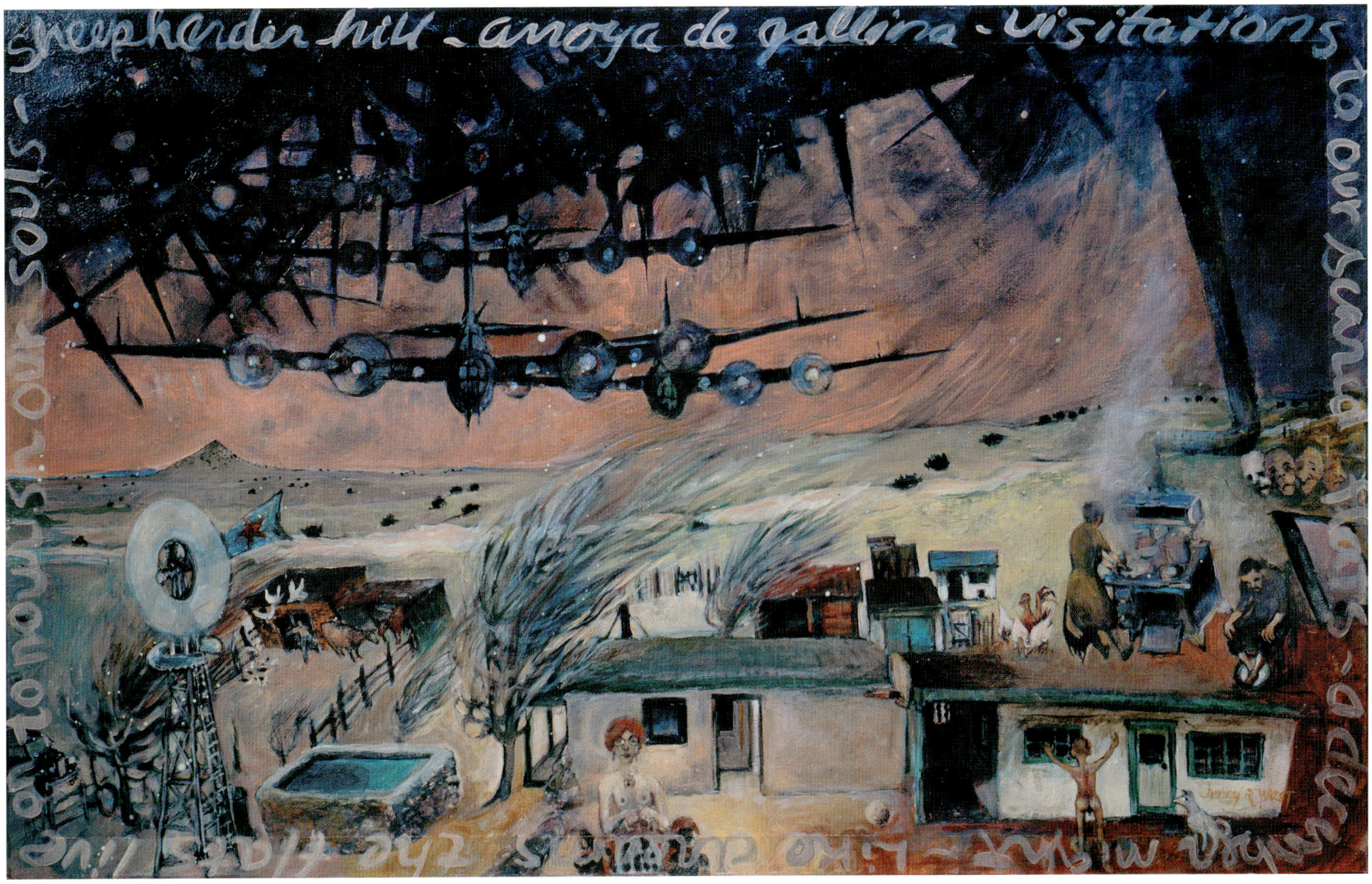
sheepherder hill - arroya de gallina - visitations

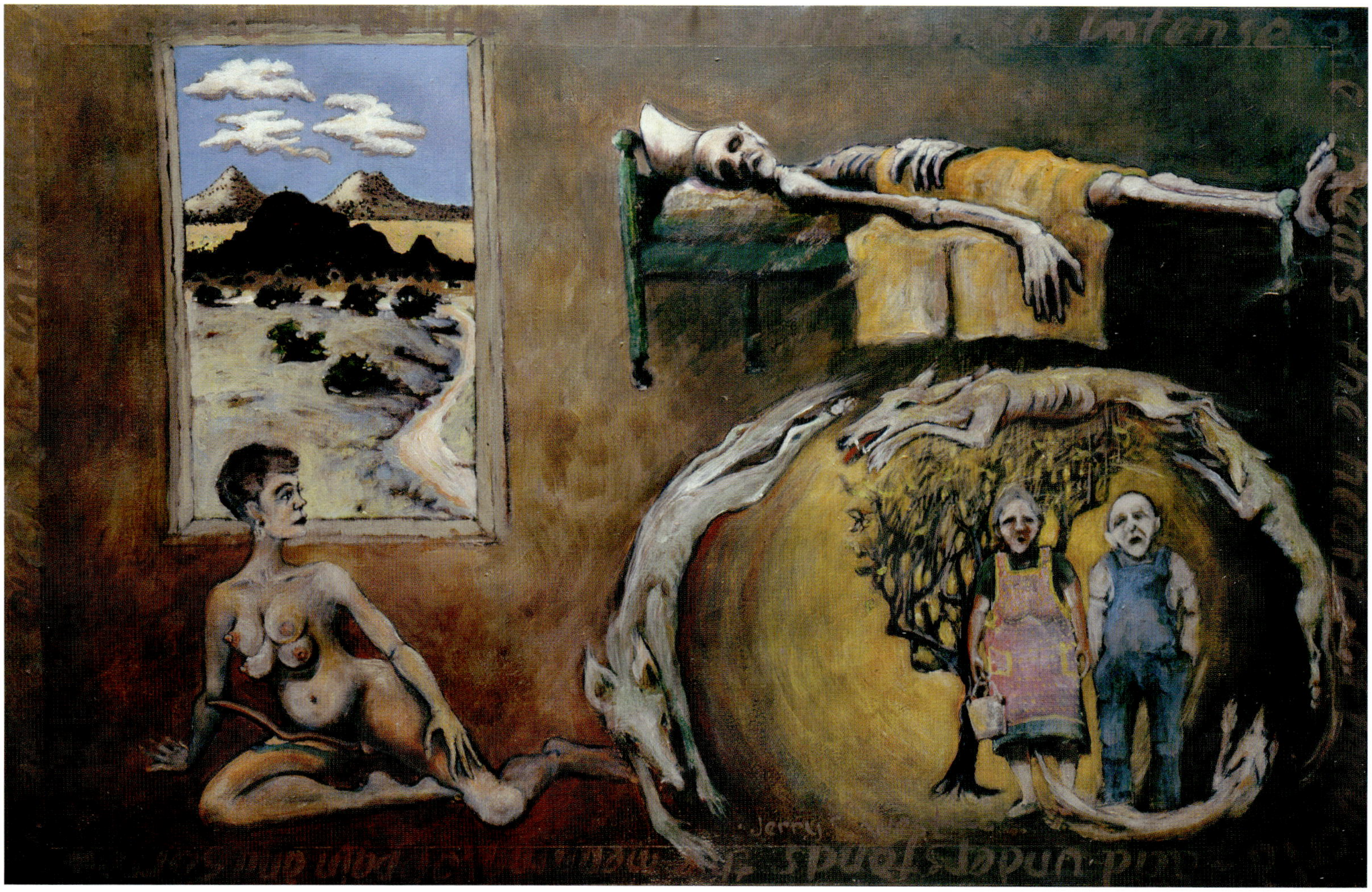

6.
To Walk over the Incandescent Dead, 1981
Acrylic on paper, 36 × 24 in.
Collection of Joe West

To walk over the incandescent dead.
To feel the stillness so intense one hears
The world and understands the meaning
of pain and sorrow.

—Henry Miller

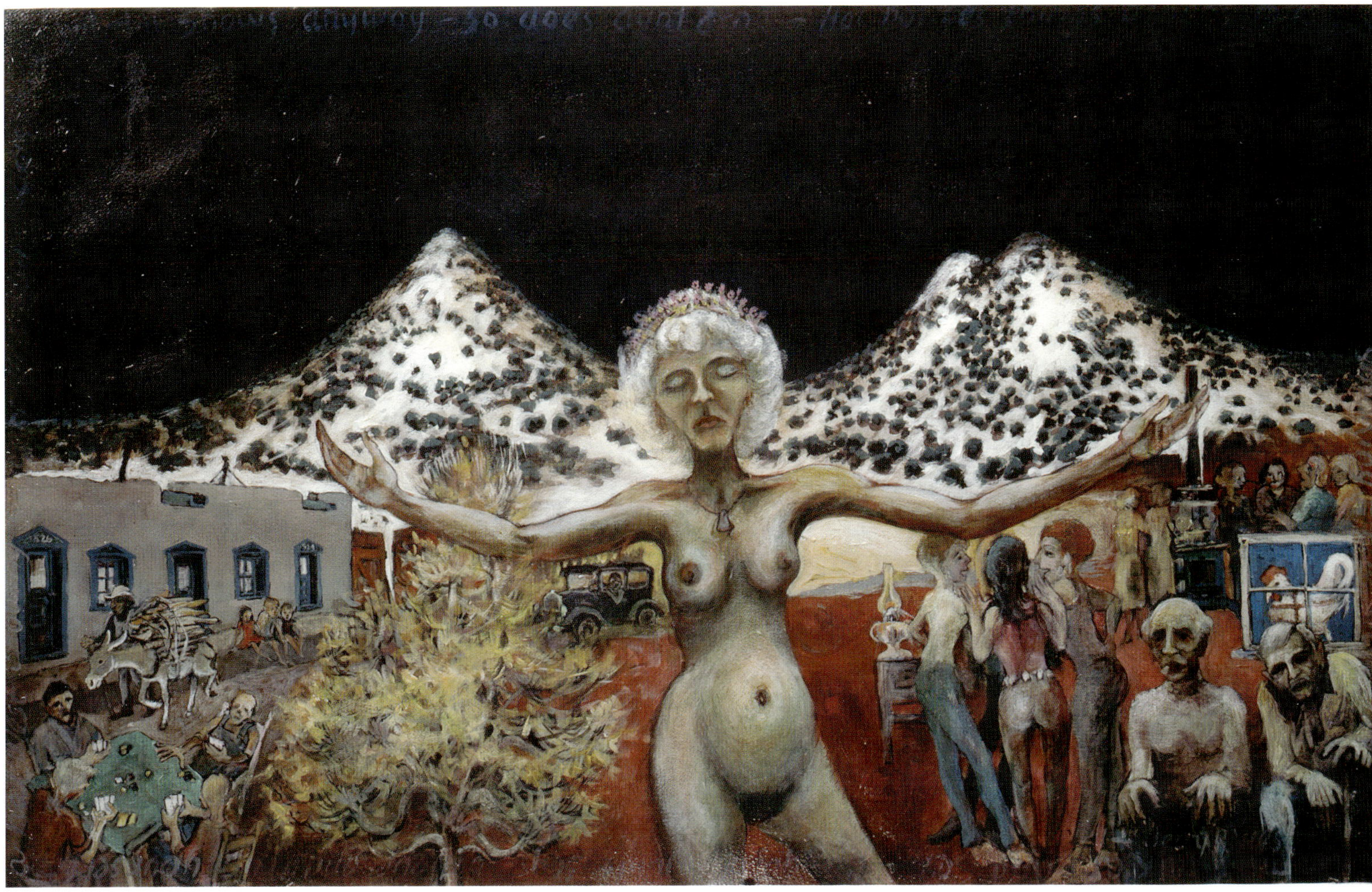

7.
A Hal West Showing, 1981
Acrylic on paper, 36 × 24 in.

In my dream, a retrospective show of my dad Hal West's paintings is being shown. Hal is dead, but he shows up anyway. He notices things about his paintings others don't. He's pleased. And though in life Hal didn't know or respect Pablo Picasso, they now sit together in the corner of the old living room, smoking and talking. The young Jewish women in the kitchen talk of art and sex. The older women near the stove speak loudly of food. Later, Canyon Road with working-class card players, Italian opera, memories, warm fall sun. A beautiful silver-haired guide meets me at the old red gate—tells me to trust myself, know my own feelings.

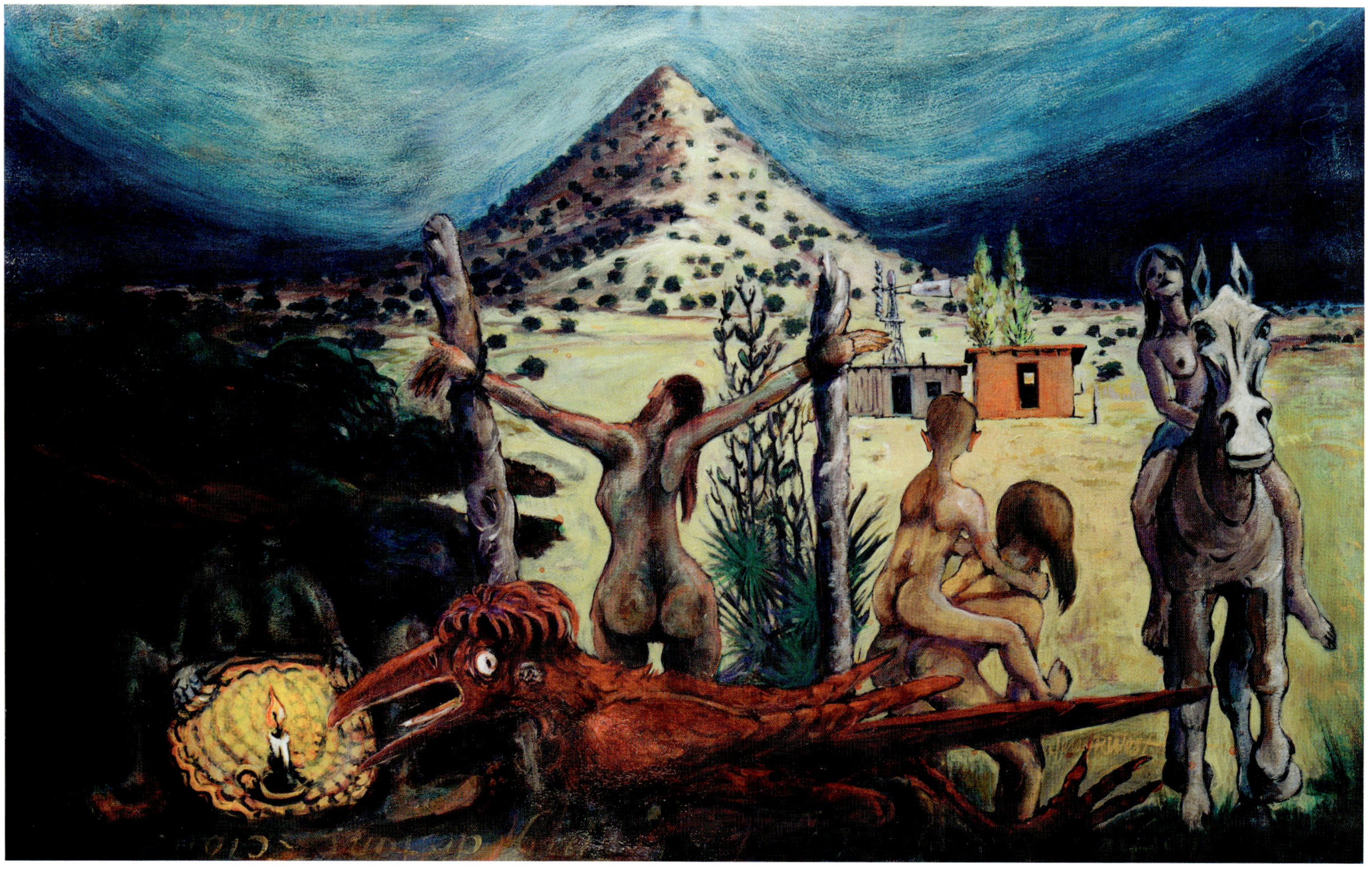

8.
August Nights, 1981
Acrylic on paper, 36 × 24 in.
Collection of Meridel Rubenstein

August Nights, a horse named Joker, a young woman called Joan, a moonless landscape,
Snipe hunt with wind and sand: oh, deceitful, cunning complicity, the roots of cruelty.
Oh, wind that washes all
Leaving no earthly shadows
Brief awakenings from eternal sleep
That carries bits of tattered clothes
Away to beckoning clouds.

—JRW

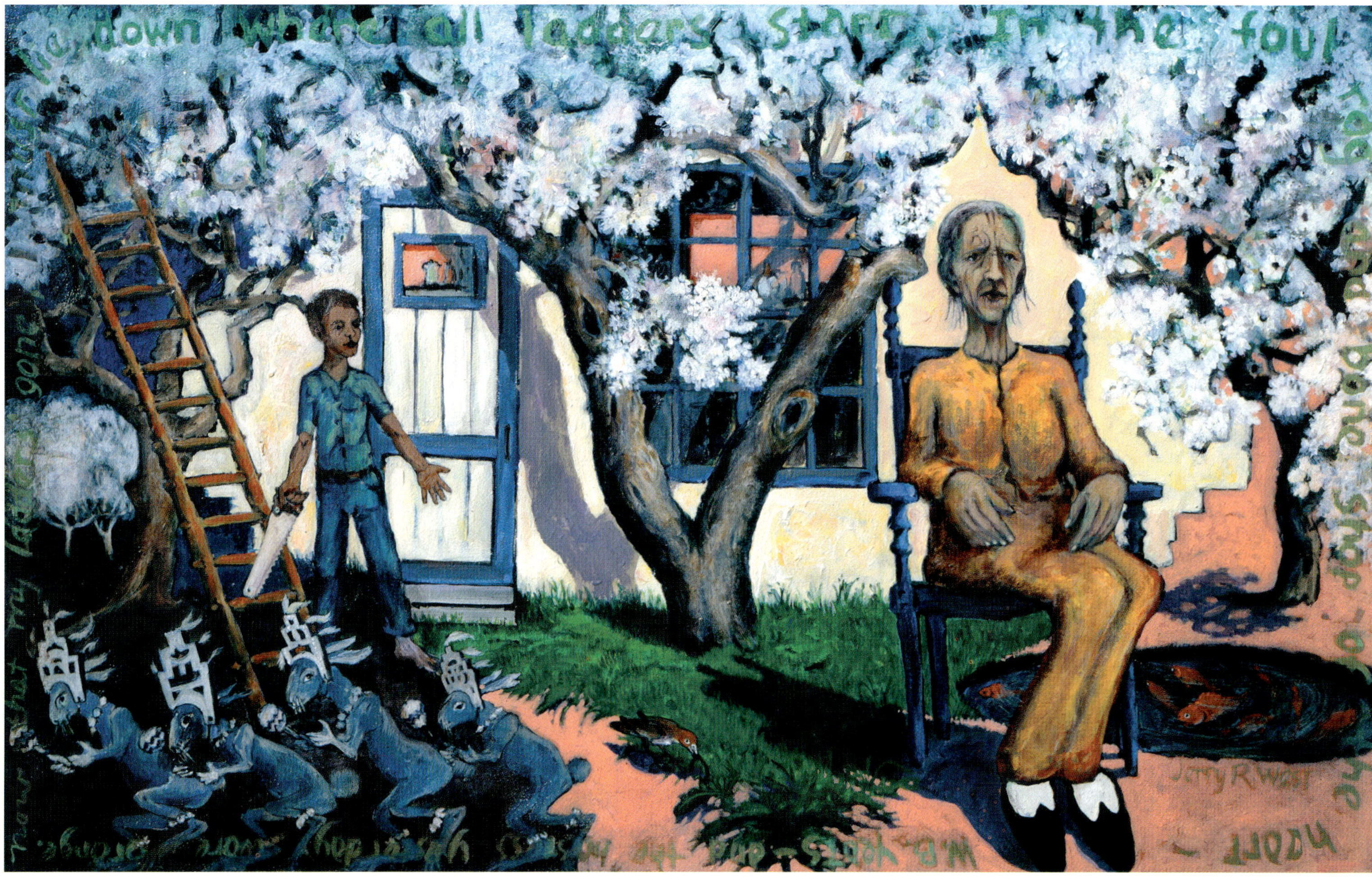

9.
The Latest in Tea Shops, 1981
Acrylic on paper, 36 × 24 in.
Collection of Tamara West Mott

10.
The Prairie World—My Coney Island of the Mind, 1981
Acrylic on paper, 30 × 24 in.
Collection of Chuck Forsman and Kristin Lewis

Oh, Prairie World—my Coney Island of the mind—the grasslands now ringed round by mobile homes, junk trailers—and rusting pickup trucks; barbed-wire enclosures with protruding power poles. Where is the warm summer day when I first saw the green sweet *vega*, with gamagrass waving and water gurgling, with butterflies alighting on clover—and yes, where do we go from here?

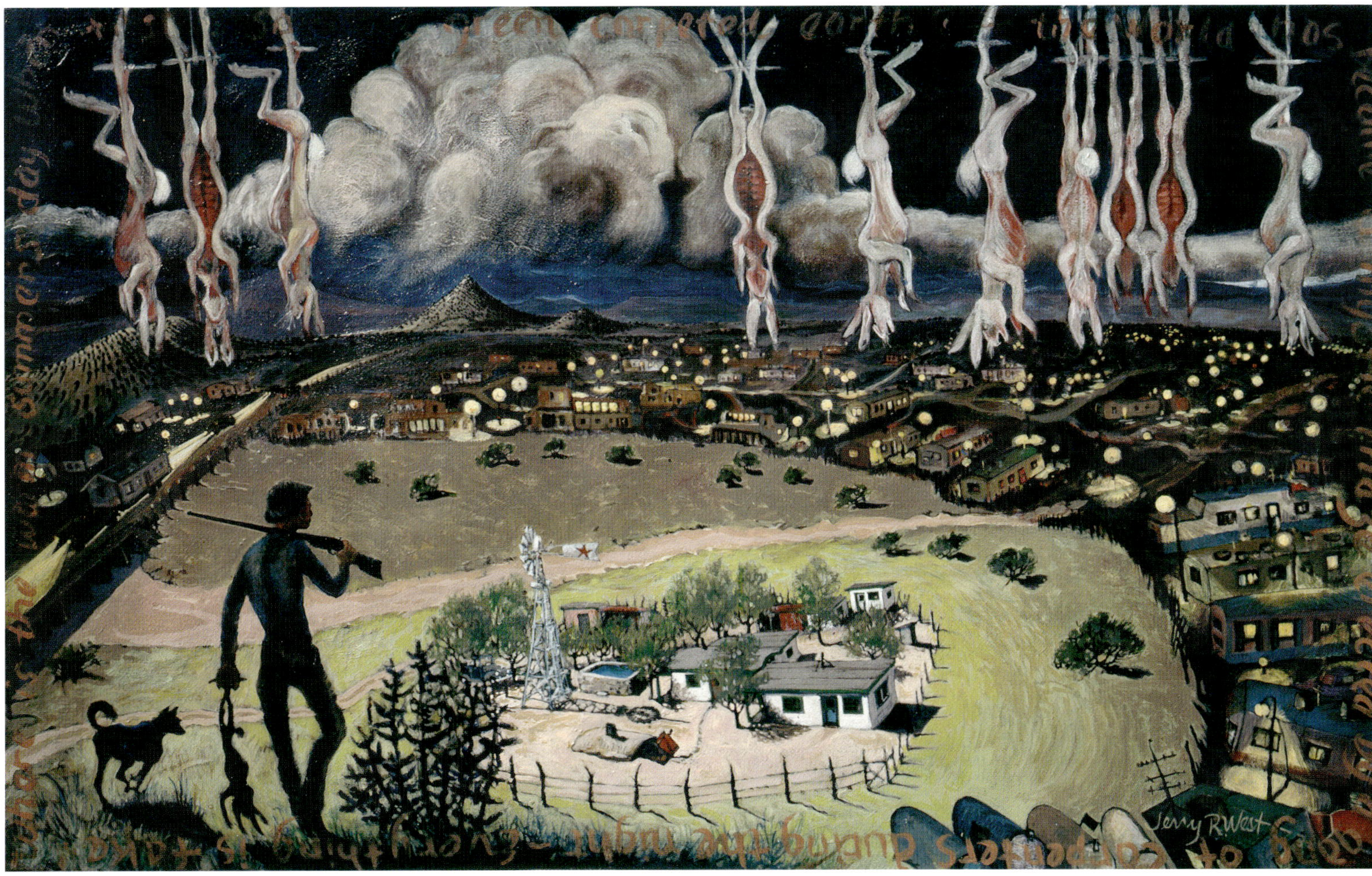
Jerry R West

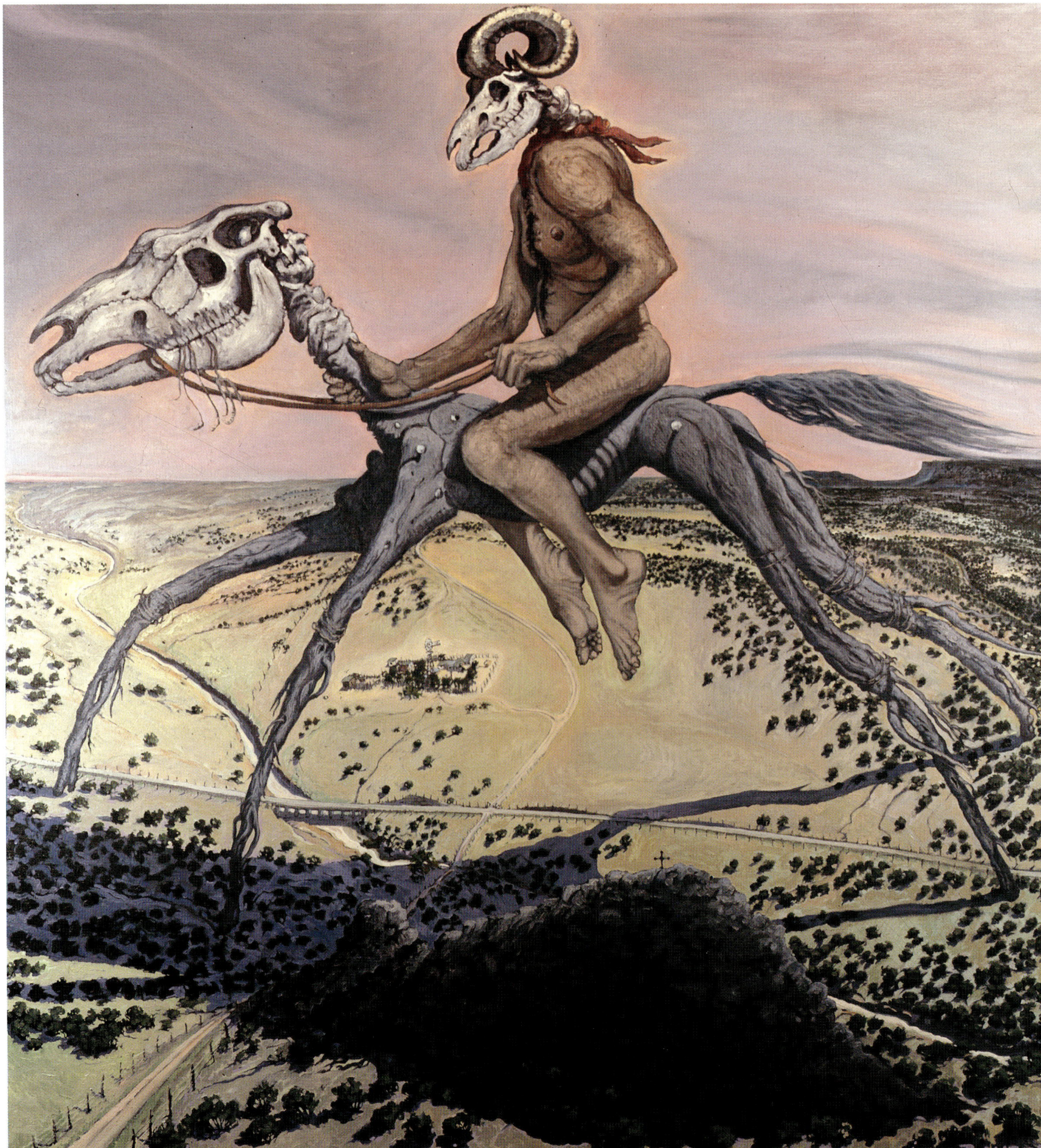

11.
Prairie Apparition, 1983
Oil on linen, 54 × 60 in.
Private collection

11. The Prairie World Revisited

Fresh from the intense dream and memory work of "A Prairie Night," I continued to paint images that conveyed deep psychological and emotional content. Still in my head were thoughts and influences from the five-year, back-and-forth relationship with Elaine Freeman and New York. There I had been greatly affected by traveling with Elaine and interacting with women deeply involved with the feminist movement. In the late 1970s and 1980s, there had been a significant counterculture movement among black, Hispanic, and Native American artists. Theirs was an art of self-expression, an art involved with a local point of view, whether emotional, psychological, or historical; theirs was an art concerned with personal mythology. I identified strongly with their efforts.

During this period I traveled to places exotic to me: various parts of the US East Coast and abroad to Mexico and Crete. Travel opened my mind and heart to new ways of seeing and being, as did working side by side with an array of international artists at Blackburn's studio.

After months of being away, periodic homecomings to Santa Fe were always challenging and emotional. Santa Fe and the West in general were changing at a rapid pace. Expensive homes and gated communities were quickly being built. More and more art galleries were popping up along Canyon Road and throughout the downtown area. What had been the clichés in local art and architecture were becoming the norm, captivating yet another band of newcomers to the scene. I knew I wanted to strike a more honest tone, a more honest way of creating an image.

Meeting Meridel Rubenstein in 1977 and experiencing her one-person show of New Mexico portraits at the Museum of Fine Arts in Santa Fe was inspirational for me. Her photographs depicted individuals from all ethnic classes, sometimes with backdrops more real than flattering, unadorned by any special attire. These were truly straightforward portraits, yet intensely psychological at the same time. Through her distilled vision of New Mexico I rediscovered my own deep affection for my home place. Together we were drawn outward as well, traveling, photographing, sketching, and painting.

In Mexico I sought out the studios of rebels Diego Rivera and José Clemente Orozco, I studied the muralists of Coyoacan and spent a magic time in the blue home of Frida Kahlo. These influences would push their way into my dreamscapes, further propelling me along on my journey I refer to as "The Prairie World Revisited."

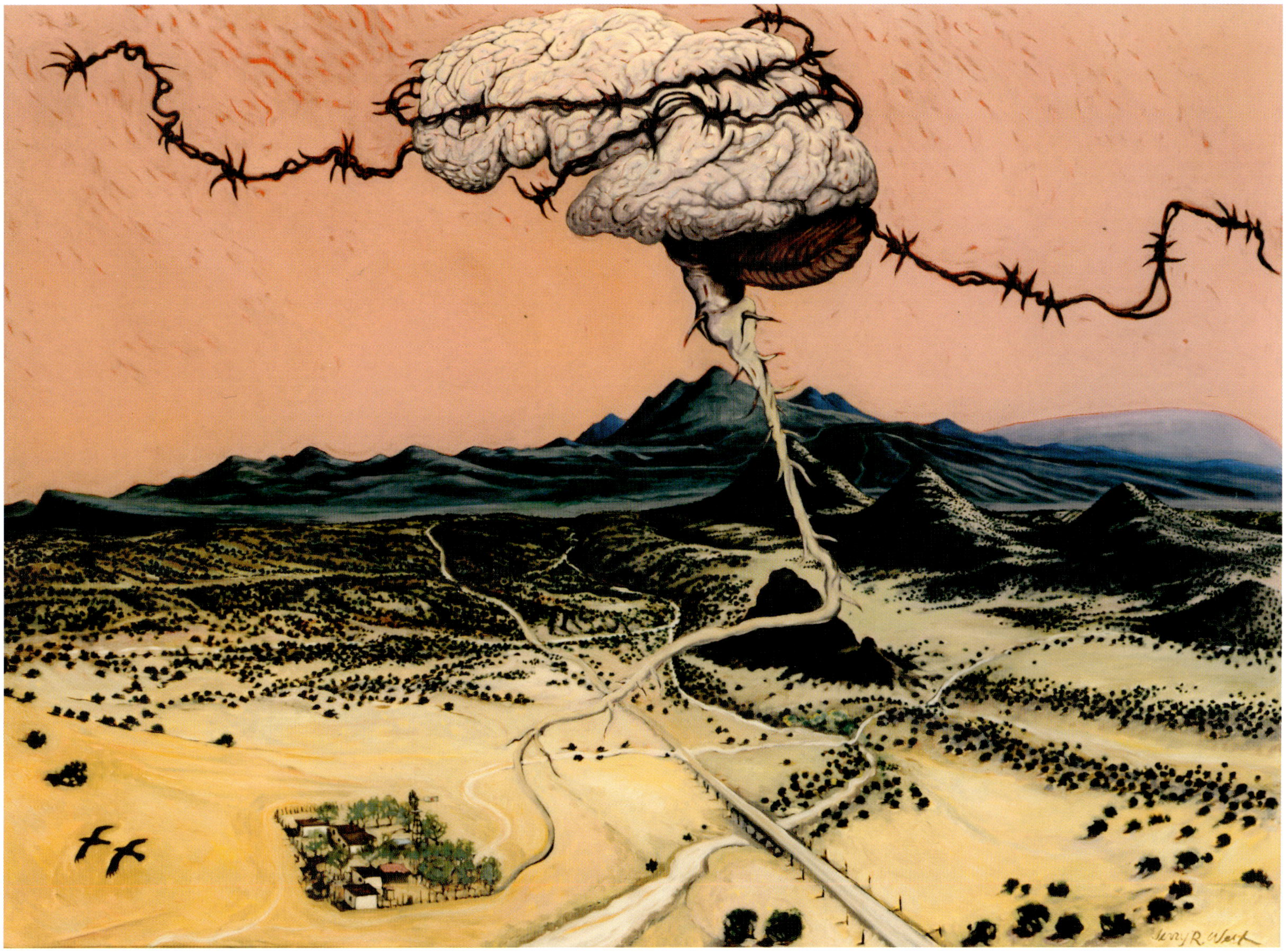

12.
Brain over Cerrillos Flats, 1984
Oil on Masonite, 48 × 36 in.

But let's not go deeper than those teeth,
nor bite into the rinds growing over the silence,
because I don't know what to say;
there are so many people dead
and so many sea-walls that the red sun used to split,
and so many heads that the boats hit,
and so many hands that have closed around kisses,
and so many things I would like to forget.

—Pablo Neruda

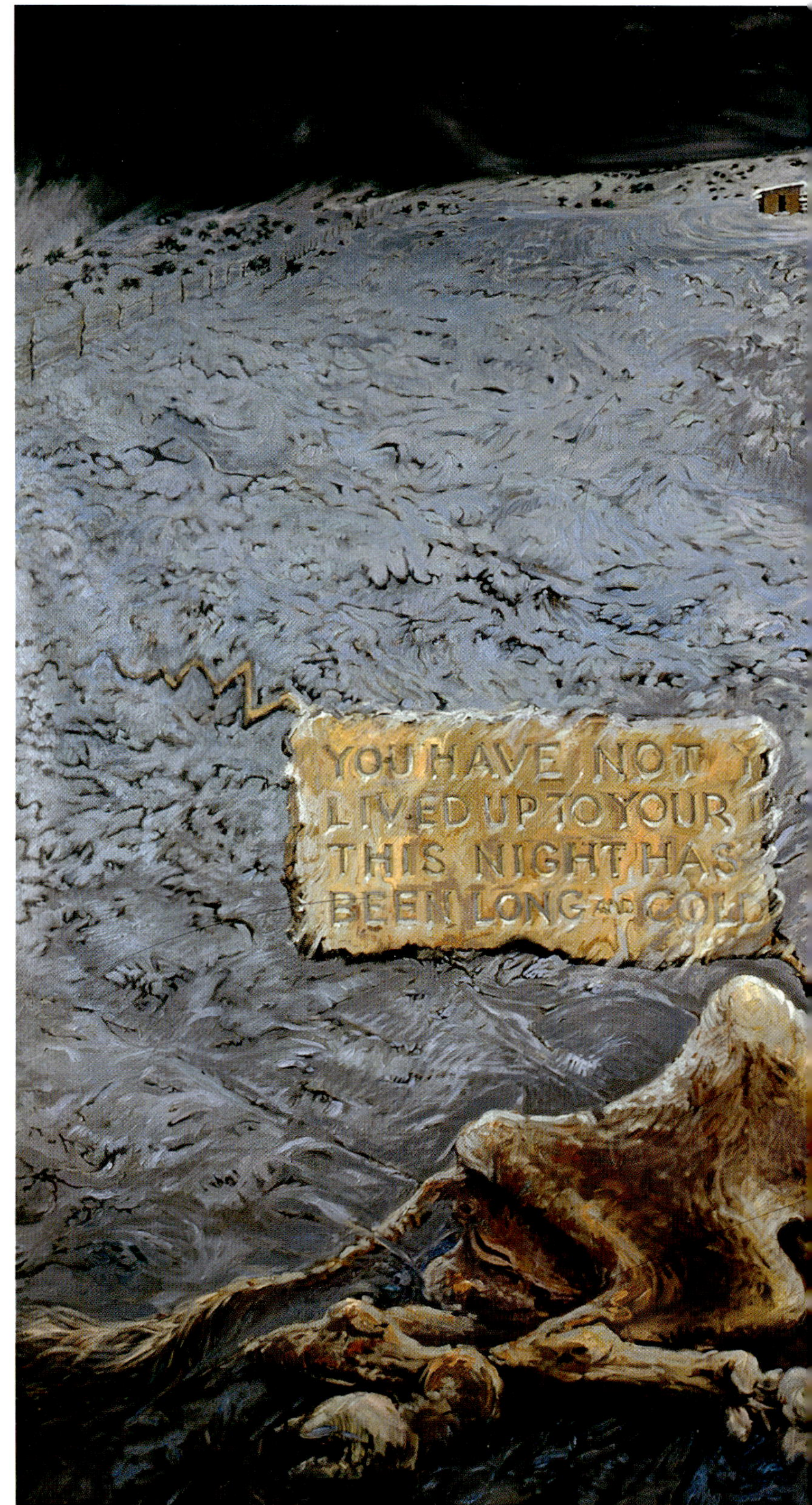

13.
Homeplace, 1983
Oil on linen, 180 × 96 in.

In the dream, my brother and I are returning home with the dogs after fetching the family milk cow, Nancy, from a faraway pasture. A violent winter storm descends on us before we reach home. It's terribly dark, windy and cold. We kill the cow so that the dogs might survive the night by crawling inside her to stay warm. My brother and I reach home and sleep in a warm house through the night. Next morning the storm has subsided, we return to the site of the killing. The "dogs" emerge from the hollowed-out cow, and out of their mouths come harsh accusations and scolding—in the form of Moses-like tablets. They reprimand us for not being more thoughtful, for being disobedient, and for not being good enough.

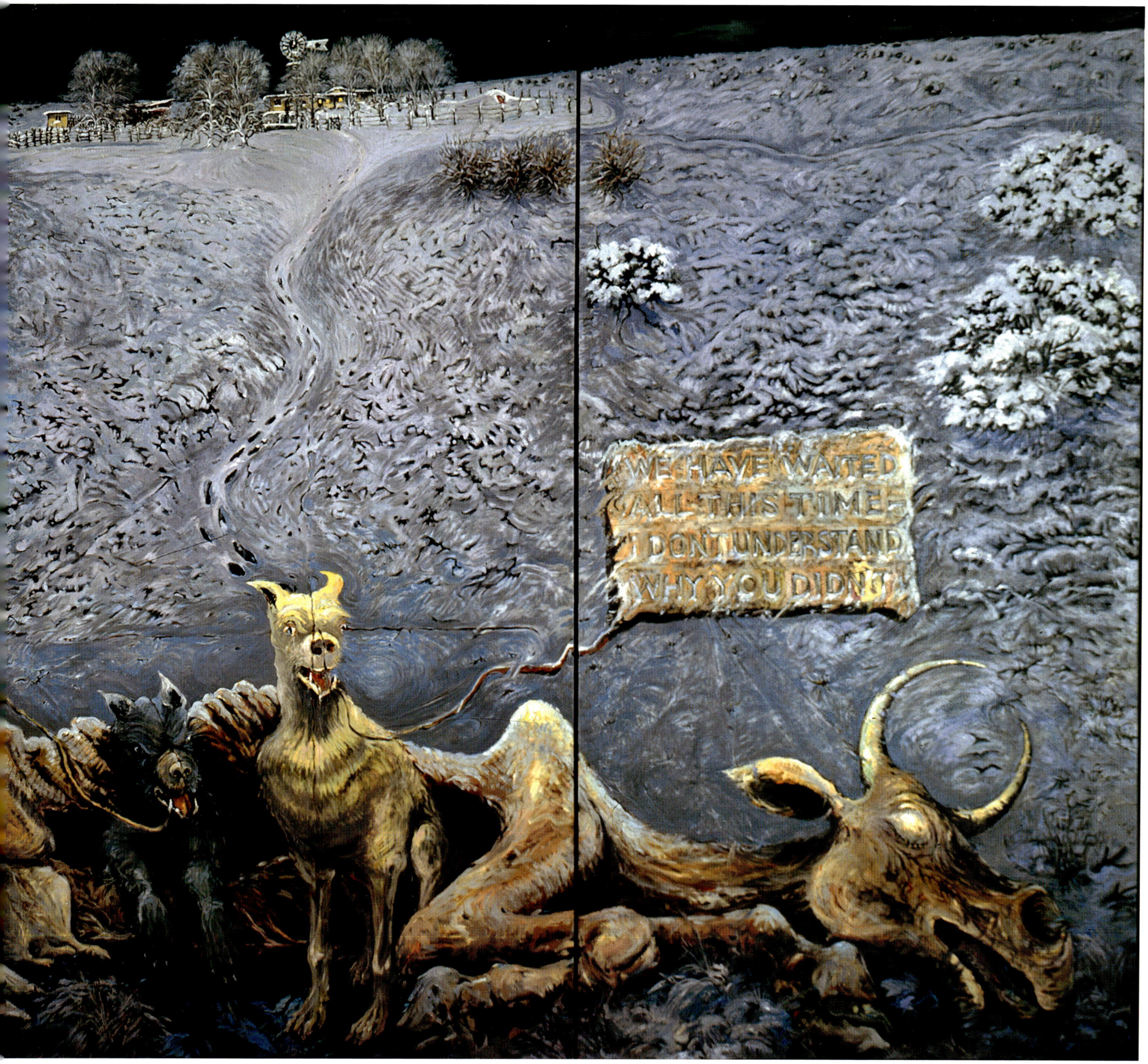
WE HAVE WAITED
ALL THIS TIME
I DONT UNDERSTAND
WHY YOU DIDNT

14.
The Search, 1983
Oil on linen, 72 × 86 in.
Private collection

The human species has for centuries attempted to gain psychological and physical insight from other animals. Unfortunately we usually need to kill them in order to make that transformation. In this painting two men dressed in bearskins stumble across a frozen landscape carrying a kerosene lantern. For we modern humans this process of becoming one with nature is a slow, plodding process.

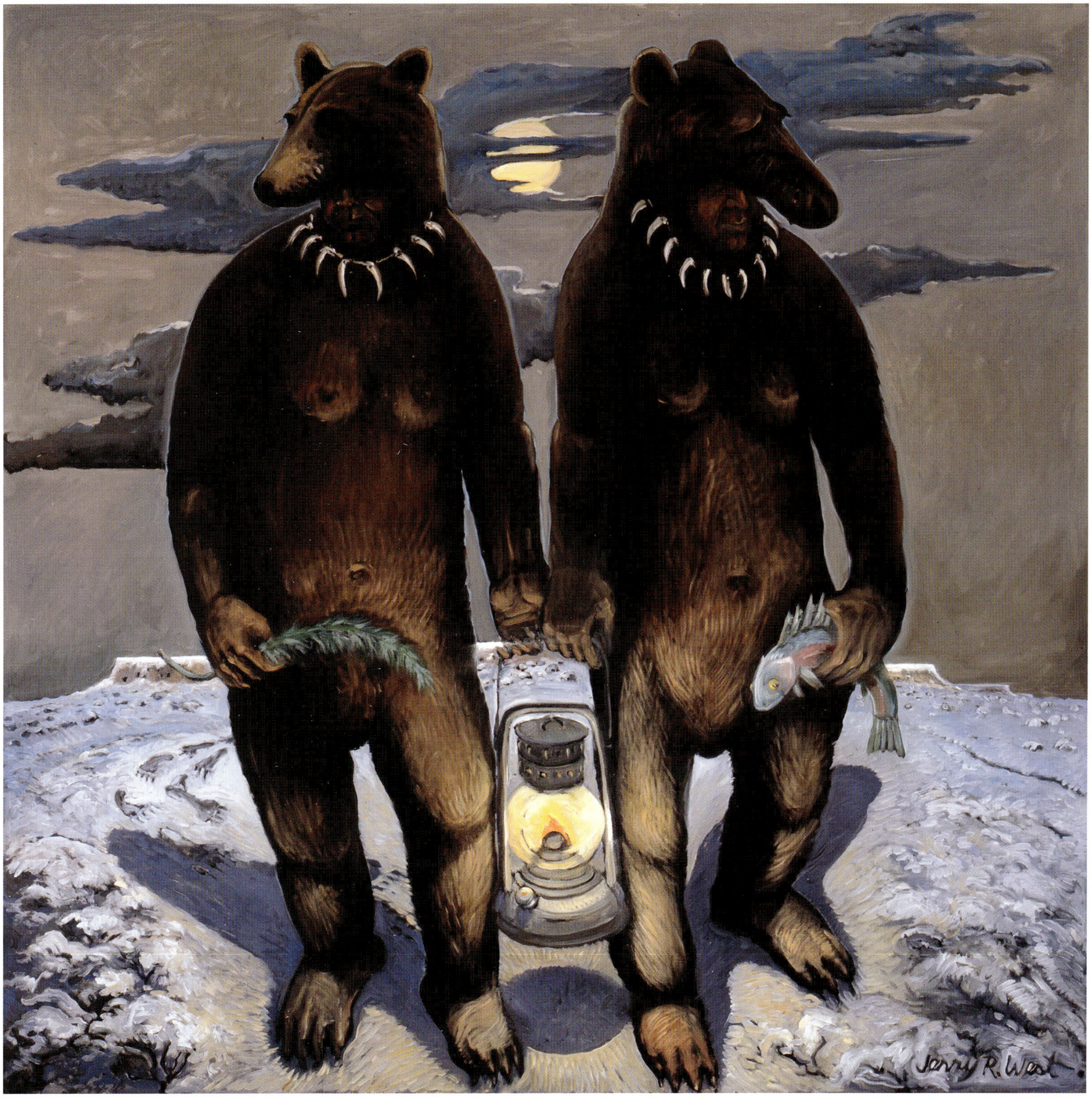
Jerry R. West

15.
Night Passage, 1988
Oil on linen, 42 × 46 in.

There was a period in the war years 1944–45 when my father was very ill. Among many other issues he had been diagnosed with a brain tumor. The tumor made him susceptible to severe convulsions that could erupt anytime, day or night. It fell to me, the middle kid, to sleep with my papa and if he had a convulsion, prevent him from choking, swallowing his tongue, or hurting his arms or head. I can clearly remember waking up in the middle of the night to hear if he was still breathing. The dogs in the painting are borrowed from the belief system of the ancients that they carried the soul off into other dimensions.

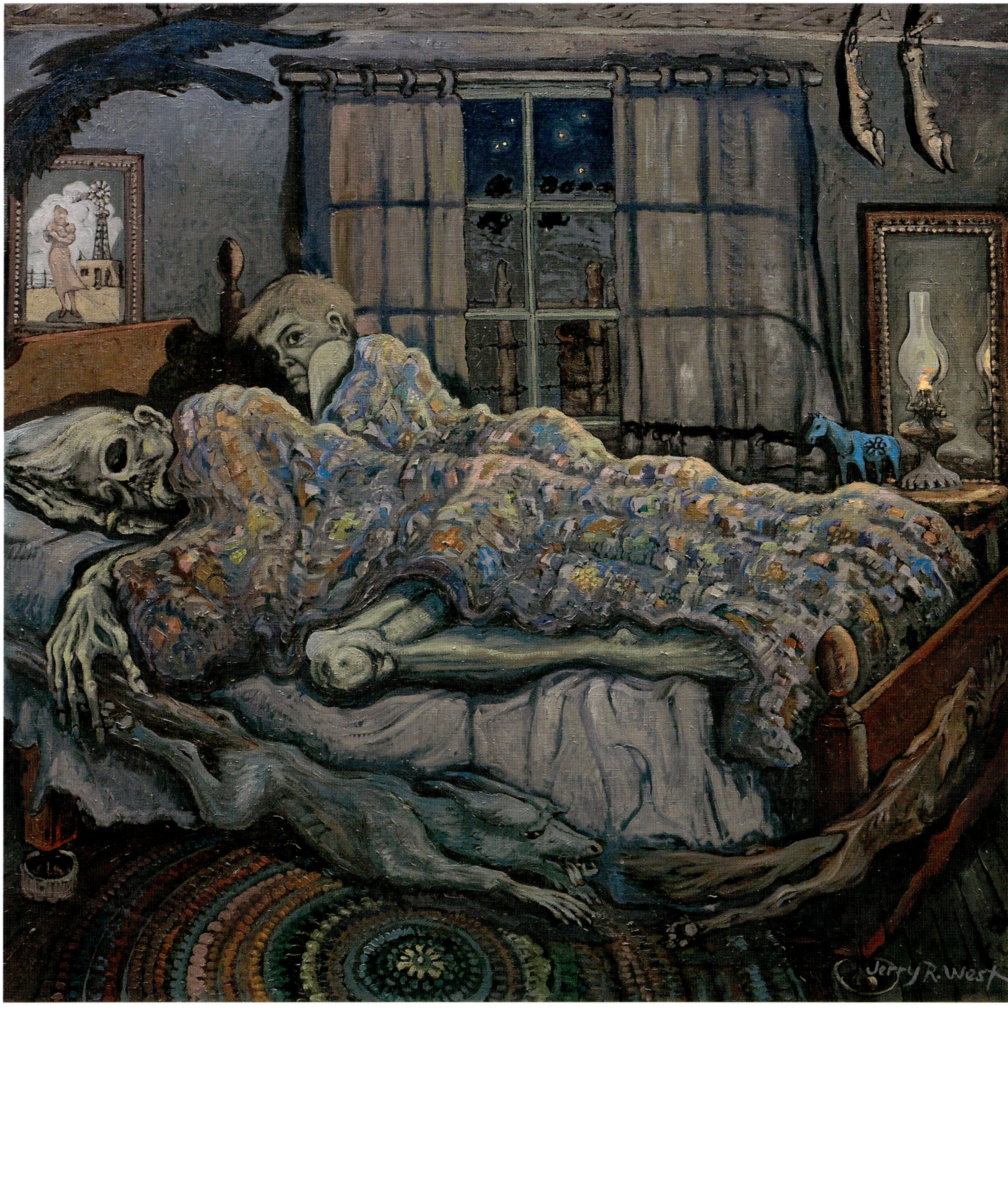
Jerry R. West

16.
Return to Milk Can Town, 1986
Oil on linen, 48 × 72 in.
Collection of Weston DeWalt

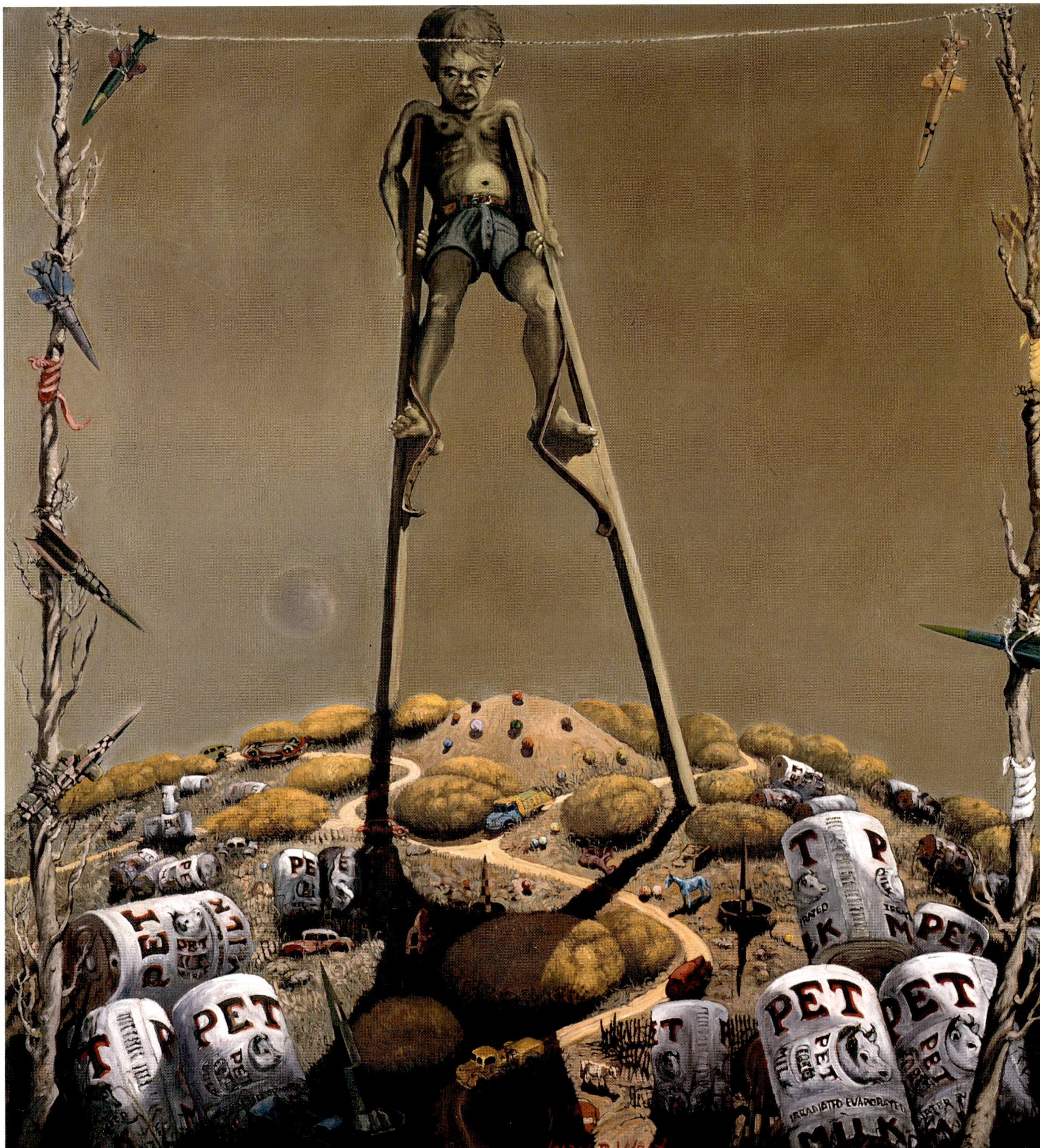
PET
Jerry R West

17.
Boy with Porcupine, 1984
Oil on linen, 48 × 56 in.
Collection of Van Deren and Joan Coke

When I was very young, my dad told me stories of killing porcupines and using them for food. Sometime in my young life, when things were very difficult at home, with my father ill and money and food in short supply, I, whose job it was to bring the cow home in the evening for milking, came across a very old porcupine. I managed to kill it with stones. I carried it home thinking I would be a hero and rewarded with kindness. Instead I was made fun of for doing the wrong thing. The whole incident greatly impacted me, and the memory of it all has never left me.

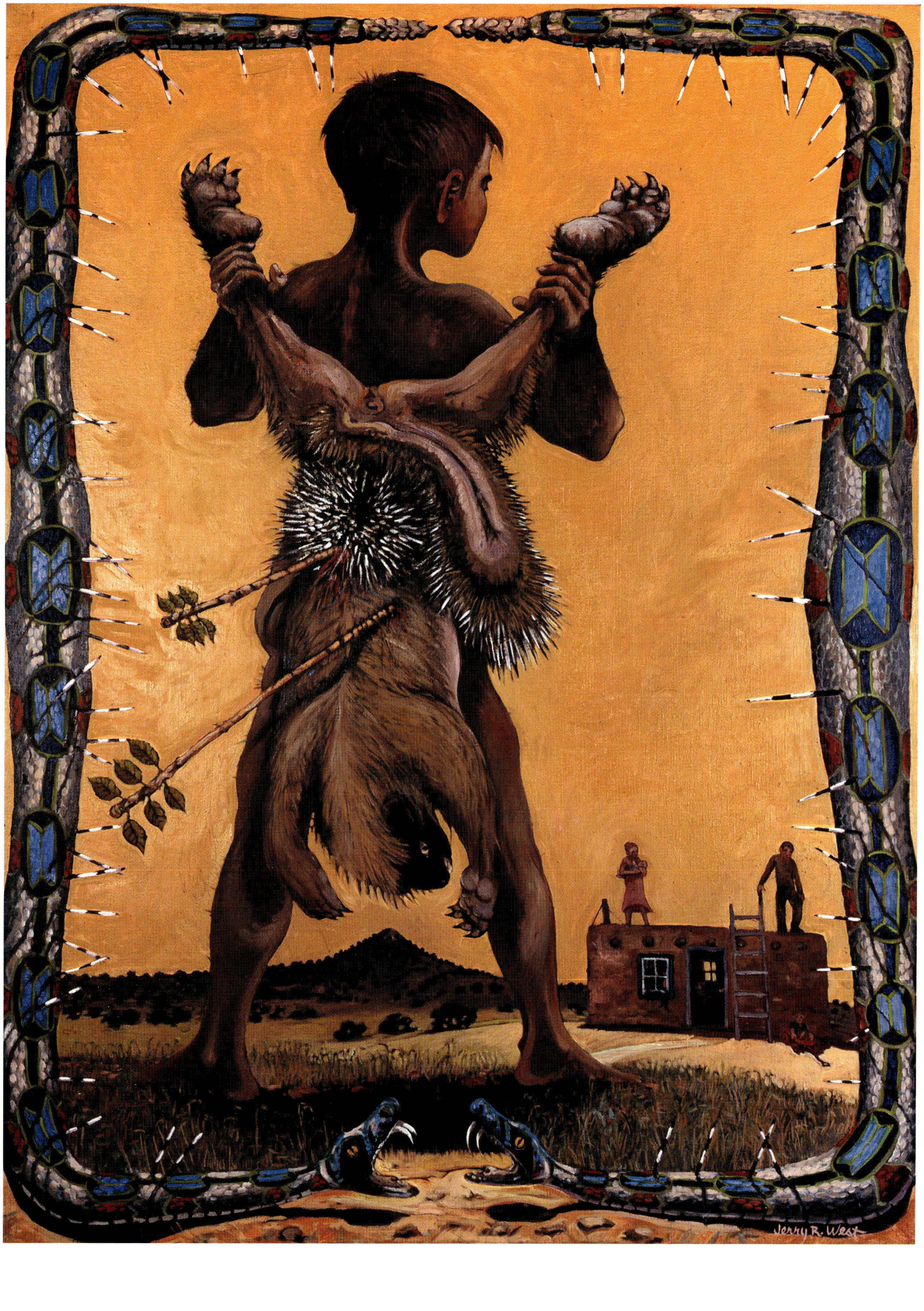
Jerry R. West

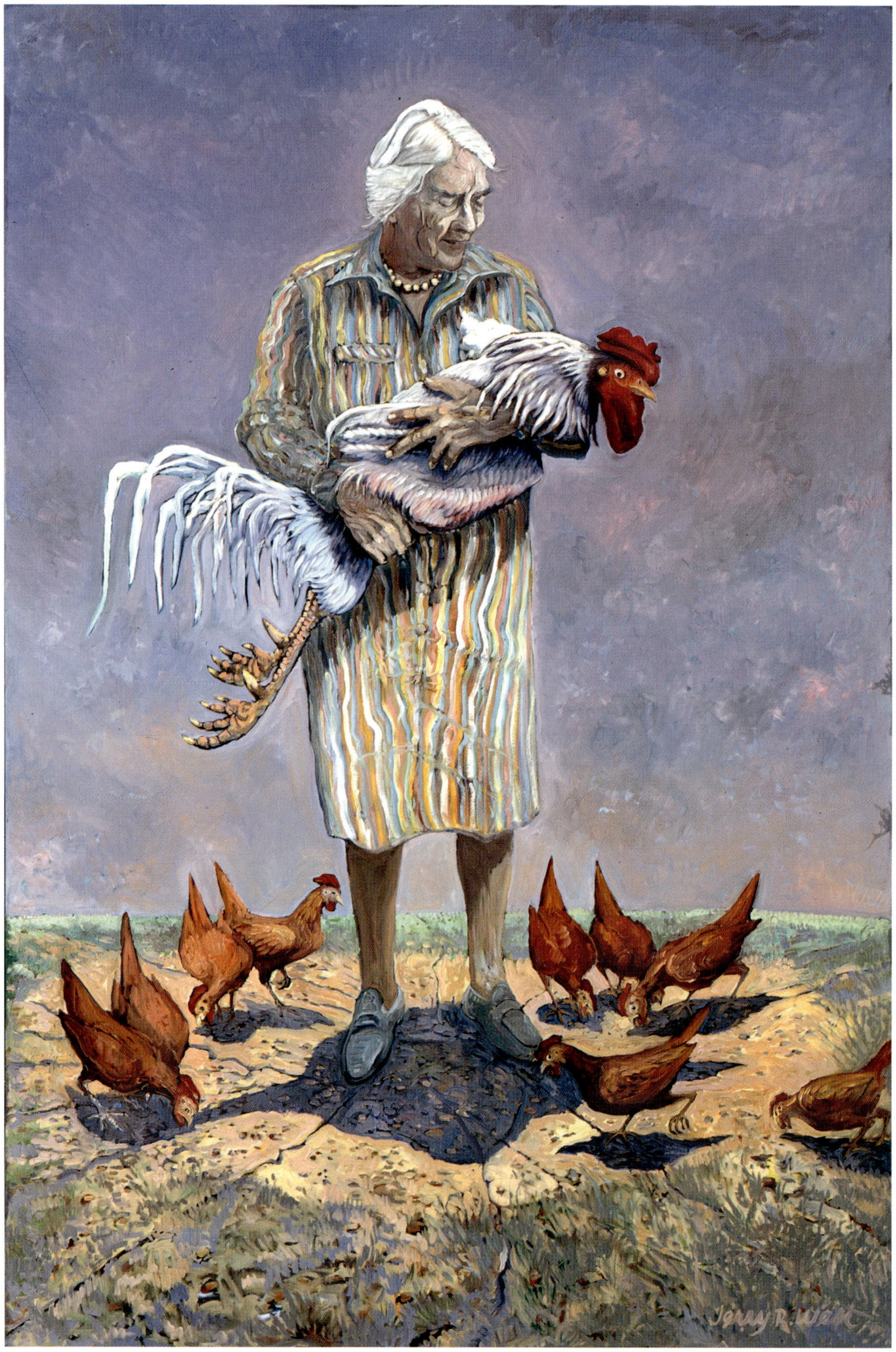

18.
Prairie Matriarch with Rooster, 1988
Oil on linen, 48 × 72 in.
Collection of Ray Graham

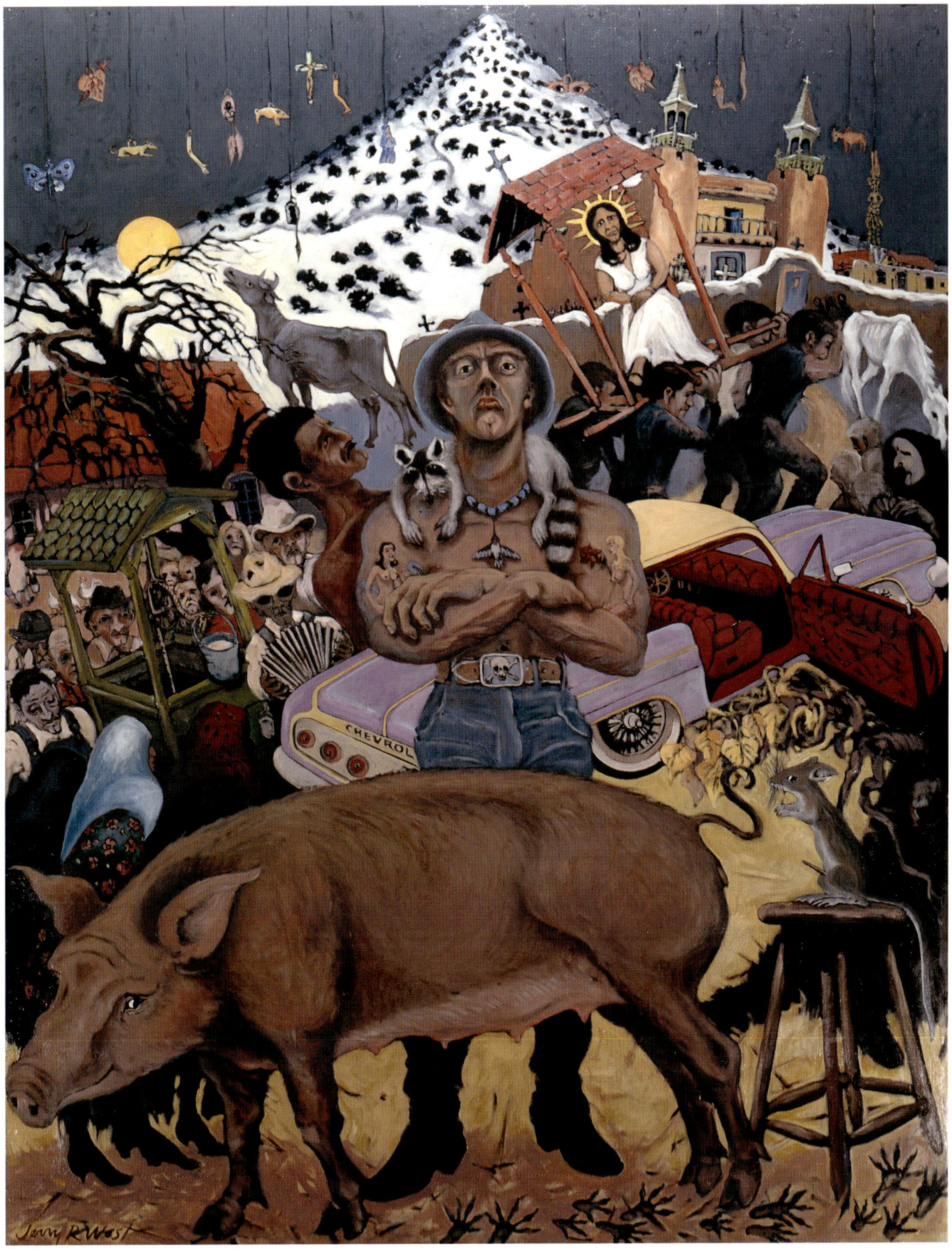

19.
A New Mexico Procession, 1984
Oil on Masonite, 36 × 48 in.
Collection of The Albuquerque Museum

20.
Flight over Juárez, 1981
Oil on Masonite, 48 × 36 in.
Collection of Barbara Gehring

In this flying dream, our dad, Hal, launches my brother, Archie, and me from the back streets of Juárez by pulling us with the old Ford, and we glide up and over the city.

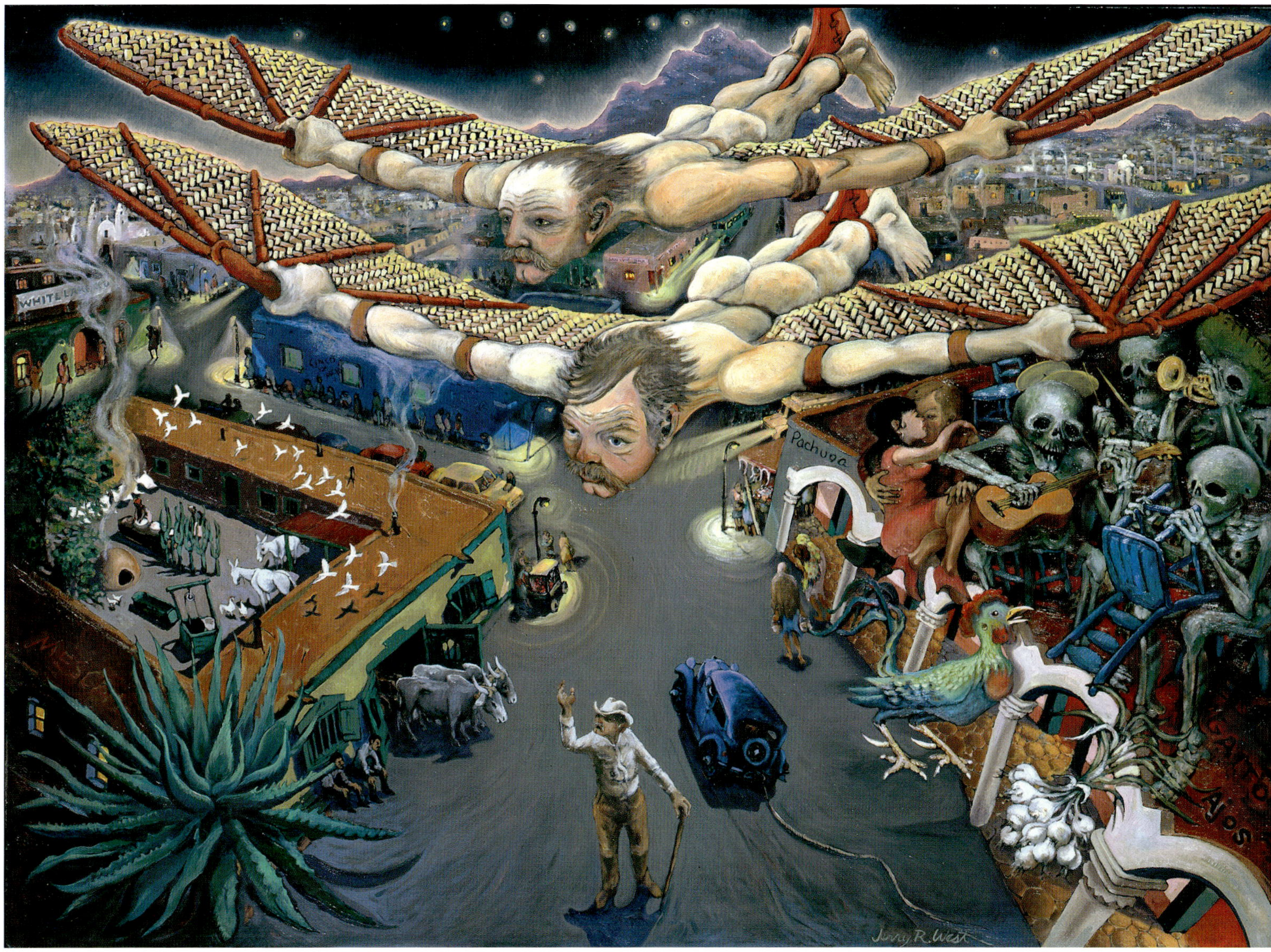
Pachuca

21.
Flight in Ice Cube over the Old Arroyo de Gallina Sheep Camp, 1990
Oil on linen, 56 × 72 in.
Collection of Ray Graham

A strange dream in which Archie and I are flying in a hollow ice cube with a small trapdoor. Archie sits quietly while I'm nervous and excited. We swoop over the prairie world and finally over the old Gallina Sheep Camp where the sheepherders would bring their sheep for the summer and camp out in the small adobe shelter. It's late afternoon, and the sheep are coming in for winter. A feeling of fear, sadness, and yet, delight.

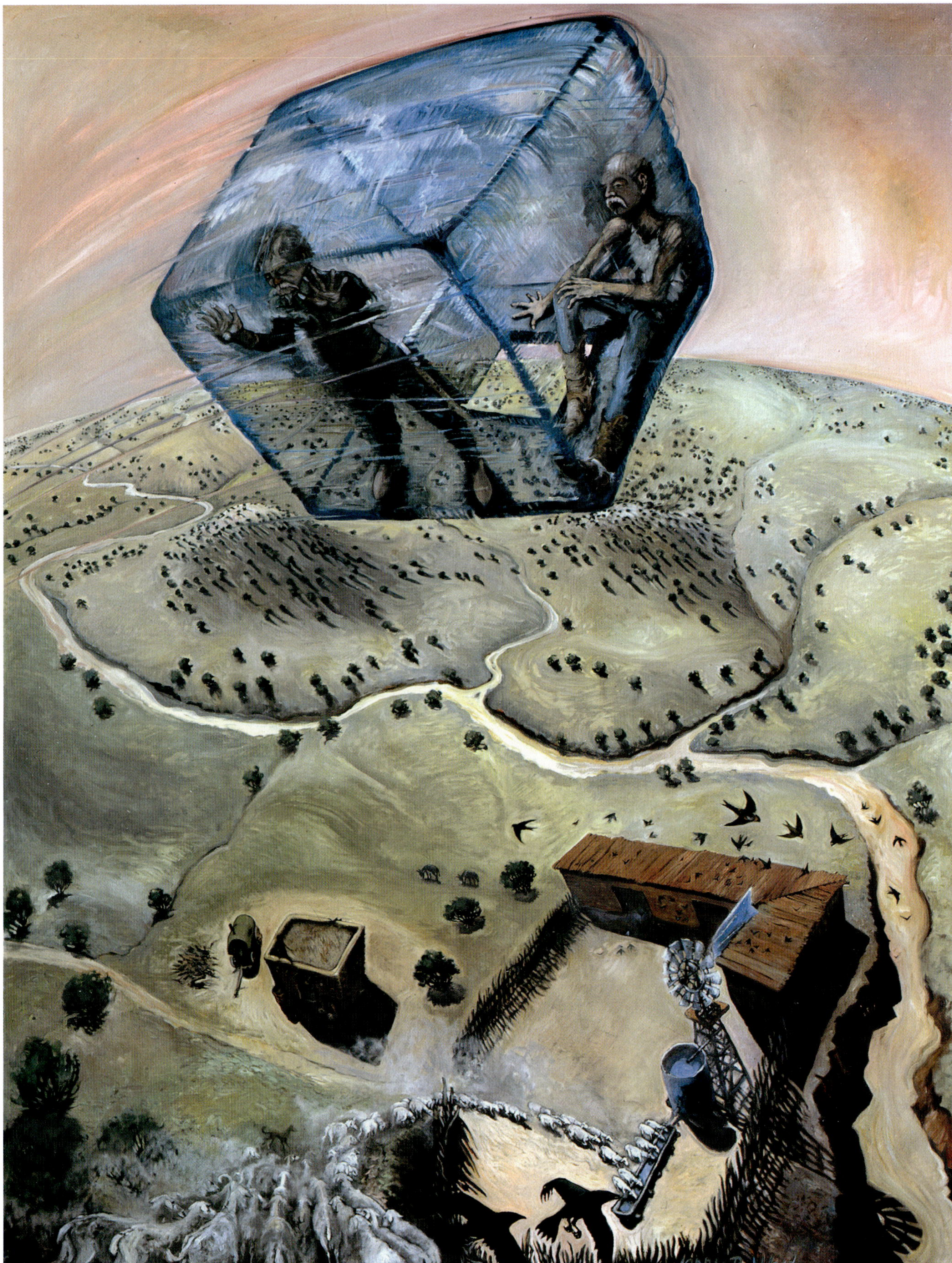
Jerry R. West

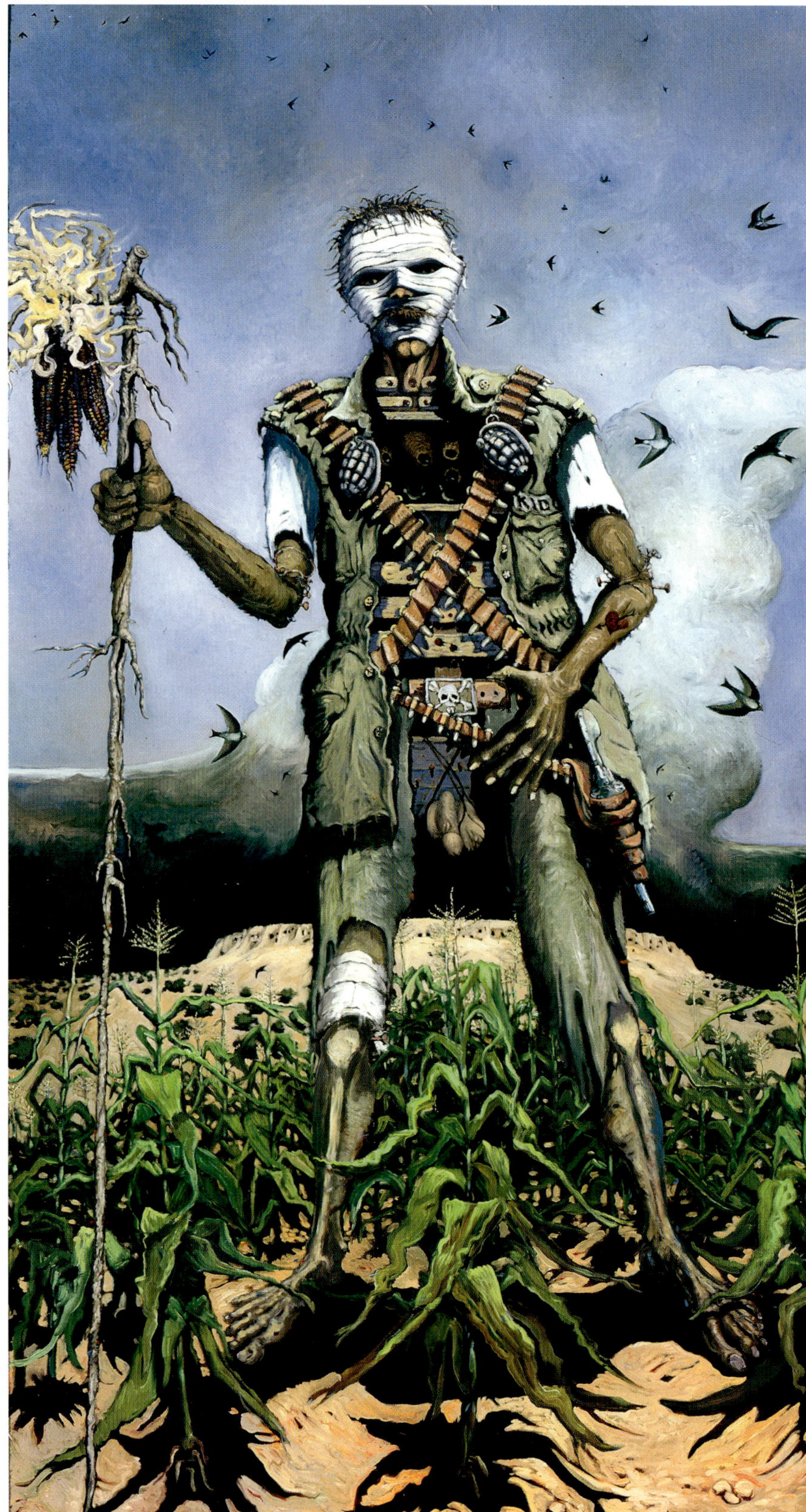

22.
Praire Scarecrow, 1989
Oil on linen, 52 × 96 in.

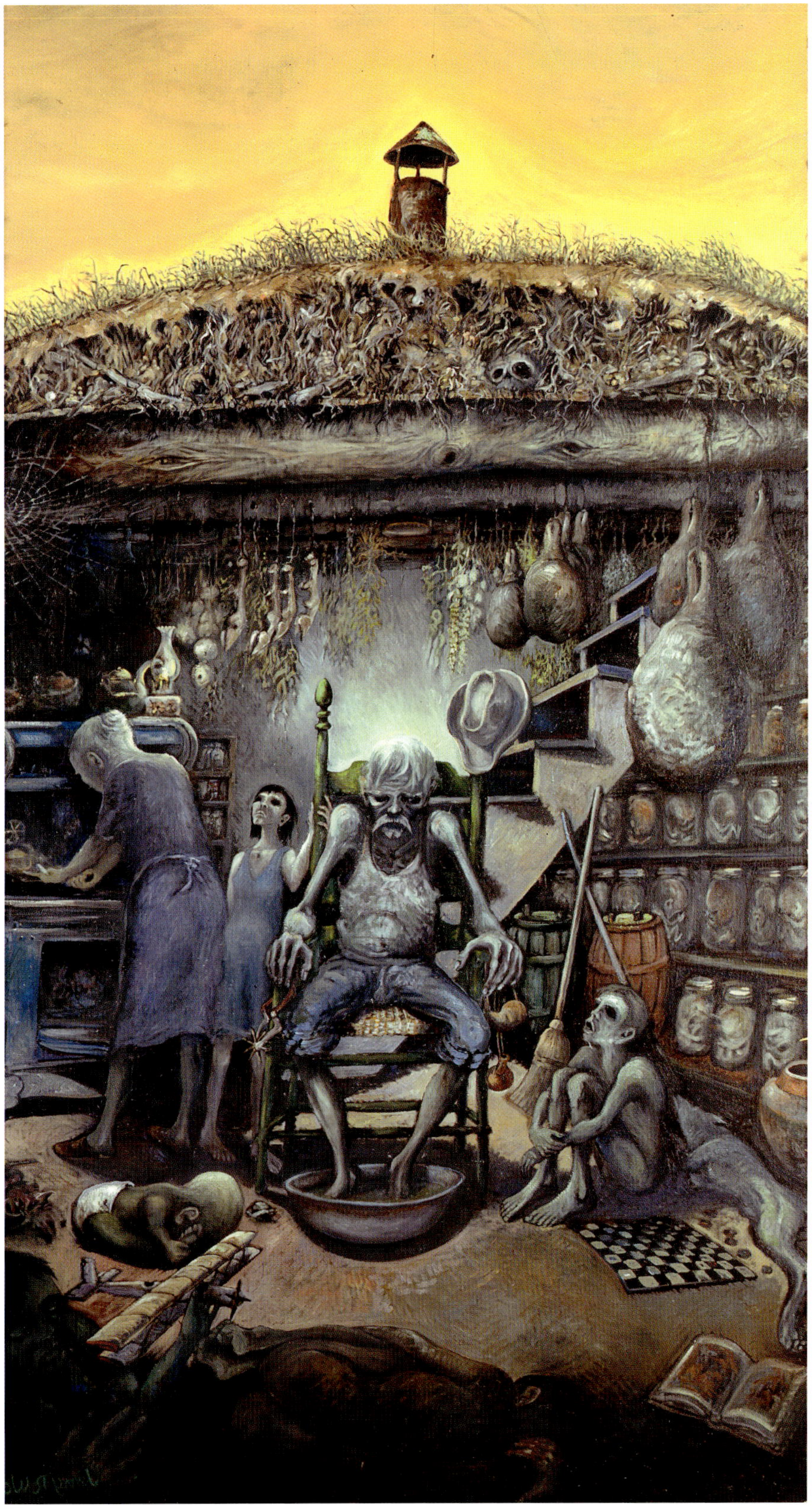

23.
Storm Cellar, Nuclear Family, 1989
Oil on linen, 52 × 96 in.

24.
The Brain and the Black Widow, 1999
Oil on linen, 48 × 72 in.

As a child, my greatest fears were of black widow spiders. In this painting, from a dream, I find myself in a narrow-walled canyon, which, while confining, is nevertheless very beautiful and covered with petroglyphs. When I did this painting, I had recently been diagnosed with an arachnoid cyst on the back of my brain, and I had experienced a claustrophobic MRI scan. The fear of finding a poisonous spider at the back of my neck is juxtaposed with the safety and beauty of the open-air canyon.

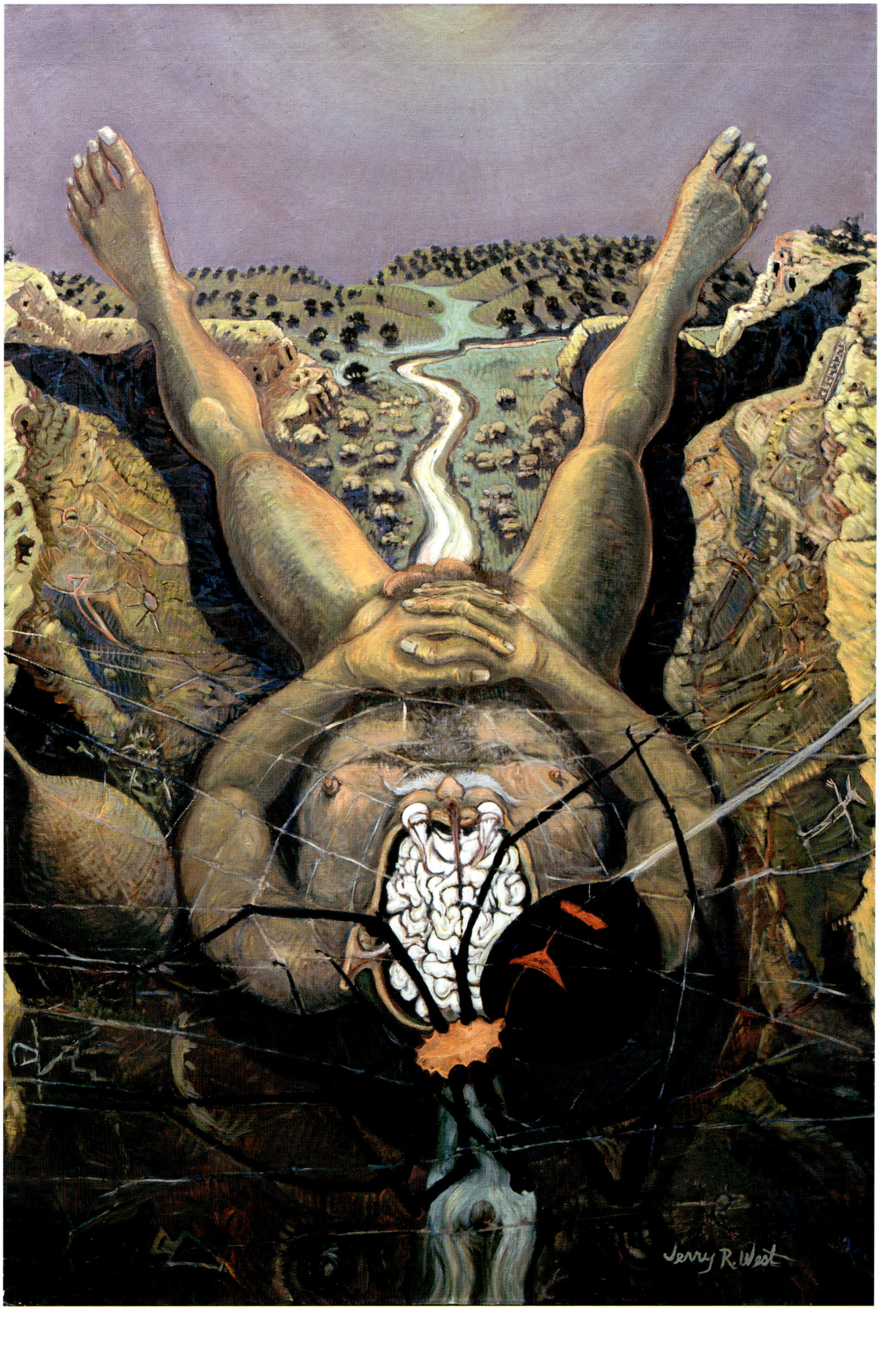
Jerry R. West

25.
Corporeal Survey, 2000
Oil on linen, 48 × 62 in.

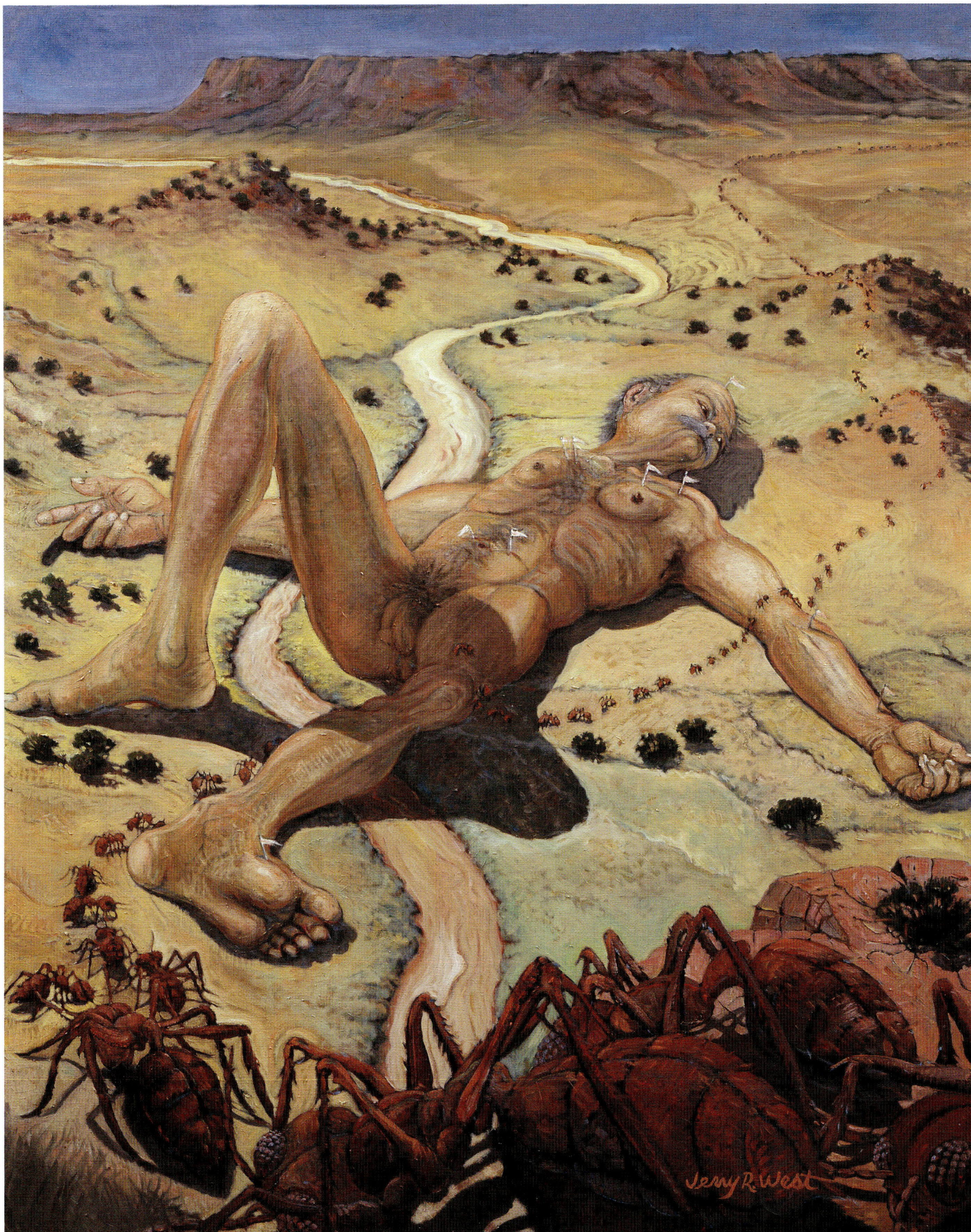
Jerry R. West

26.
The Voyage, 1988
Oil on linen, 48 × 72 in.
Private collection

In *The Voyage* I have painted a symbol of the fragility and the strength of humankind. Both female and male figures cling to each other and to the giant fish. Surrealistically, it flies over the arroyos and the prairie world. Symbolically, it may be read as a powerful sexual energy, perhaps of love and deep caring, and a confirmation of a vital life force.

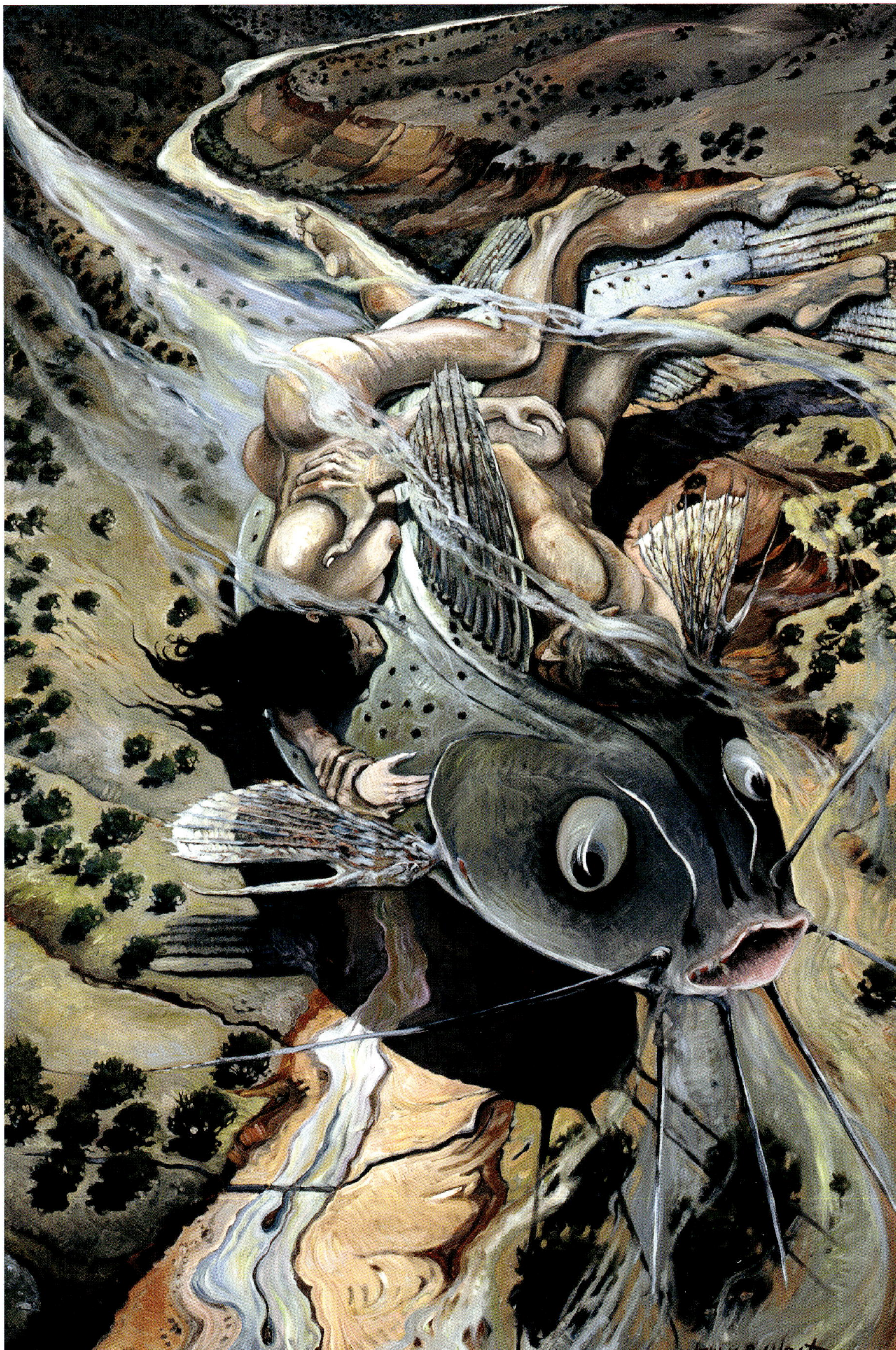
Jerry R. West

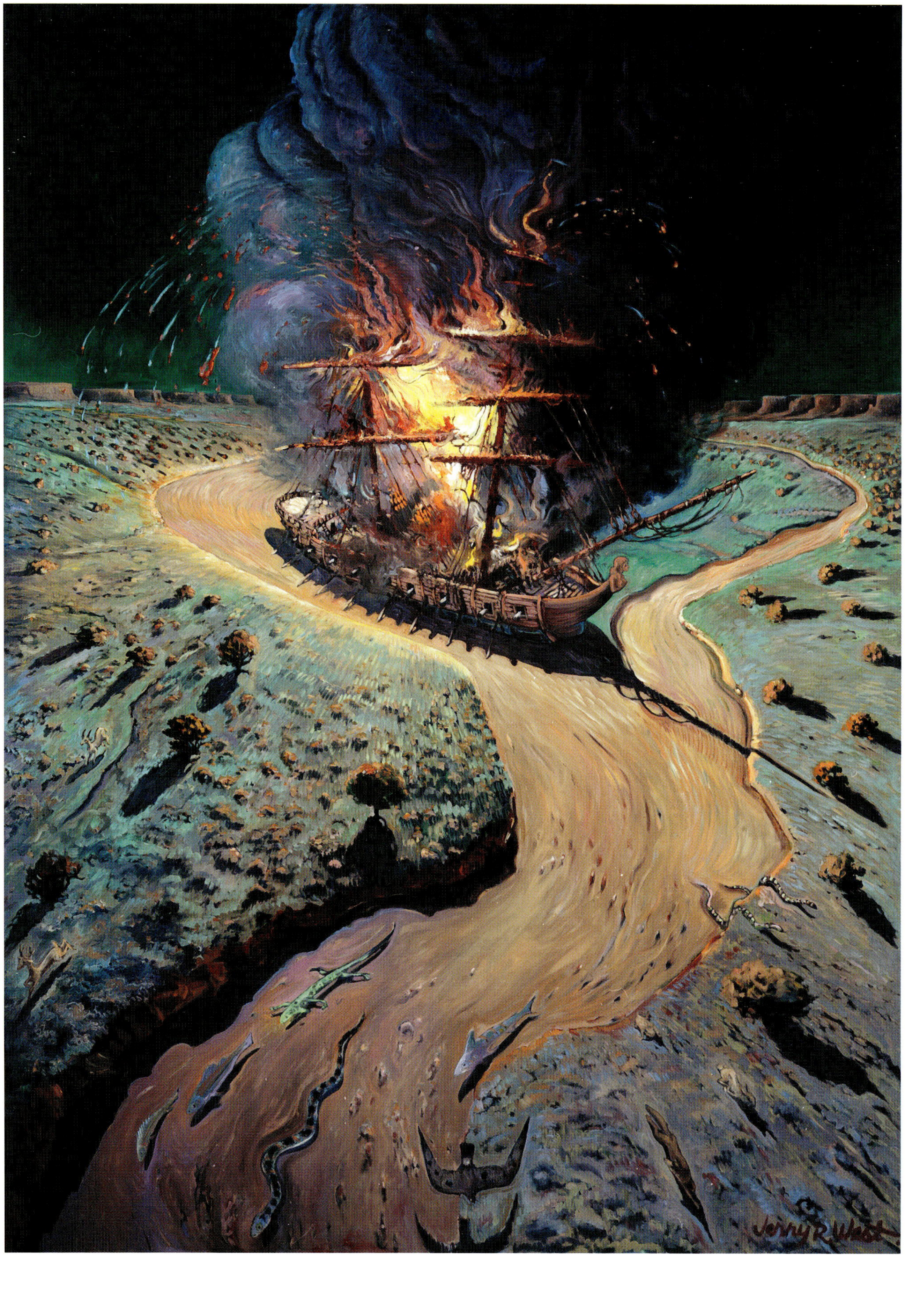
Jerry R. West

III. Of Fire and Other Instrusions

In the 1980s, when my work was being exhibited in Santa Fe at Arlene LewAllen's gallery, my practice was to put together shows that generally followed a theme or had an overall philosophical intention. Ideas associated with fire have always intrigued me. Throughout my life I have witnessed evidence of fires out of control. I have seen forest fires and smoke from a distance and walked through burned forests. When I was young, I kept company with Lipio Gonzales, a Forest Service fire lookout, up in his fire tower high on Puyé Mesa. I have hiked or ridden horseback across the prairie and seen evidence of burned-out homes, sheds, and mining shacks. I've hiked to ancient Pueblo Indian sites and found evidence of burnt corn and timbers, often the remains of entire pueblos that had burned. My Uncle Gene West's house burned in the mid-1940s, probably the result of a poorly installed chimney. As a child I accidently set fire to grasslands and watched, horrified, as it spread with uncontrolled speed.

Through the years I have been interested in paintings about fire and in exploring the psychological and philosophical dimensions of the subject. I think the complexity of what fire is capable of can never be exhausted. Since the invention of gunpowder, firepower has only escalated.

Los Alamos National Laboratory, the birthplace of the atomic bomb, is part of the environment of northern New Mexico. On my birthday, July 13, 1945, Robert Oppenheimer and his team drove the nuclear material for Fat Boy through the Santa Fe Plaza in the trunk of an old Chevrolet. Less than a week later they dropped the test bomb in Oscuro in the Tularosa Basin north of White Sands. A few weeks after that the United States dropped atomic bombs on Hiroshima and Nagasaki. Ever since those events we have been trying to mitigate the ever-present threat of nuclear war. All of this has led to

27.
Prairie Fire Beginning, 1988
Oil on linen, 60 × 80 in.
New Mexico Capitol Art Collection,
New Mexico State Capitol, Santa Fe

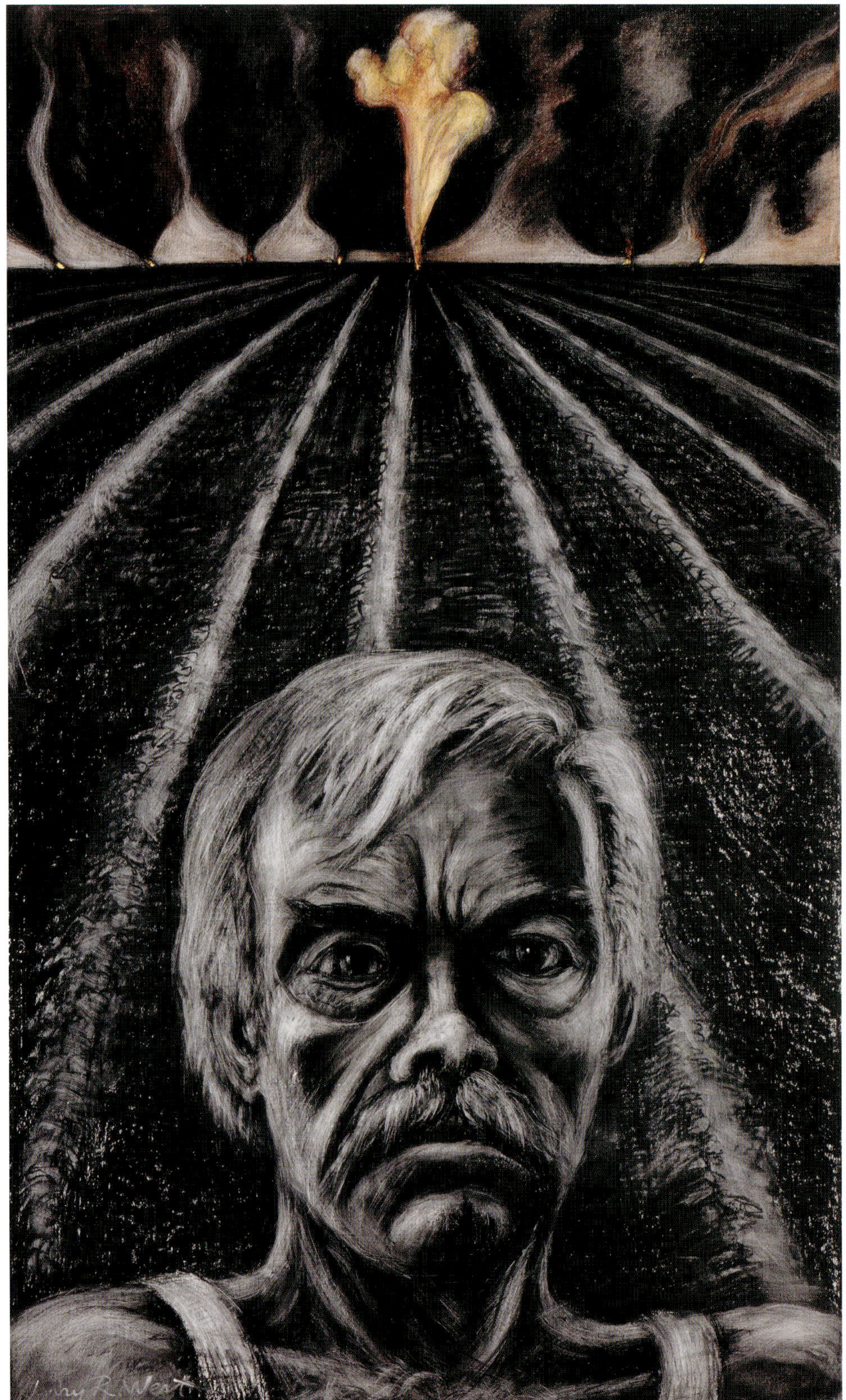

28.
Gulf Fire with Man, 1991
Charcoal and pastels, 36 × 60 in.

an amazing alteration of the human psyche, a deep and overarching angst that has affected humankind the world over. I join many artists who have, over the years, attempted to deal with this colossal change and the enormous threat to life on this planet.

In some of my paintings, I have returned to old memories of fire in an attempt to find metaphors that express my own thoughts on this subject. I offer up a selection as part of my meditation on the subject of fire and other intrusions.

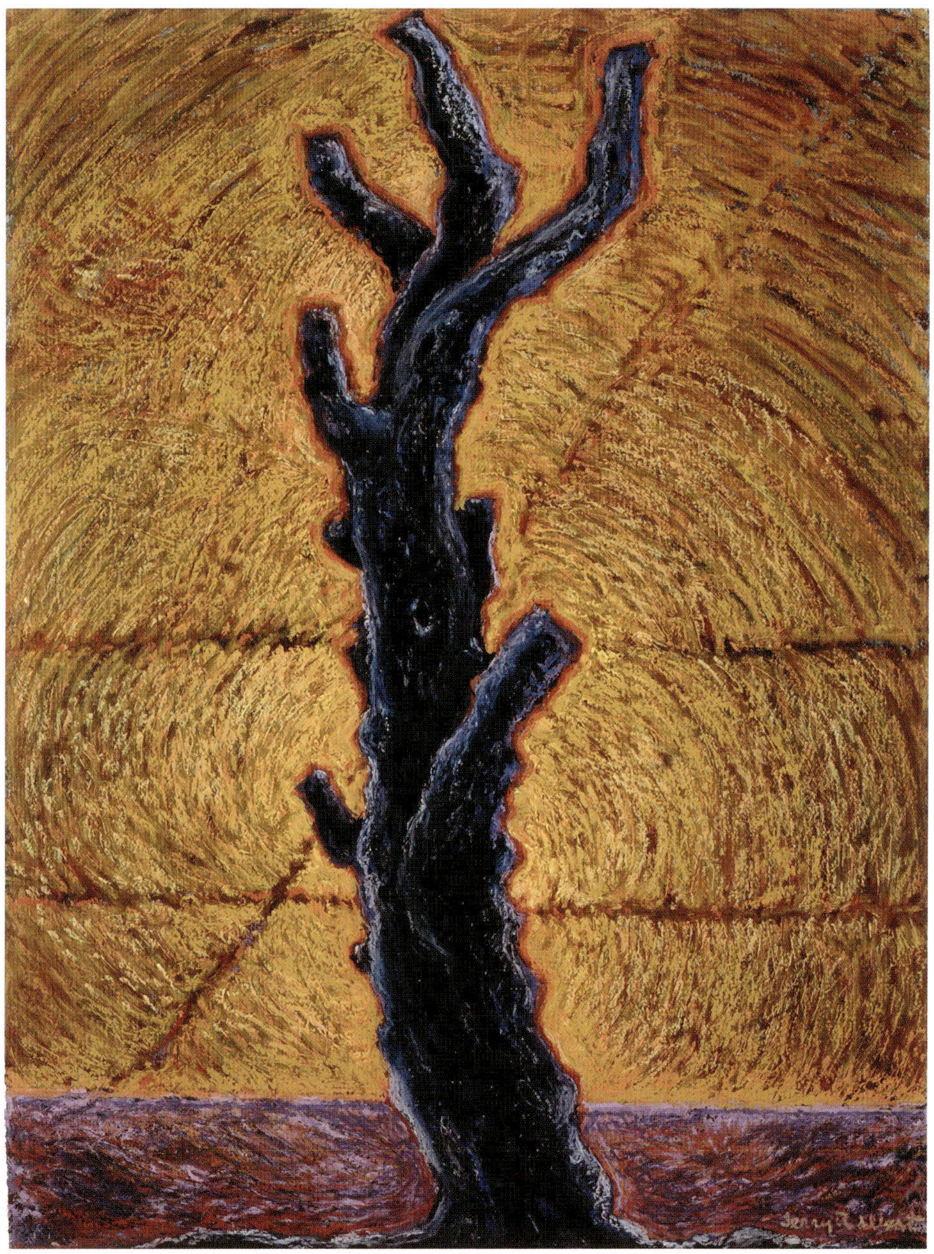

29.
Tree Icon, 1990
Oil stick on paper, 18 × 26 in.

30.
Prairie Fire with Homestead, 1991
Acrylic on paper, 36 × 24 in.
Collection of Celia and James Medrano

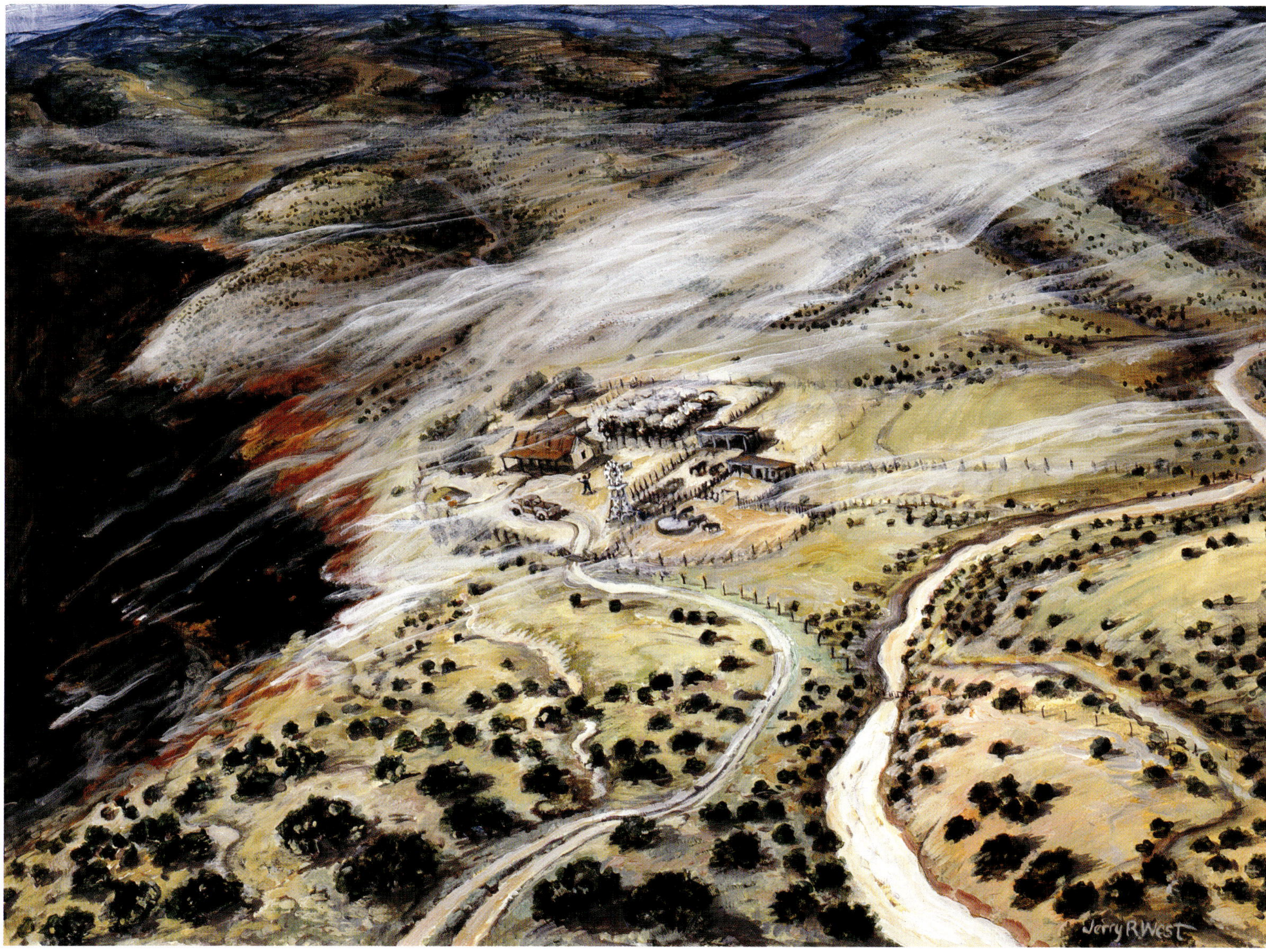
Jerry R West

31.
Exodus from Kosovo, 1999
Oil on linen, 60 x 72 in.

During the war in Kosovo in 1998, and after a trip to India where I had fallen in love with camels, I painted this image of people leaving devastated homes, taking what is necessary. I put myself in this painting as a little boy leading the family camel—the camel carrying the family bones. The bones are an image I borrowed from Faulkner telling of one of the Snopes offspring who returns from his adventures in the West carrying only a bag of family bones. And I also am pushing my mother in a wheelbarrow.

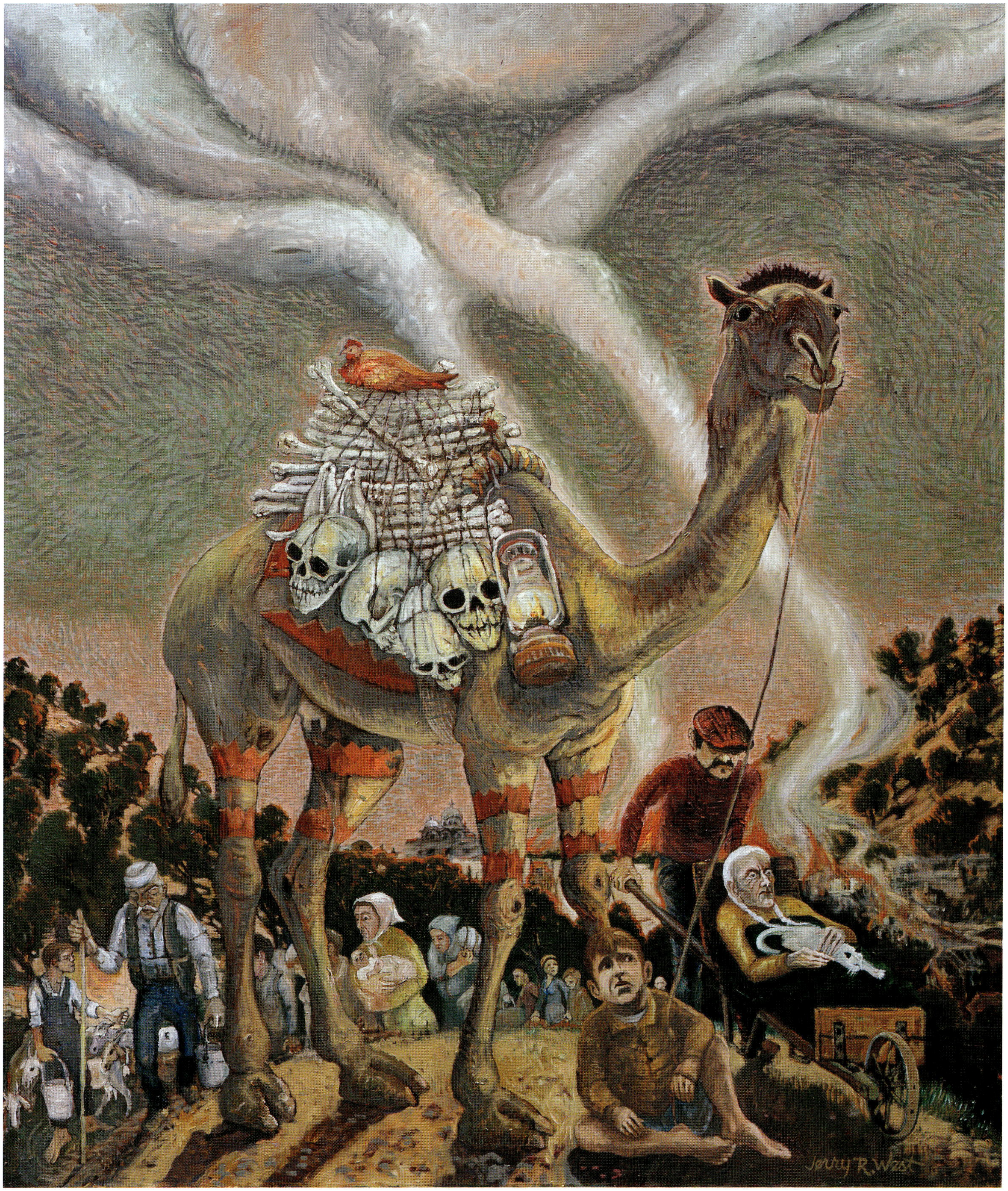
Jerry R. West

32.
Rocking Horse with Prairie Fire, 1991
Oil on Masonite, 24 × 38 in.
Collection of Paris Brisko

In the mid-1940s Uncle Gene West's house caught fire—probably the result of a poorly designed chimney—while he and his family were away on a short errand. They returned just in time to gather a group of well-intentioned neighbors, and with the old-fashioned system of a "water brigade" they passed buckets from a distant small pond we knew as Coyote Springs. How terrible and pathetic, their attempt to put out a huge roaring fire with tiny buckets of water.

When they all finally gave up and were gathered at a safe distance from the burning house, my father did a strange thing. He suddenly grabbed a blanket and rushed into the building. We all stood amazed and anxious, hardly breathing. He—after what seemed ages to me—reappeared carrying only a small rocking horse. Hal had designed that little horse and rocker, and his brother Gene had built and carved it. It had been a Christmas present for Gene's son, my little cousin Russell.

Russell would eventually grow up, to be a bronc rider, a rancher, father, and a family guy. He was in many ways an amazing person but forever troubled. His life ended too soon. This painting served as a metaphor for the collective tragedies that so many families have had to endure.

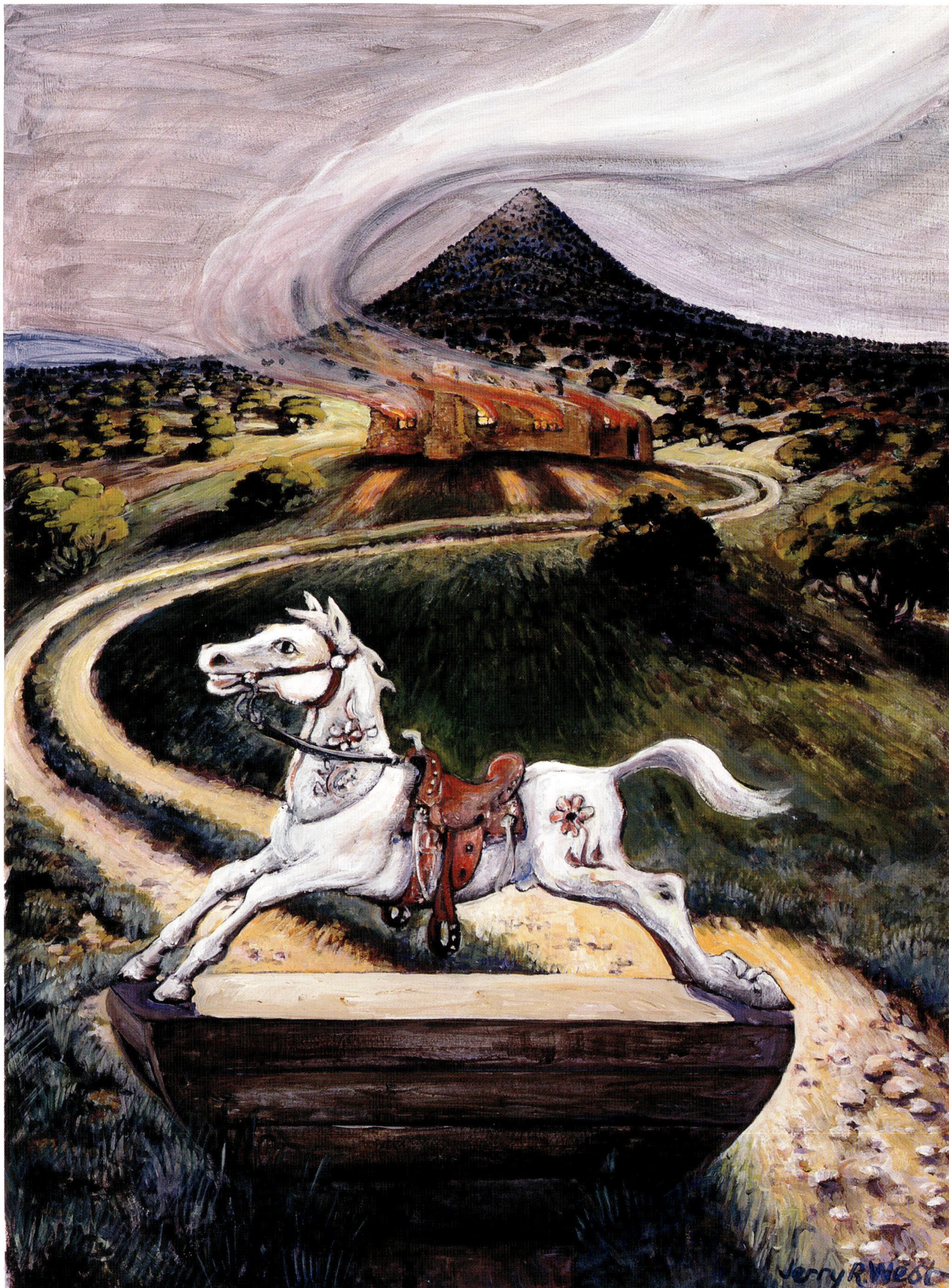
Jerry R. West

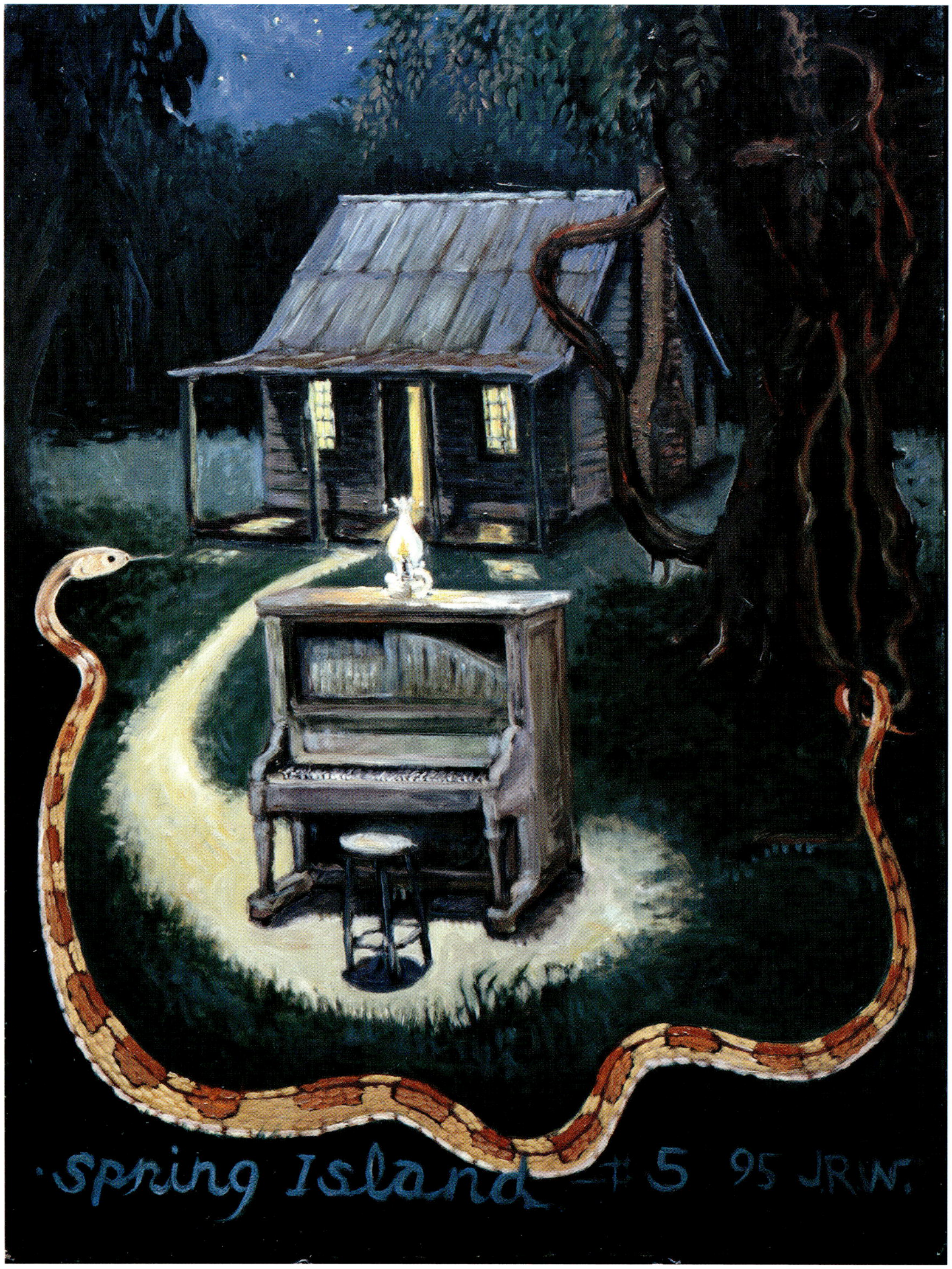

33.
Spring Island: Old Slave Cabin with Snake and Piano, 1995
Oil on Masonite, 24 × 30 in.
Private collection

34.
Living on the Edge, 2002
Oil on linen, 48 × 56 in.
Collection of Povi LaFarge Bigbee and John Bigbee

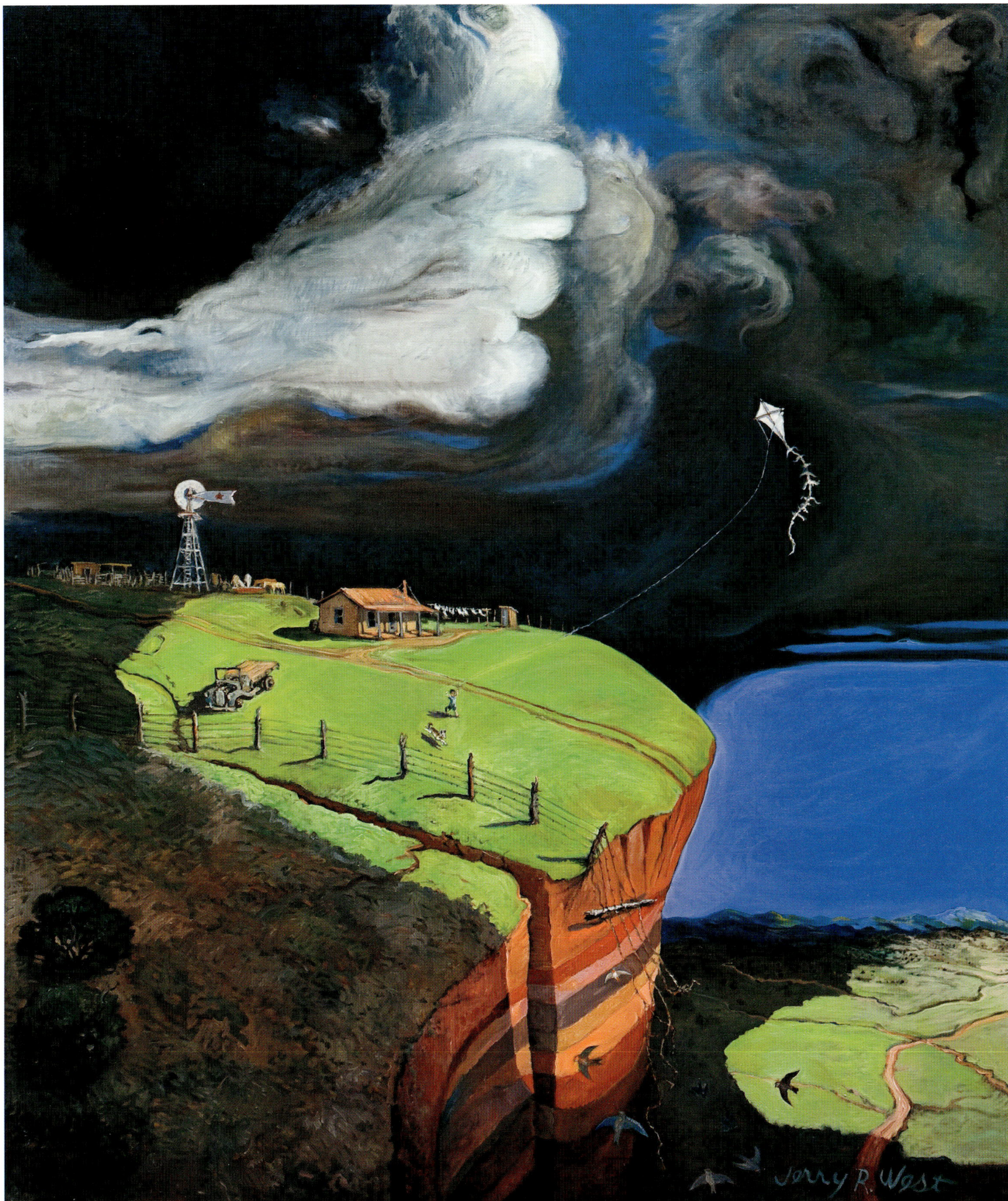
Jerry R. West

35.
Prairie Pillars with Five Ravens, 2003
Oil on linen, 50 × 72 in.
Collection of Charlie Ramsburg and Michele Zackheim

In my dream, I am walking down a row of old homestead fence posts. Suddenly, I realize the posts begin to resemble sculptured pillars that represent my parents. In the background there is an old adobe homestead on fire. The five ravens could represent the five offspring of those "two prairie pillars."

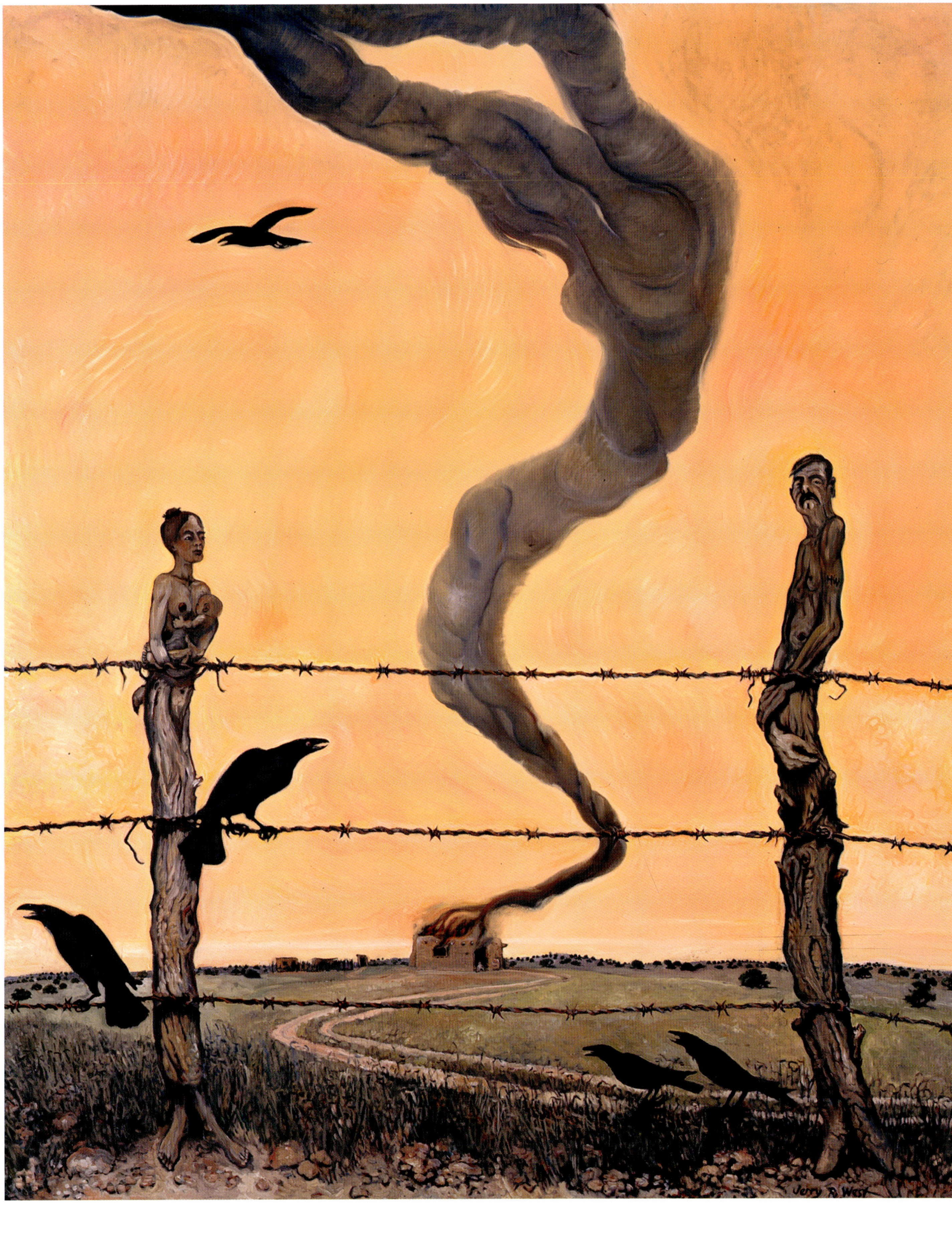
Jerry R West

36.
The Gift Horse, 1988
Oil on linen, 56 × 72 in.
Private collection

Most of us are complicit in the human urge to "help," which has unintended consequences when it becomes something forced on others. And yes, it doesn't matter whether the gift is medicine, technology, food, guns, democracy, or religion—the results are often unpredictable, the gift sometimes an intrusion.

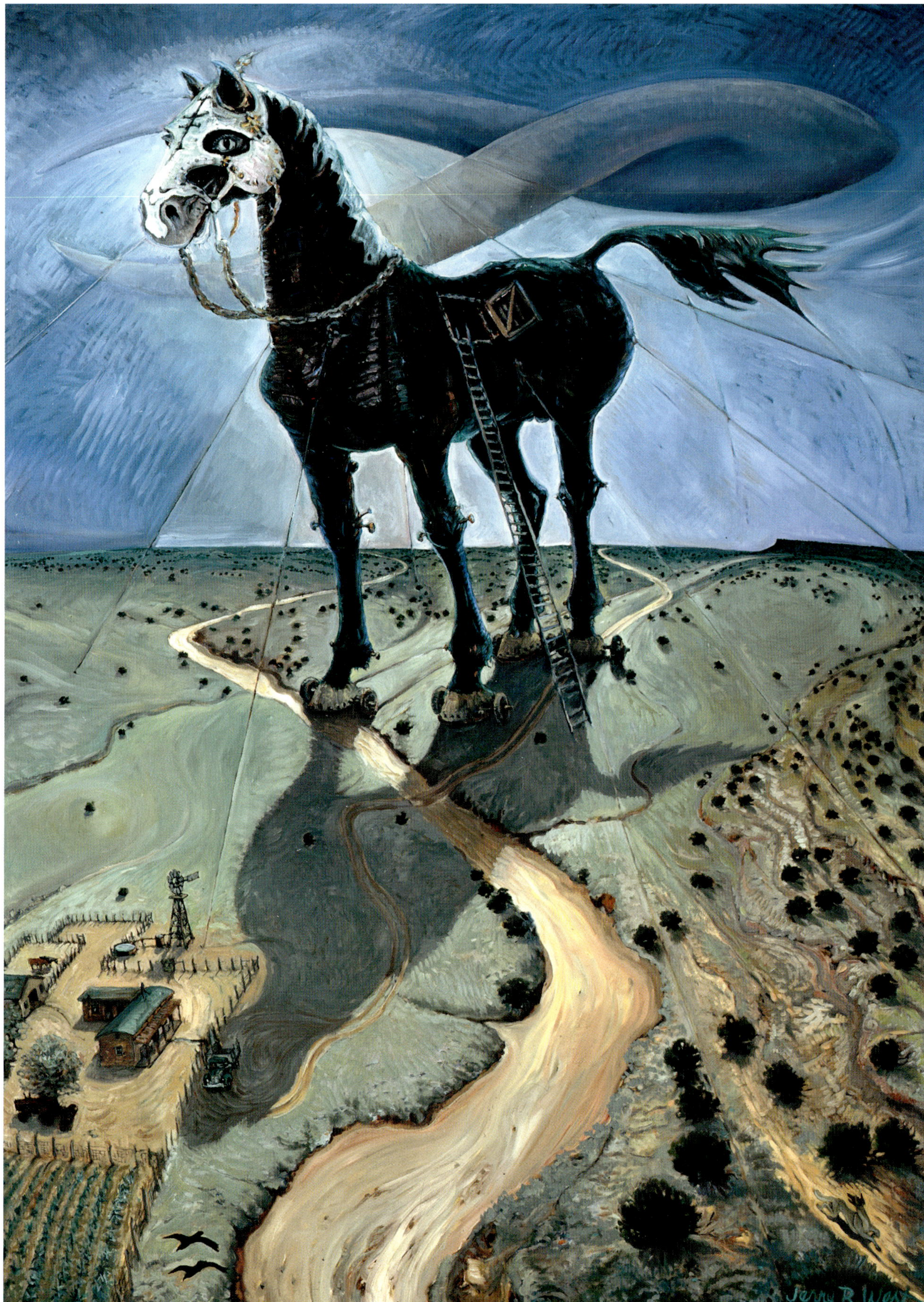
Jerry R. West

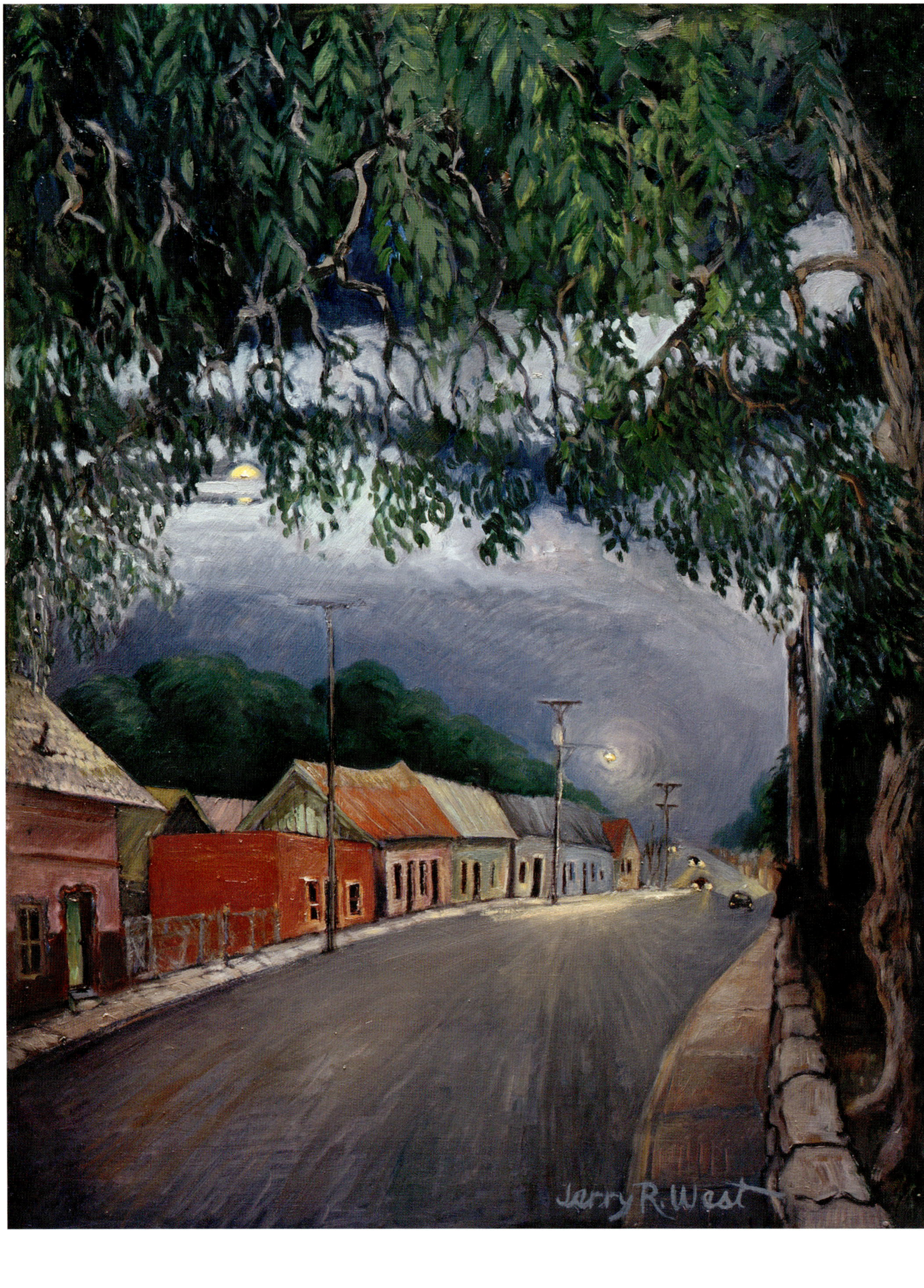
Jerry R. West

IV. Las Vegas Interludes

I have had a long love affair with Las Vegas, New Mexico. I like the color and character of the town, which was a railroad town in decline after World War II. It never became much of a tourist town, and it still struggles with its deep roots of cultural conflict that remain, however, part of the vibrant energy of the place. It has been an influential and reliable element in my painting life. I fell in love with a place and a time, and I fell in love with the decision that led me there: to be an artist.

I arrived in Las Vegas on a shoestring with no place to live in the summer of 1964. A profound personal transformation began. I was stimulated by students and teachers practicing art and by lovely people from the town's long history of political activism. Fundamentally, I underwent an identity renaissance. I made lifetime friends.

Living and working with artists at Highlands University on and off for four years changed my focus completely. I deeply respected my professors there. I will always remember the intense, happy times spent with Elmer Schooley in the etching studio. I was seriously introduced to modernism and grew to respect its tenets, but it was not my path. My path became narrative storytelling.

These years were my Las Vegas interludes. In my art, I sought to capture the magic of that picturesque, historically idiosyncratic environment. After 1980, I continued to maintain a studio in the old Railroad Roundhouse for over two decades. As the years have gone by, I have evolved both personally and artistically, and yet, even after many travels and adventures, Las Vegas still exerts a magnetic influence.

37.
Las Vegas Row Houses under a Full Moon, 1990
Oil on Masonite, 24 × 36 in.
Private collection

38.
Red Car at Columbia Crossing, 1994
Oil on Masonite, 24 × 36 in.
Private collection

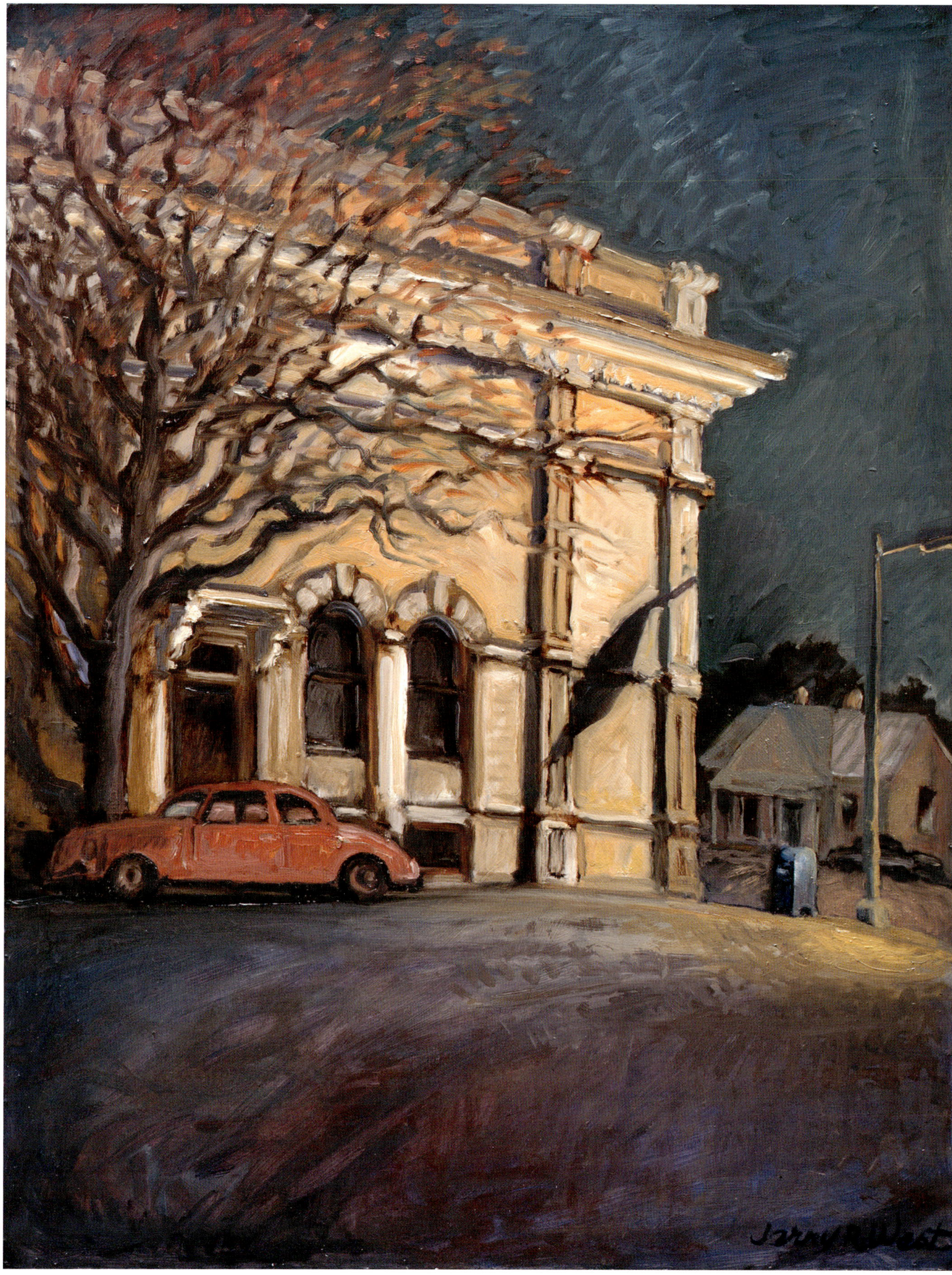

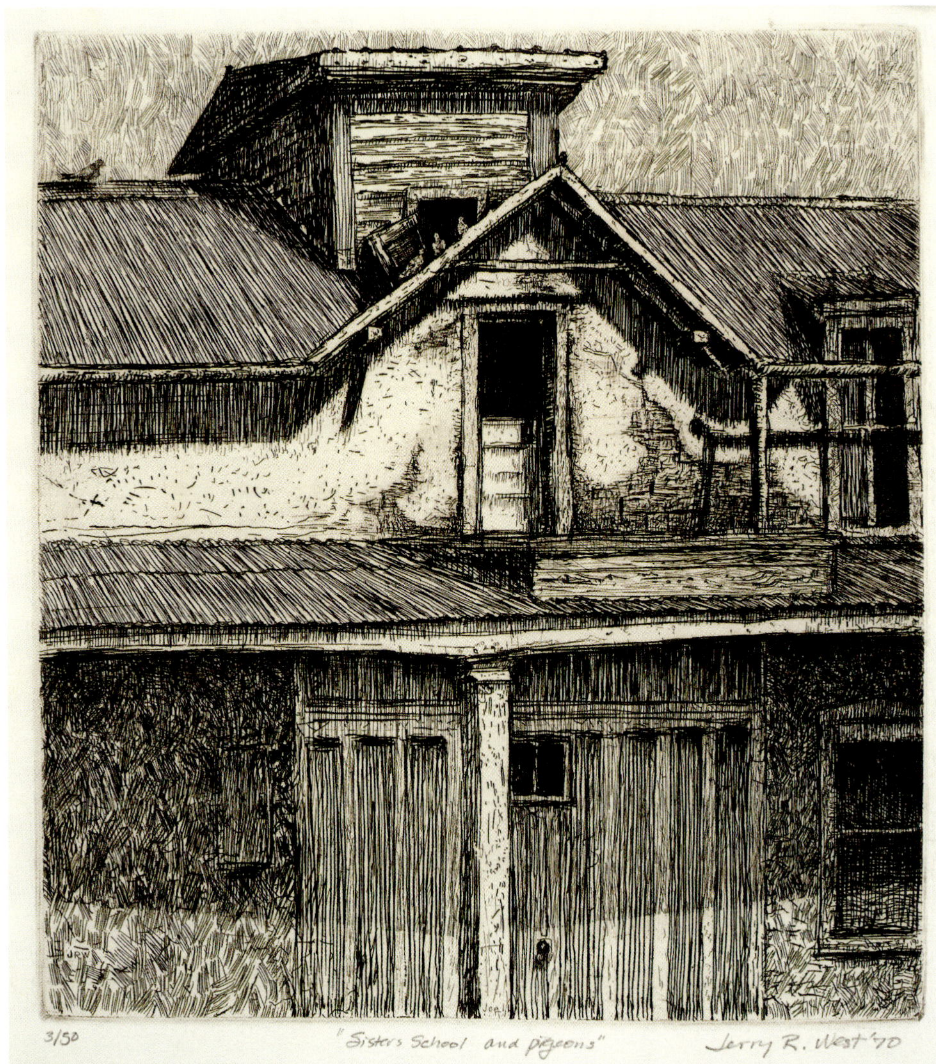

39.
Sisters' School with Pigeons, 1970
Copper plate etching, 9 × 12 in.
Edition of 20

How does a painter look at a town? Jerry West has looked at Las Vegas and seen the people in the context of their struggles, and he found his place in the town by getting to know them, listening to the people who live there, appreciating their stories, appreciating the architecture of the town. He has a sincere curiosity about, and interest in, everyone he meets. For Jerry, everyone has a story, and everyone is part of a greater story. These stories often figure in his work and contribute to the fullness of his imagery, sometimes figuring in his dreams as well. The affection he has for Las Vegas shows in the paintings and etchings that he has produced there. Las Vegas, New Mexico, is my old hometown, and he has shown me another way to look at the place where I grew up.

—Bernie Lopez

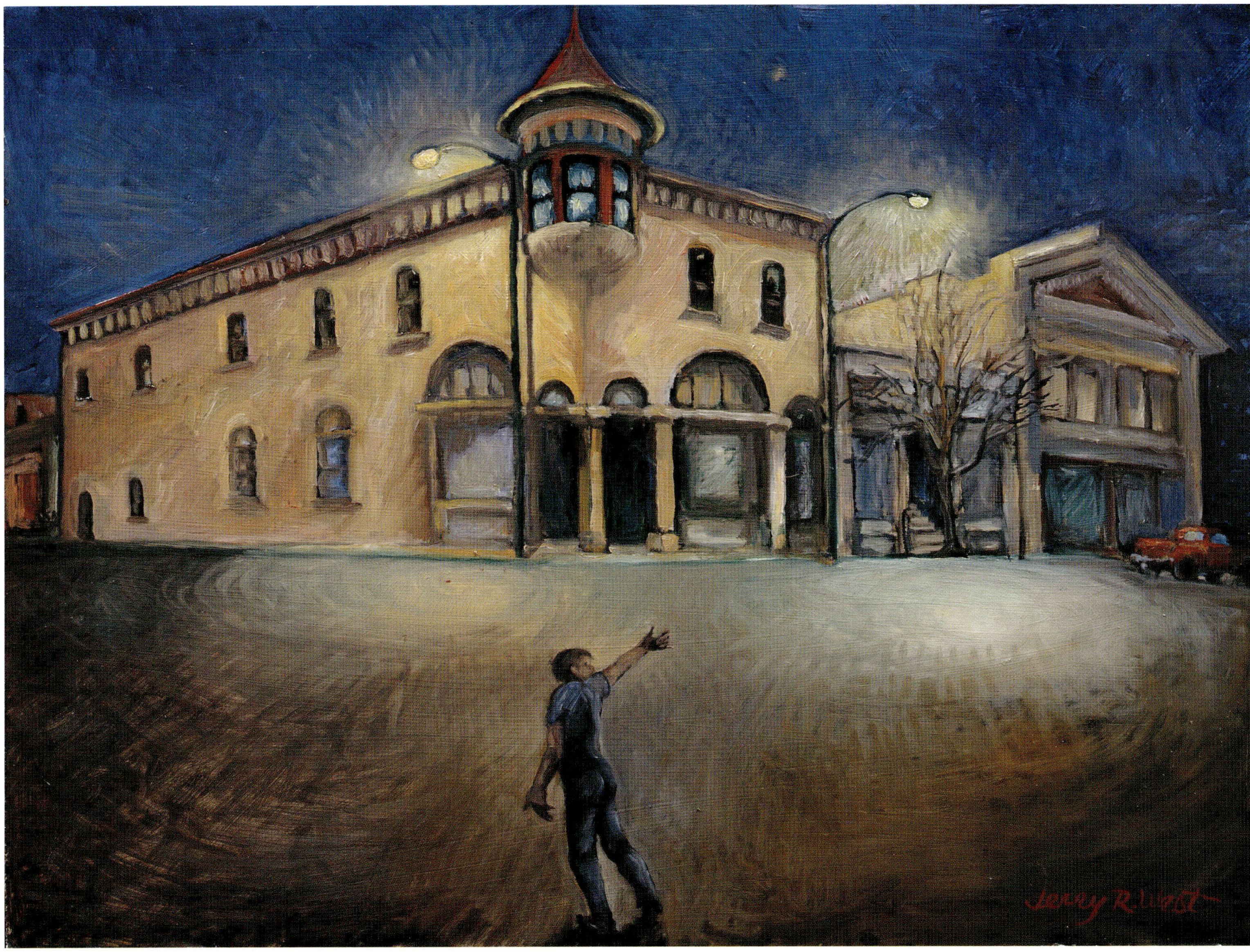

40.
Night Watch, 2002
Oil on linen, 32 × 24 in.
Collection of Wid Slick

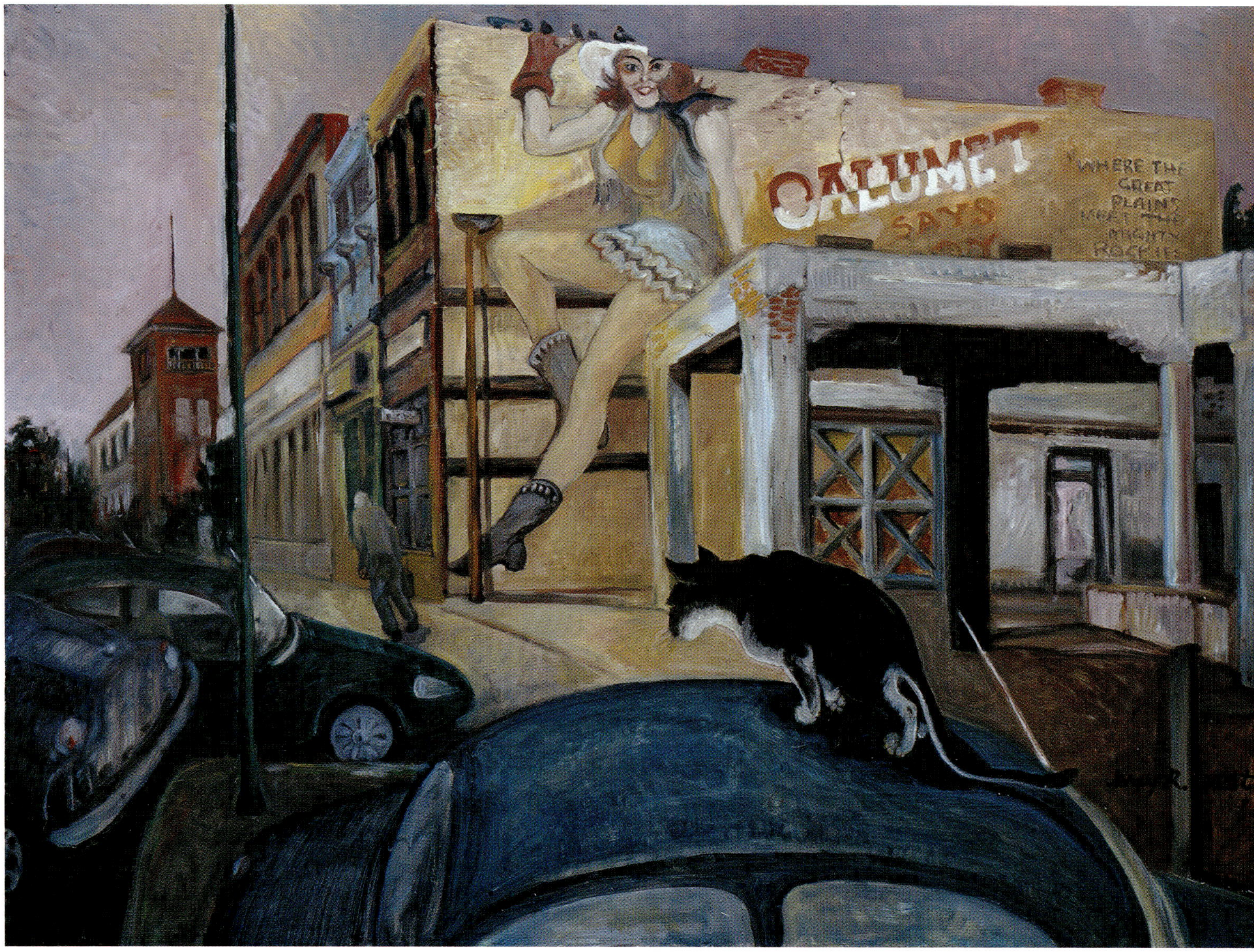

41.
Calumet Woman with Cat, 2000
Oil on Masonite, 32 × 24 in.
Estate of Kak Slick

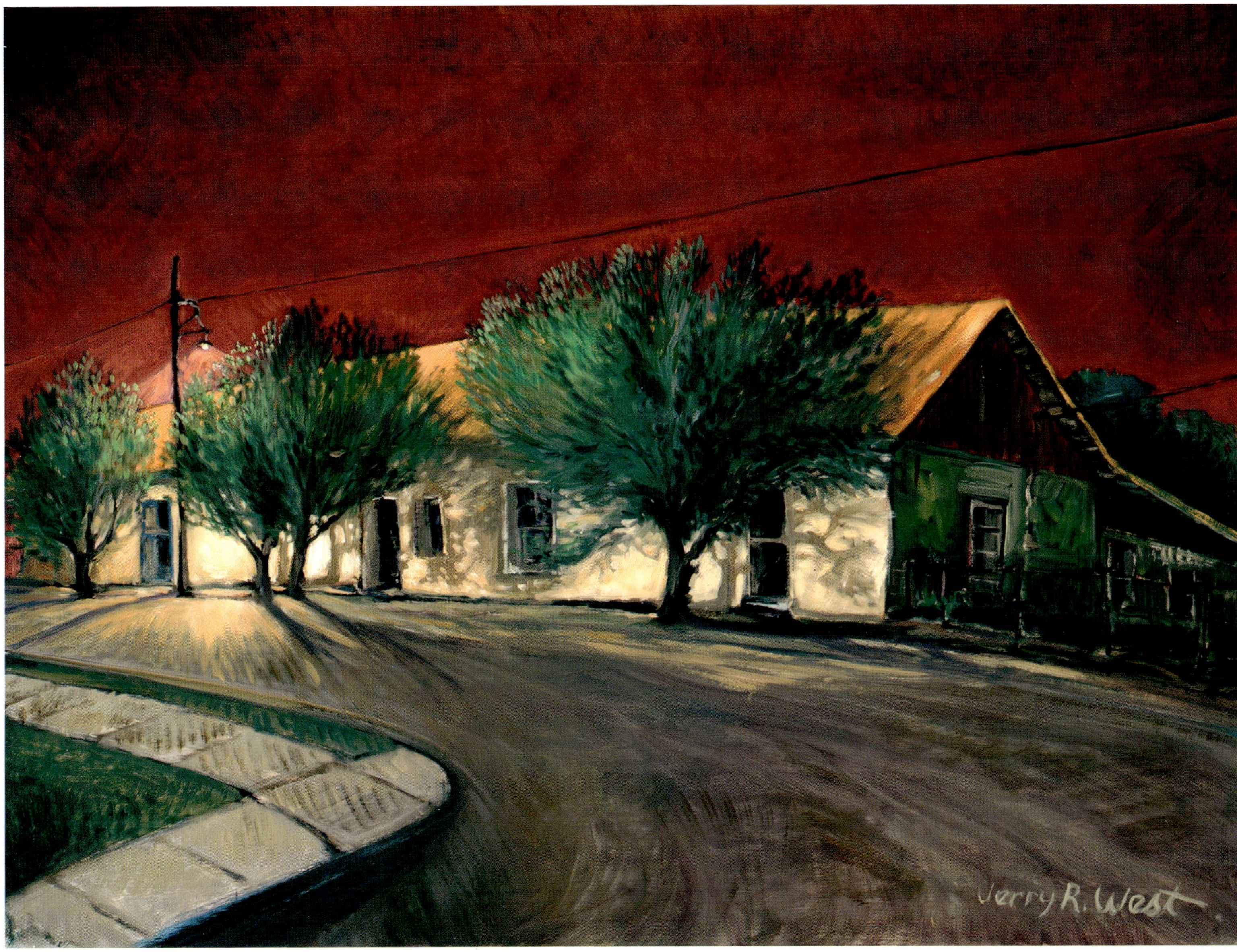

42.
Red Sky at Evening, 1995
Oil on Masonite, 32 × 24 in.
Private collection

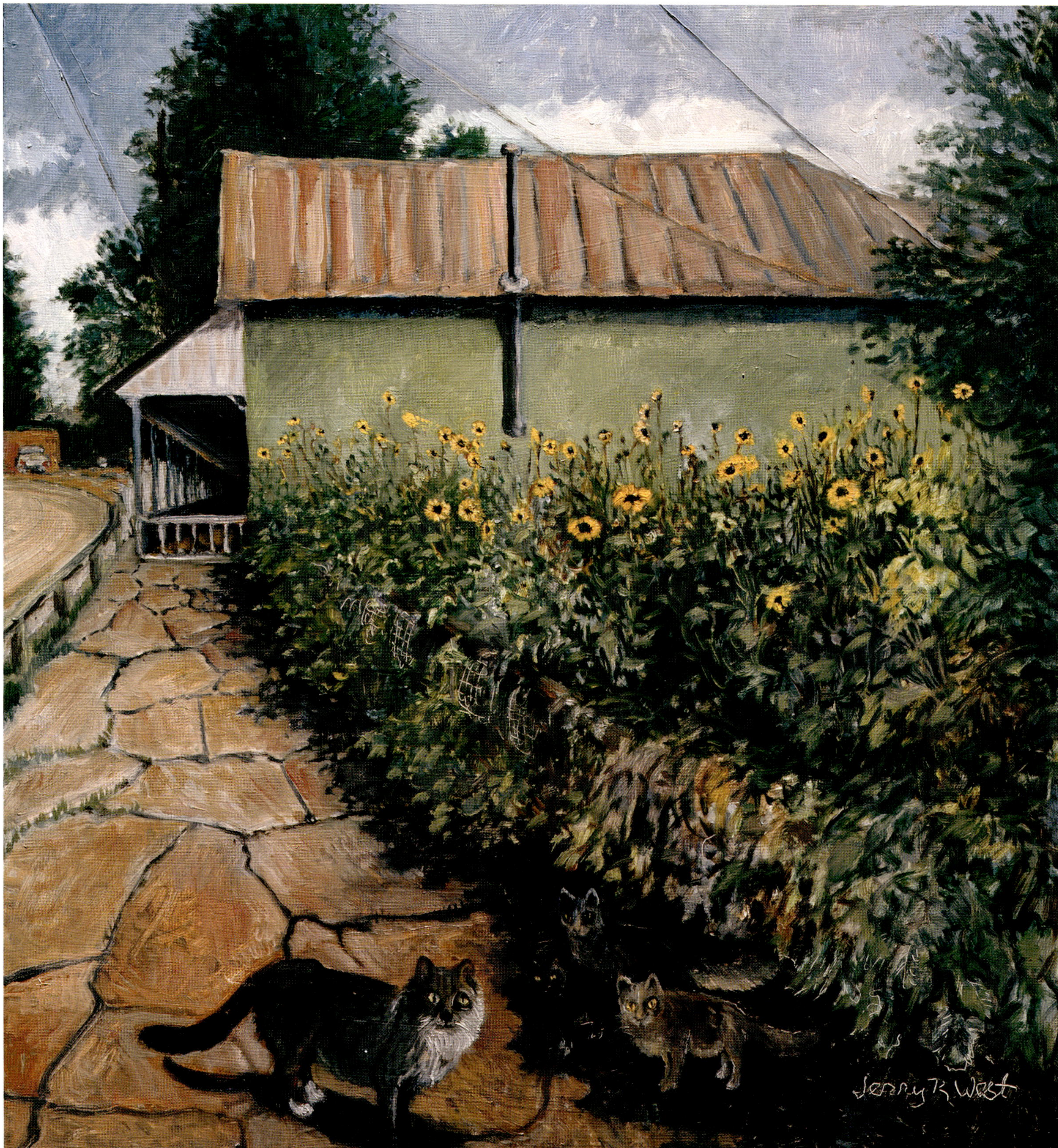

43.
Cats on South Pacific, 2001
Oil on Masonite, 26 × 38 in.
Private collection

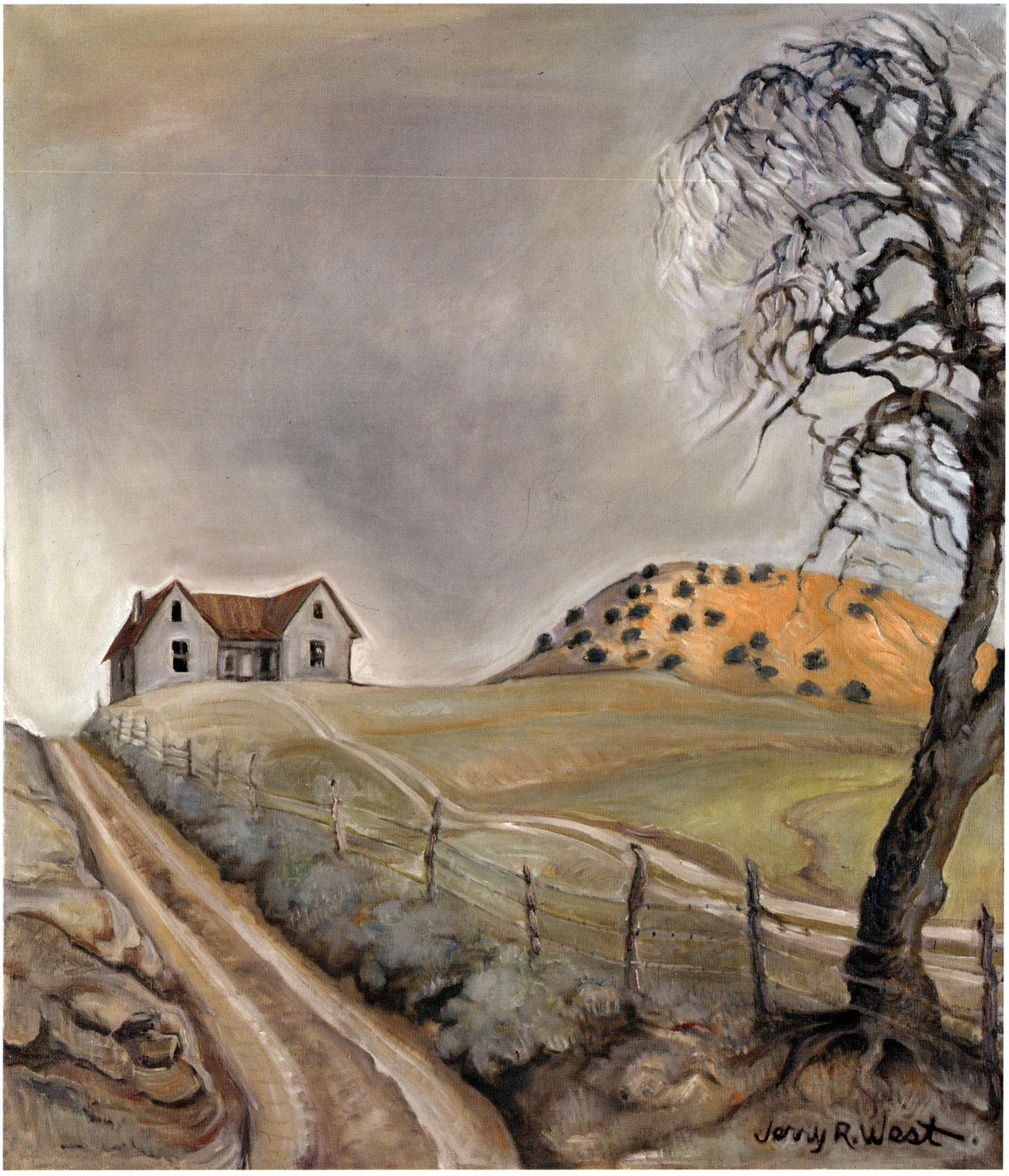

44.
Upper Las Vegas House, 1992
Oil on Masonite, 24 × 32 in.
Collection of Ray Graham

45.
Mora Mill with Sheep, 2001
Oil on Masonite, 26 × 32 in.
Collection of Mitch Marti

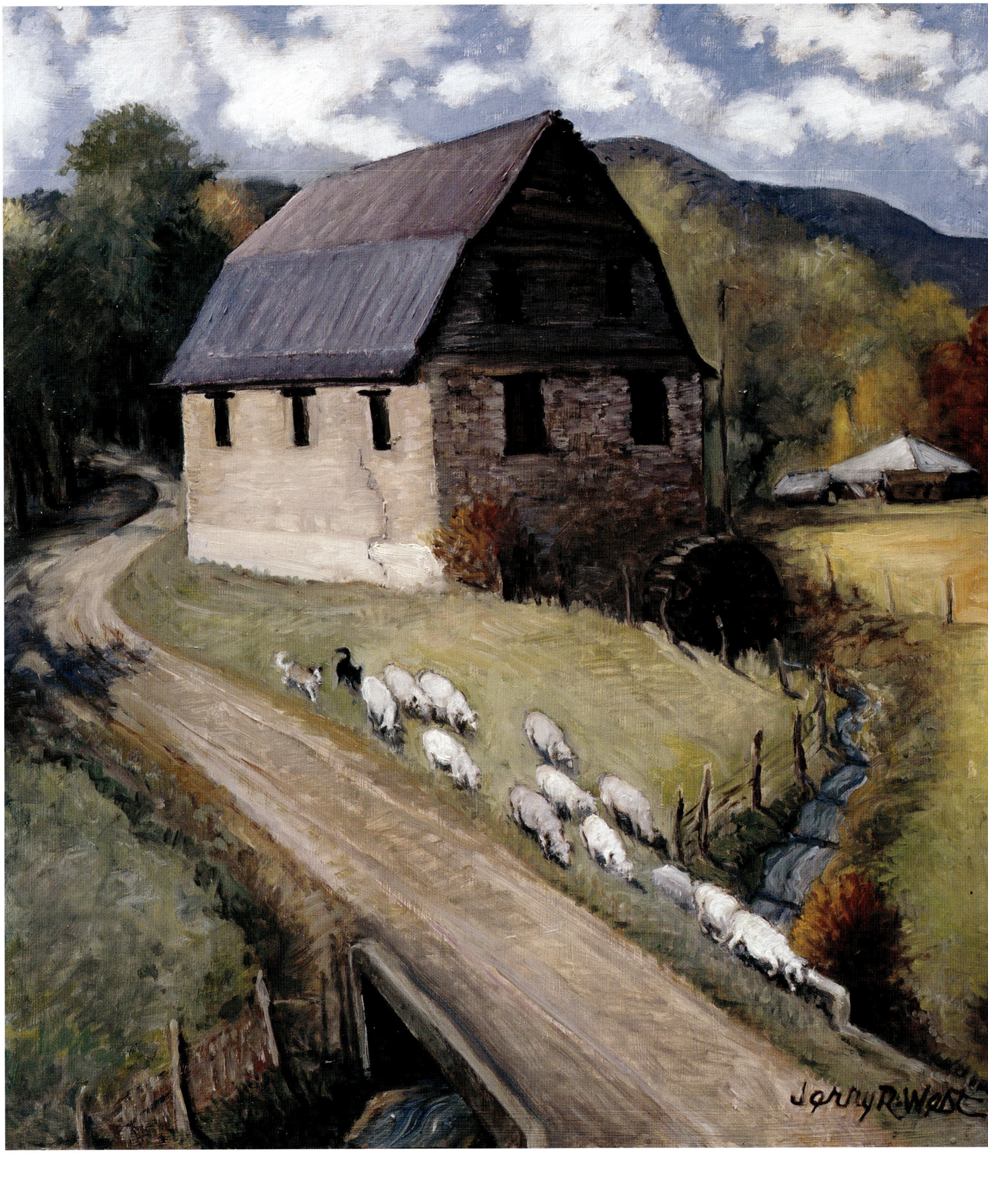
Jerry R. West

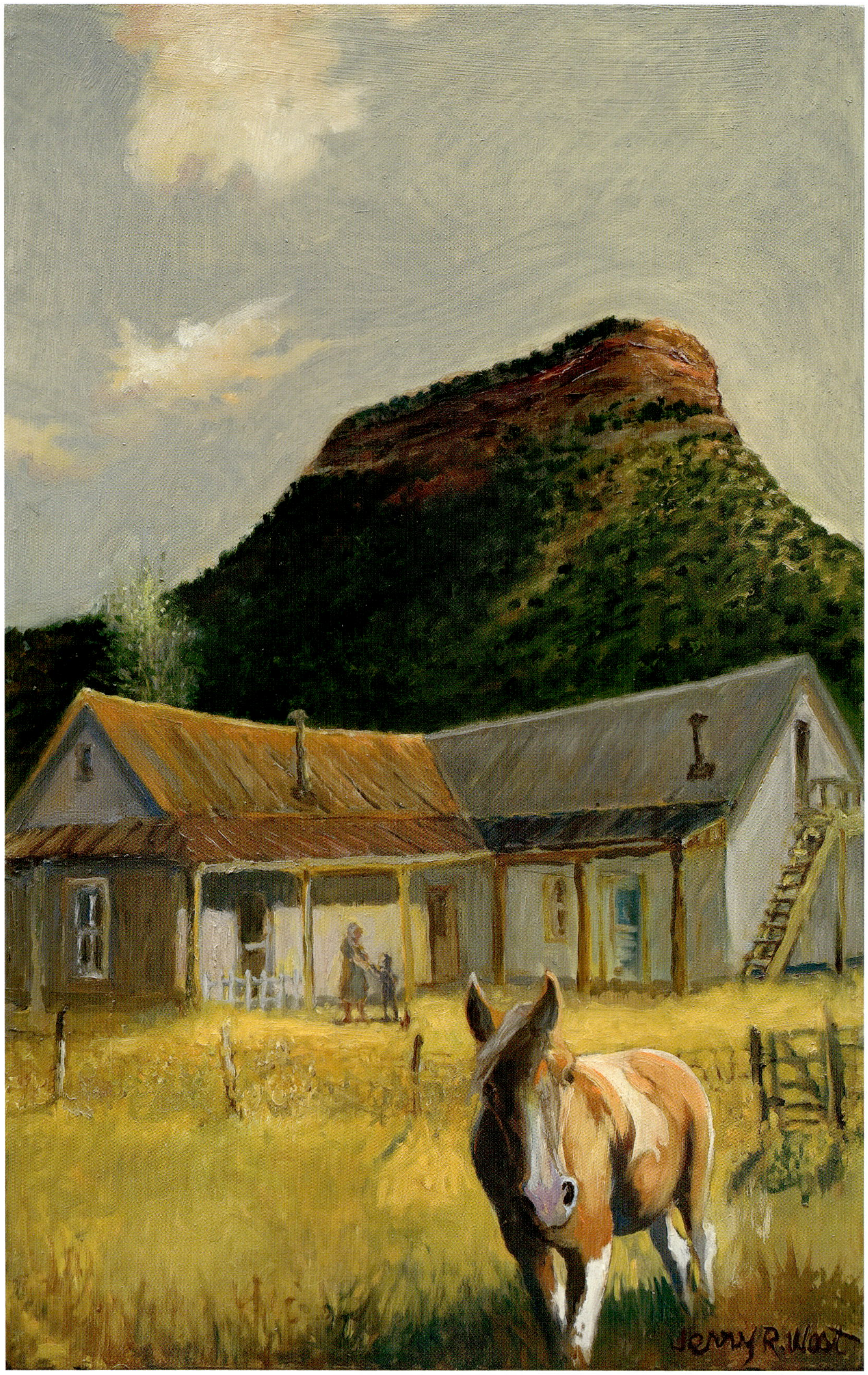

46.
Pinto Pony, Grandmother and Grandson, 2002
Oil on Masonite, 26 × 34 in.
Private collection

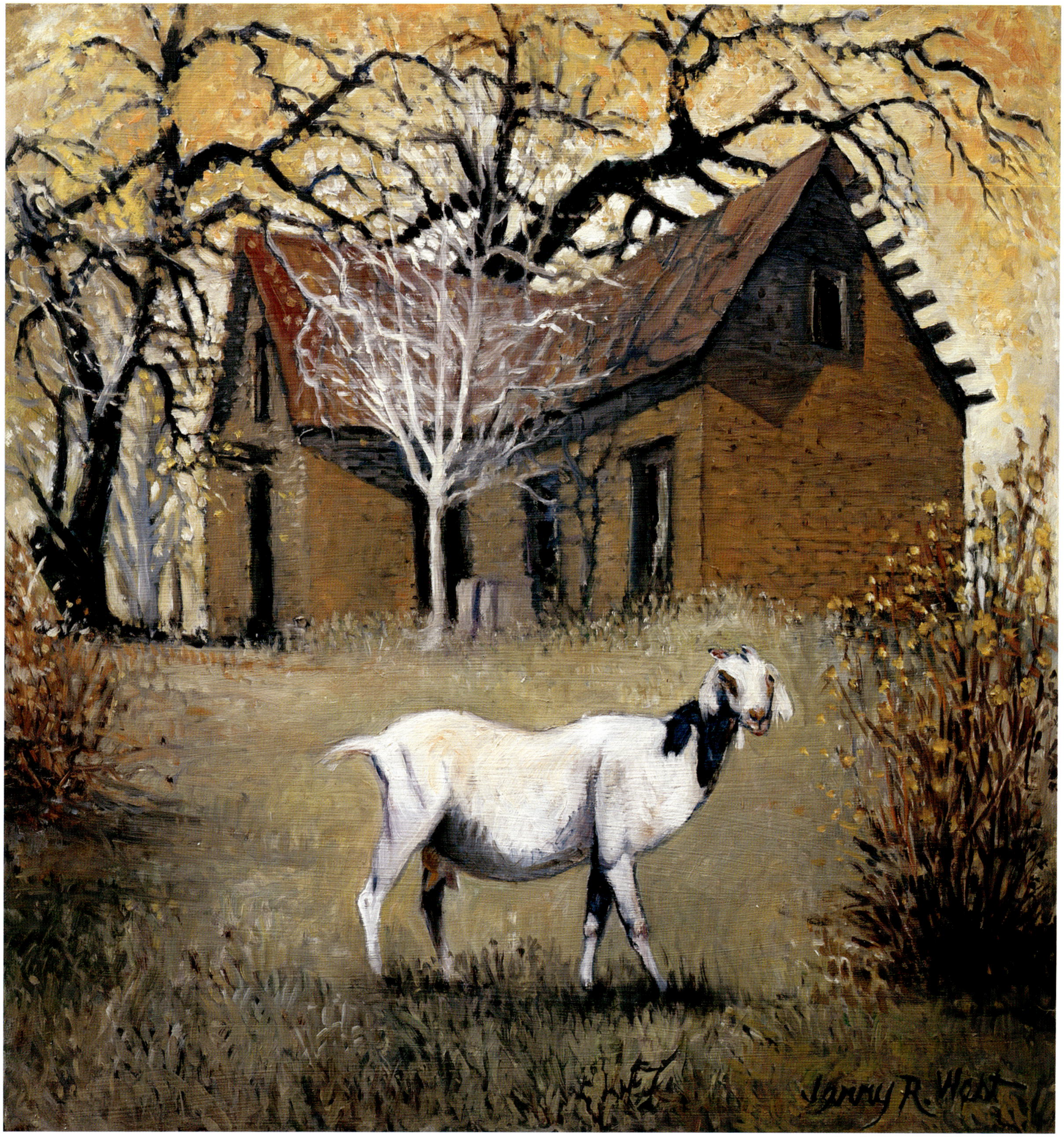

47.
White Goat with Adobe House, 2003
Oil on Masonite, 28 × 38 in.
Collection of Tina Davila

48.
Two Ravens over Blanchard, 1990
Oil on linen, 72 × 72 in.
Collection of Ray Graham

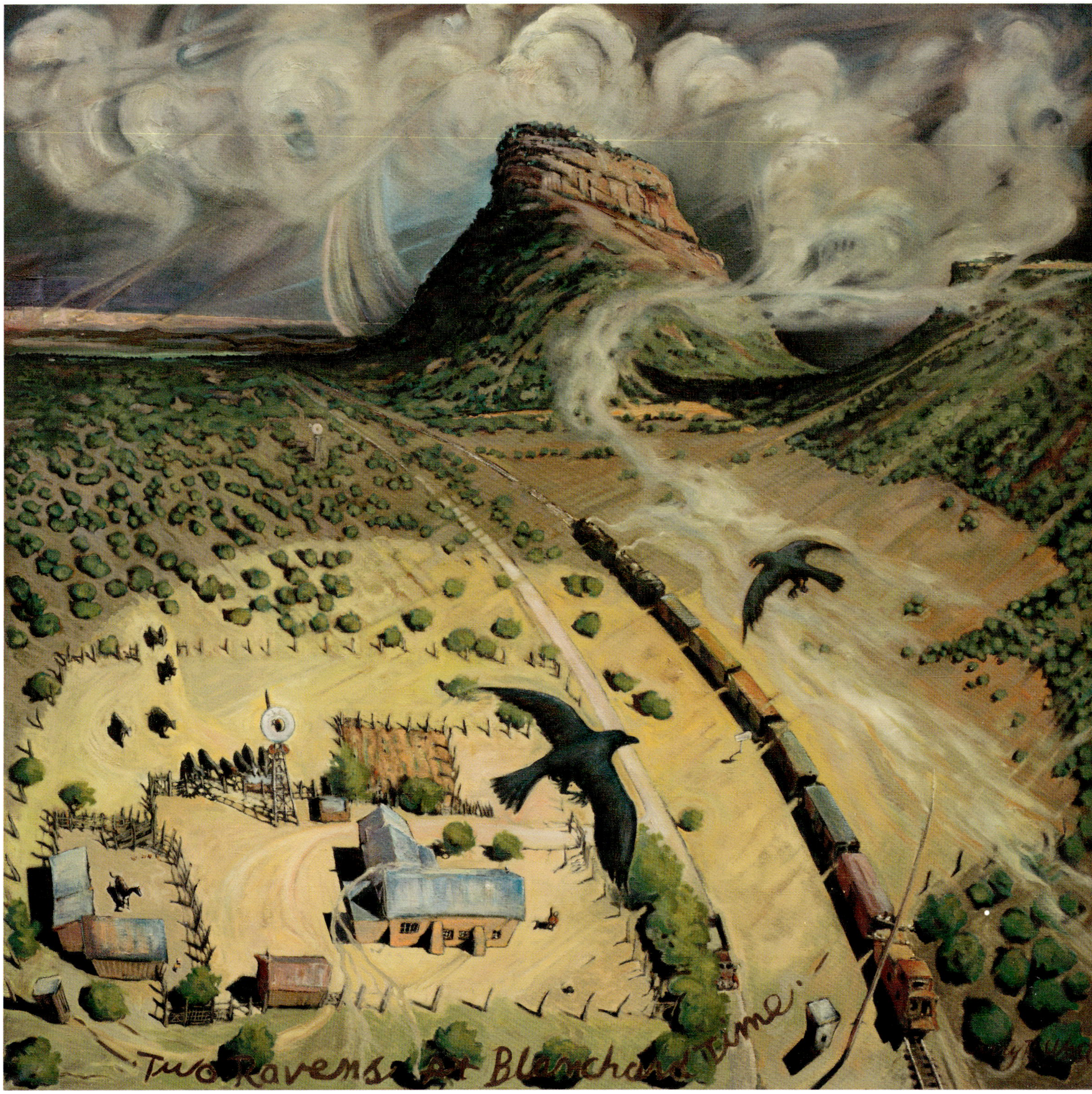
Two Ravens at Blanchard time.

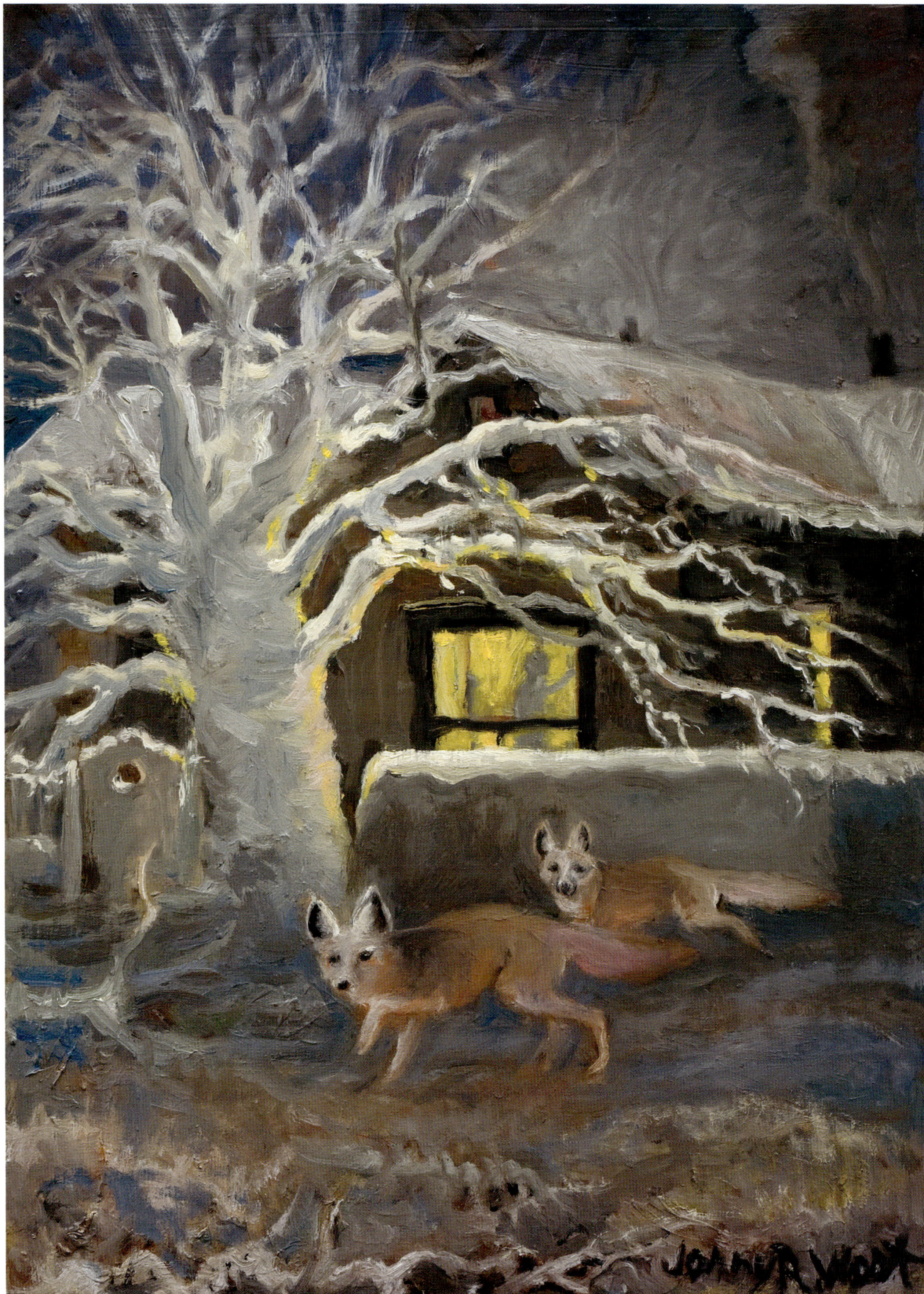

v. Winters of Malcontent and Serafina Mysteries

Beginning in the fall of 2008 I lived and painted for four years in an adobe house in Serafina, west of Las Vegas. The house stands next to an unpaved frontage road that parallels the Amtrak rail line that runs between Chicago and Los Angeles. Daily, at about 1:30 pm the westbound train would rumble by, and then at 3:30 pm the eastbound could be heard: first a long, loud whistle, then the laboring diesel engines lugging up the long, steep grade from Pecos, finally reaching the level grade of Serafina, changing the gear ratio and reducing the engine sounds. Then except for the few sounds of local cars, some ranch trucks, and the rumble of the school bus twice a day, all was relatively quiet. Of course, there was always the wind: tree limbs scratching on a tin roof, squeals and hissing of the wind around the eaves and edges of the house, and the knocking of the screen door. And, too, the local coyotes spent much time talking back and forth, keeping each other located and in touch, with the neighborhood dogs always getting into the action. There were also sounds from the mice and wood rats, the usual scampering and shuffling. And always the haunting cries of birds in early mornings and late afternoons—piñon jays in great flocks, blue birds, robins, magpies, flickers, warblers—and always, the mysterious talking of the ravens.

Because I helped with the restoration and remodeling of the old adobe house back in 1980 when Ray Graham bought the ranch on which the place stands, I have always revered this house for its surroundings and the great view of Starvation Peak and Rowe Mesa. And because through those intervening years I assisted Ray in keeping the house rented I continued to take great interest in the place. The four-year period from 2008 to

49.
Artist at Studio Window with Two Kit Foxes, 2009
Oil on Masonite, 18 × 24 in.
Private collection

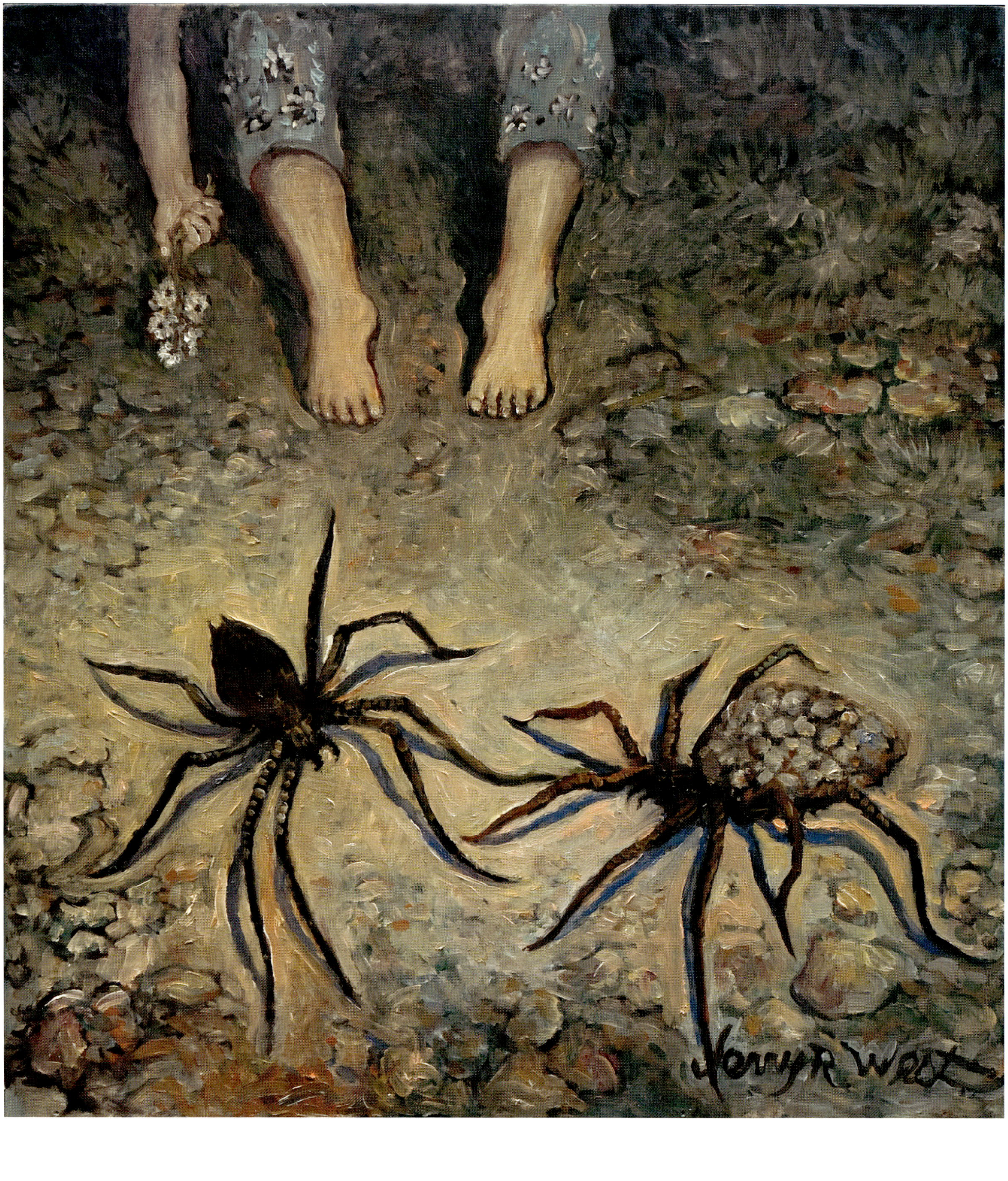
Verny R West

2012 was the first time I personally occupied the space and experienced the full range of moods of each season, with all the amazing weather that can happen in northern New Mexico.

Winters of malcontent included cold weather and stormy moods. I cut wood and kept the kitchen range going. I cooked great stews and delicious beans and chile. I read, listened to music and the news once in a while, watched the skies, and walked the grassy meadows and the piñon- and juniper-studded hills. But mostly I listened to the wind and painted.

Each spring I would have a studio open house. I'd show paintings in every room of the house. We'd eat and drink, talk and listen to music, and dance. During these four years at Serafina I had many good friends and family come visit and a lover now and then. But mostly I had alone time: a thoughtful, meditative time for painting.

I will always miss Serafina: the quiet place, with glimpses of the moon through the limbs of a dying cottonwood; the glowing sunsets and scattered clouds; the windmill sounds; the strange and delightful critters with their special private languages, squeaks, and whispers; the mystery of the silent rooms with what always seemed to be far-off voices and laughter. The overall magic of the place has never let go of me.

50.
Clementine with Wolf Spiders, 2011
Oil on Masonite, 18 × 24 in.
Collection of Andrew Gelatley

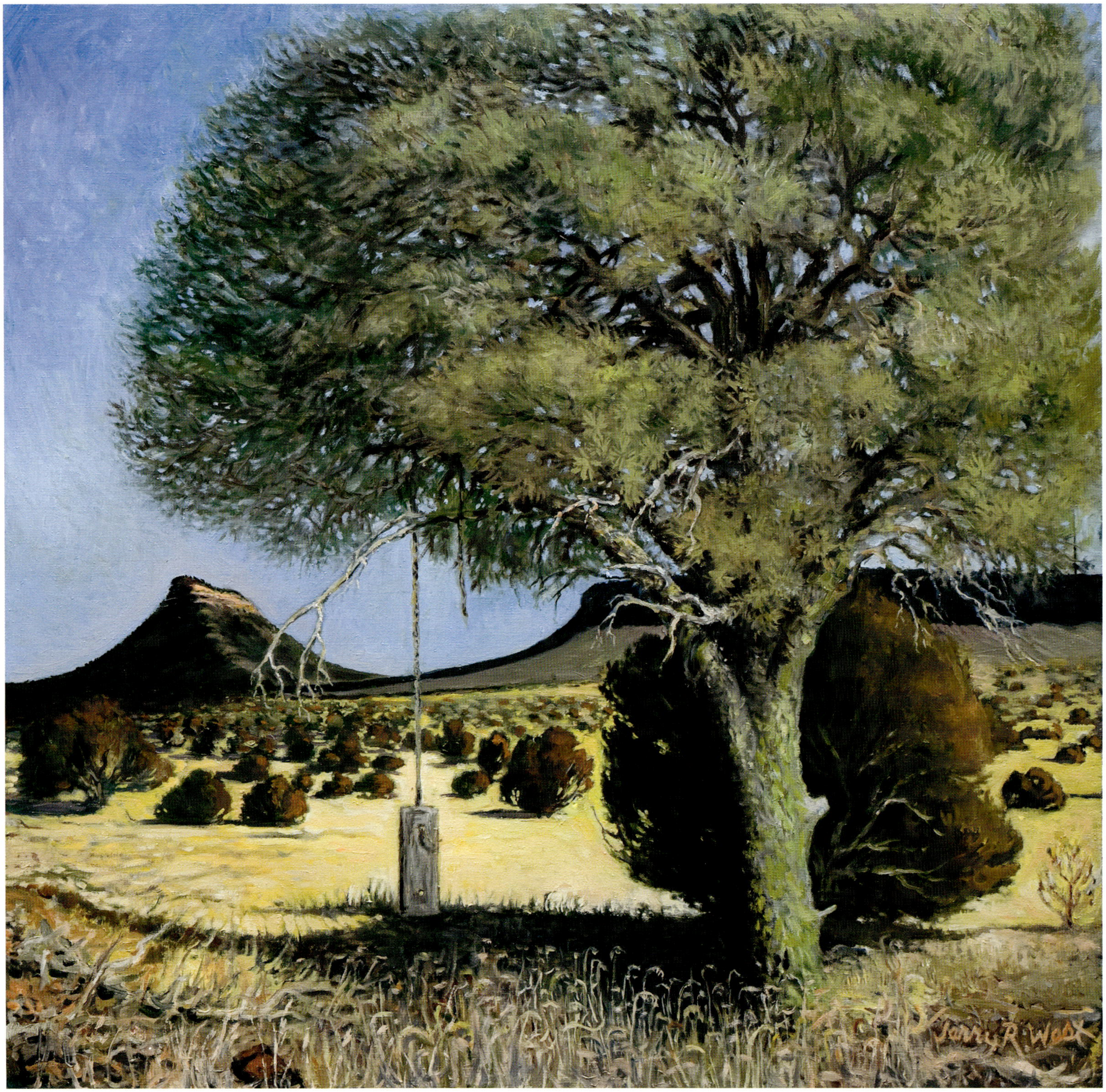

51.
Old Piñon with Broken Swing, 2010
Oil on linen, 36 × 40 in.
Collection of Tom Shehan

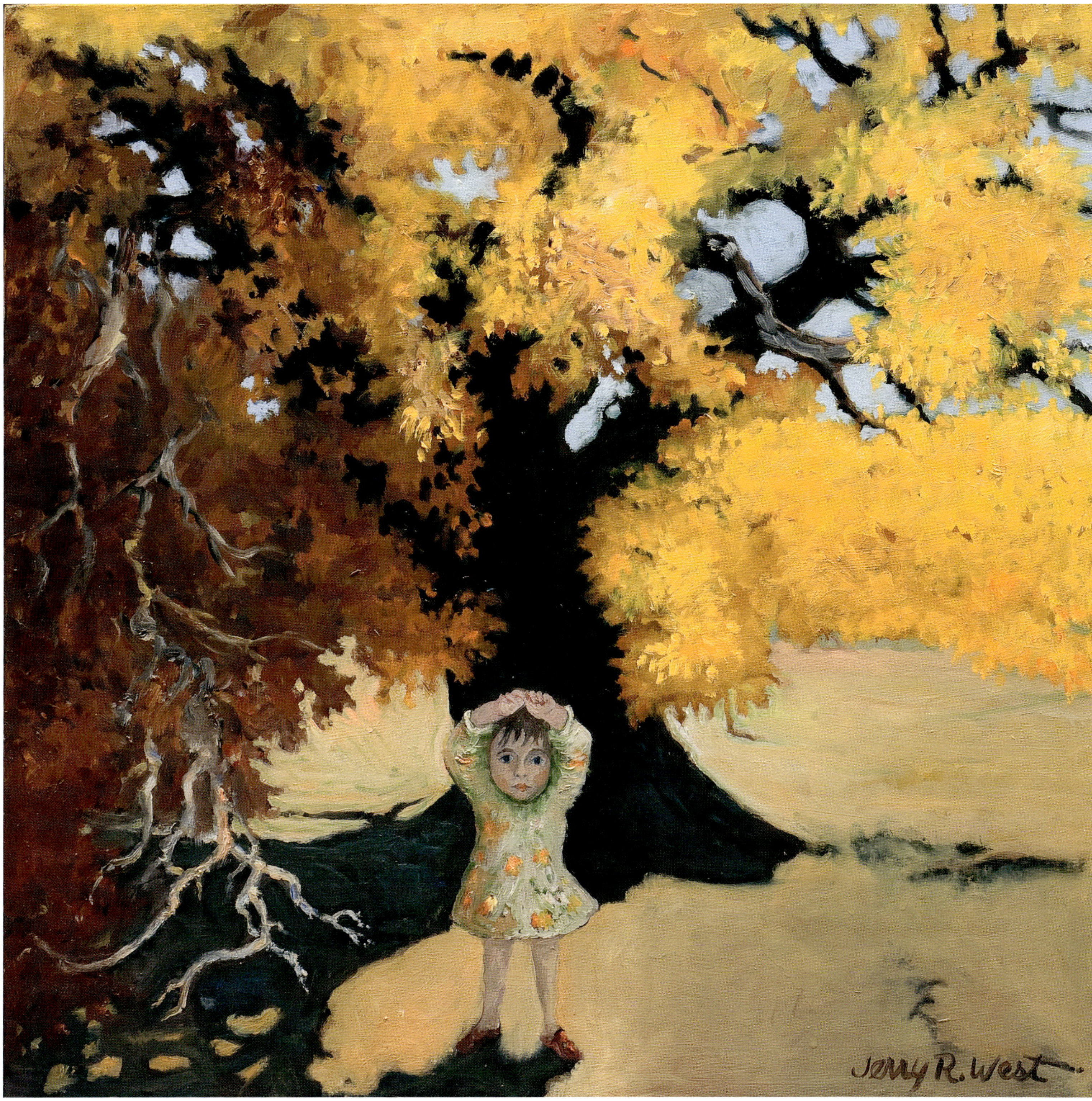

52.
Little Girl Hugging—Clementine O'Shea West, 2009
Oil on Masonite, 24 × 30 in.
Collection of Doris Martin

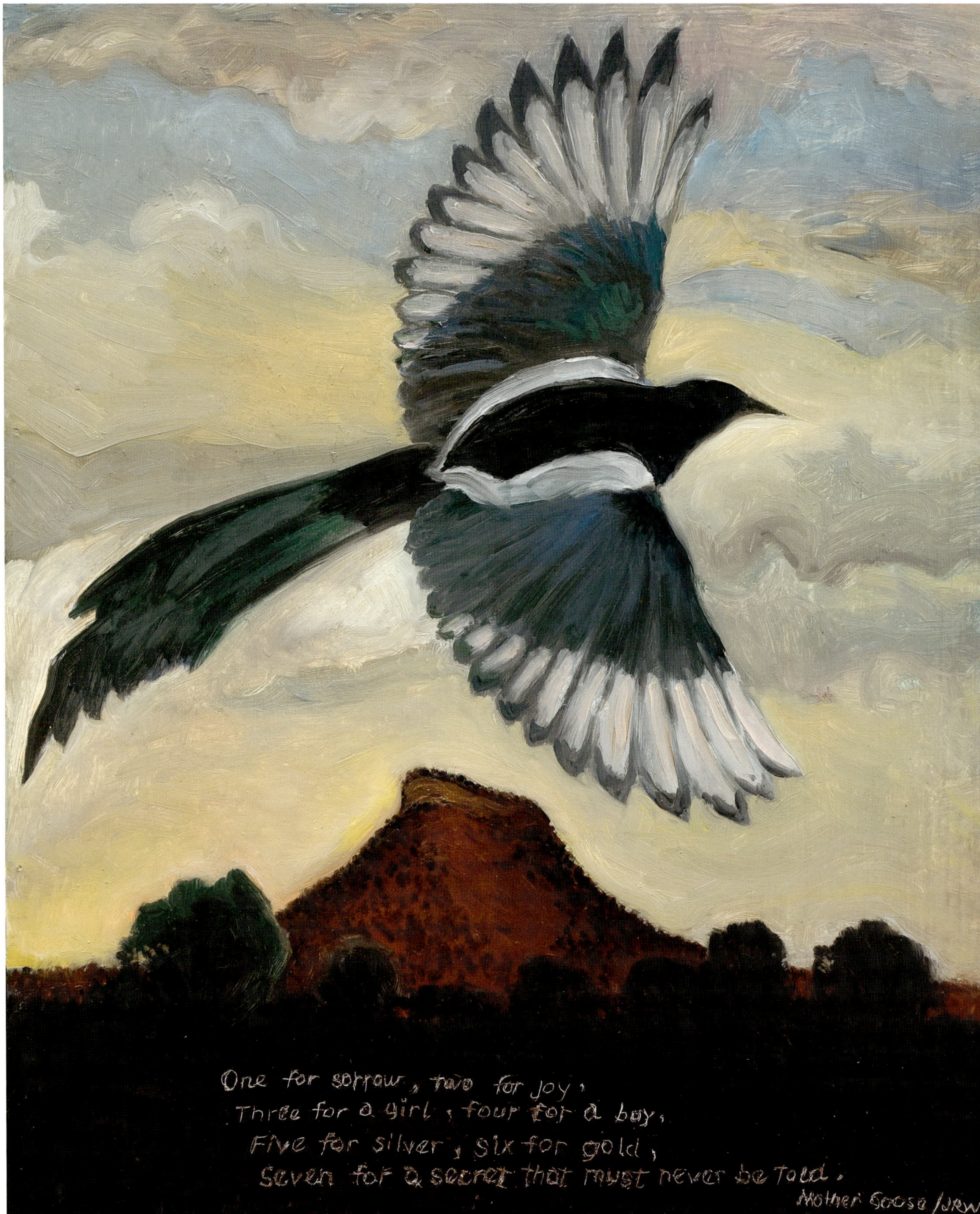
One for sorrow, two for joy,
Three for a girl, four for a boy,
Five for silver, six for gold,
Seven for a secret that must never be told.
Mother Goose / JRW

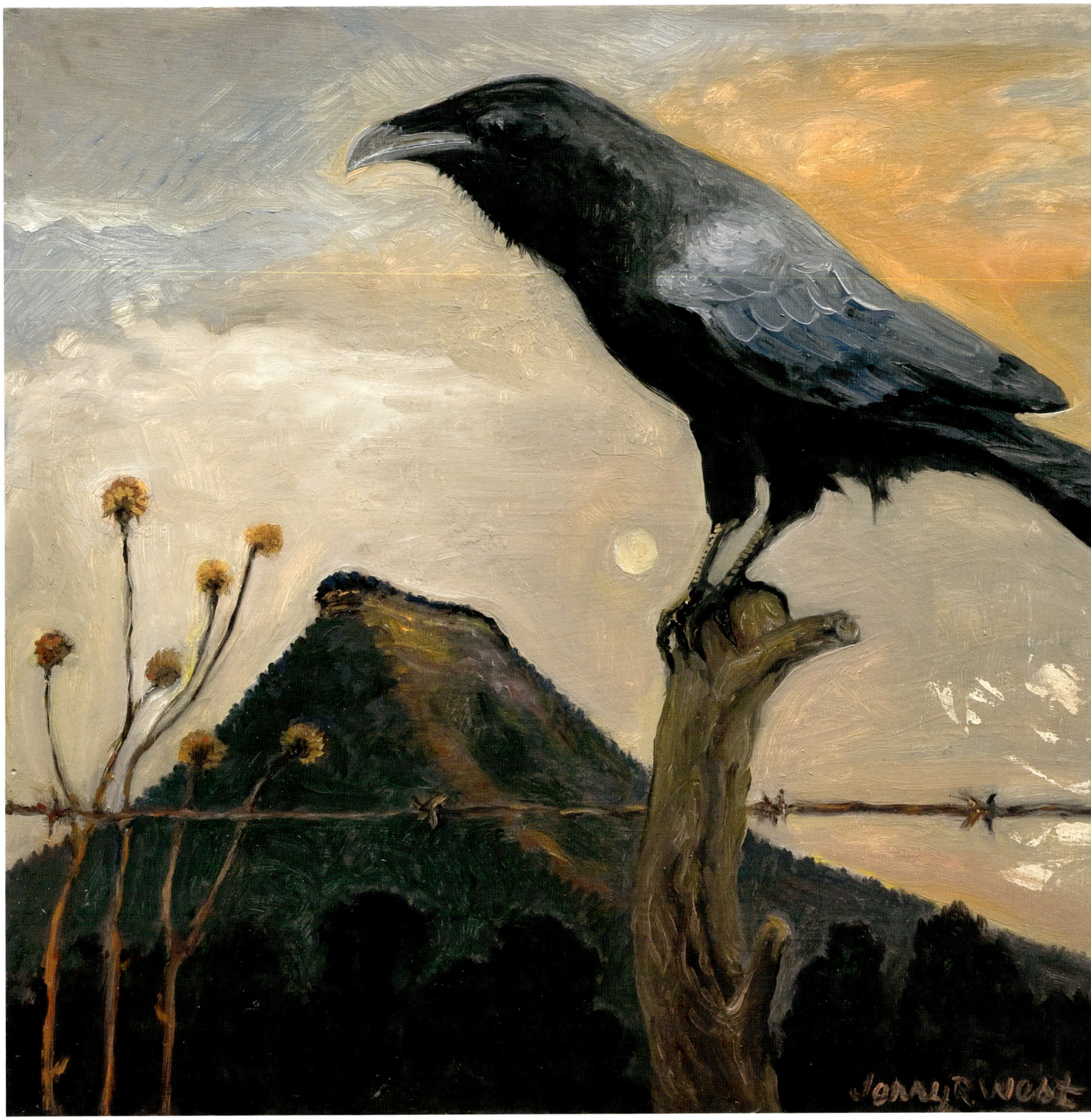

53.
Magpie over Starvation Peak, 2008
Oil on Masonite, 24 × 30 in.
Collection of Susan Dunshee

54.
Raven of Starvation Peak, 2009
Oil on Masonite, 26 × 26 in.
Collection of David and Marilyn Salman

55.
Cow Creek Camp with Angel Wing Cloud, 2010
Oil on linen, 30 × 40 in
Collection of Anne Pedersen and Mark Donatelli

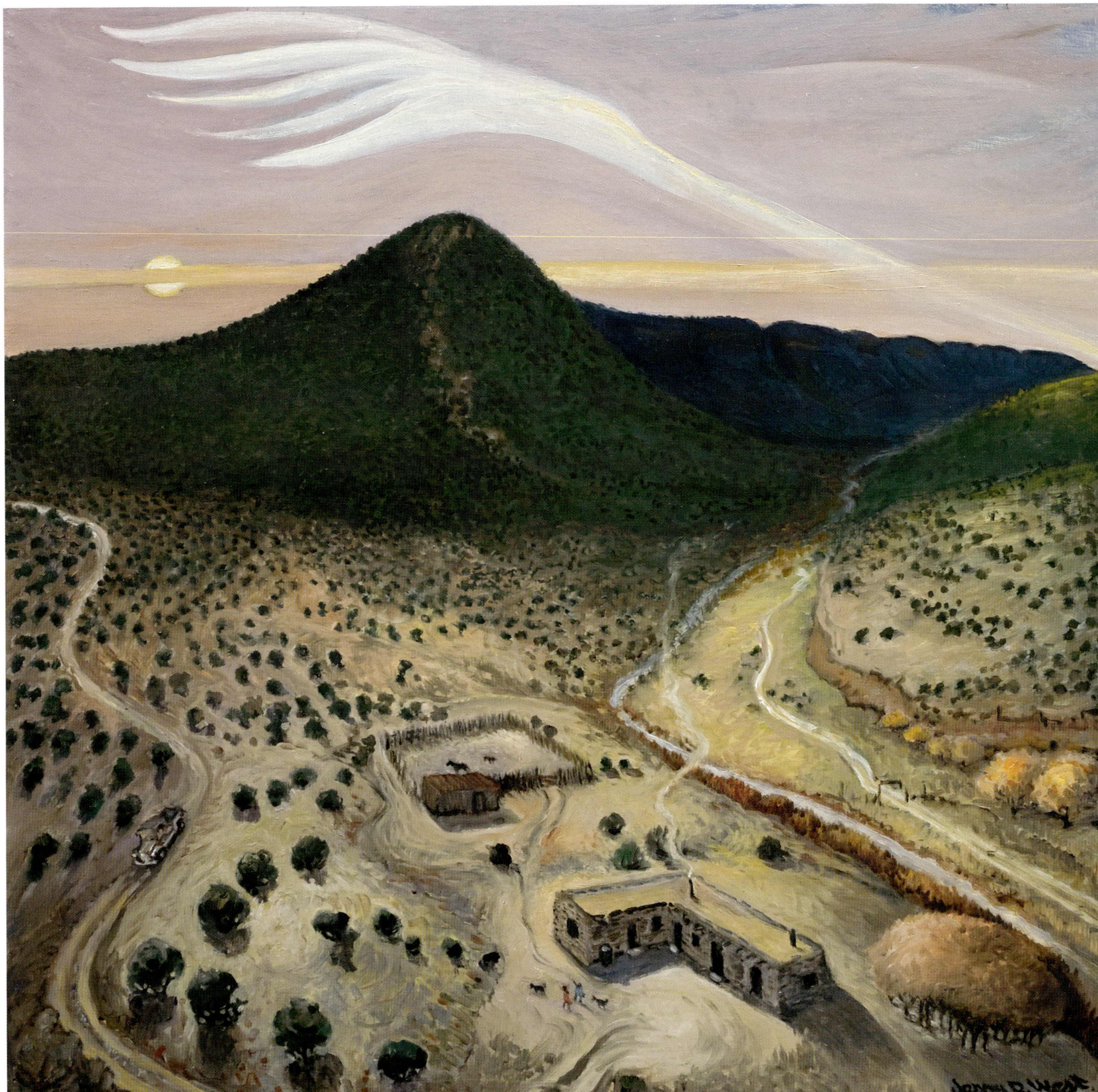
Jonny R. West.

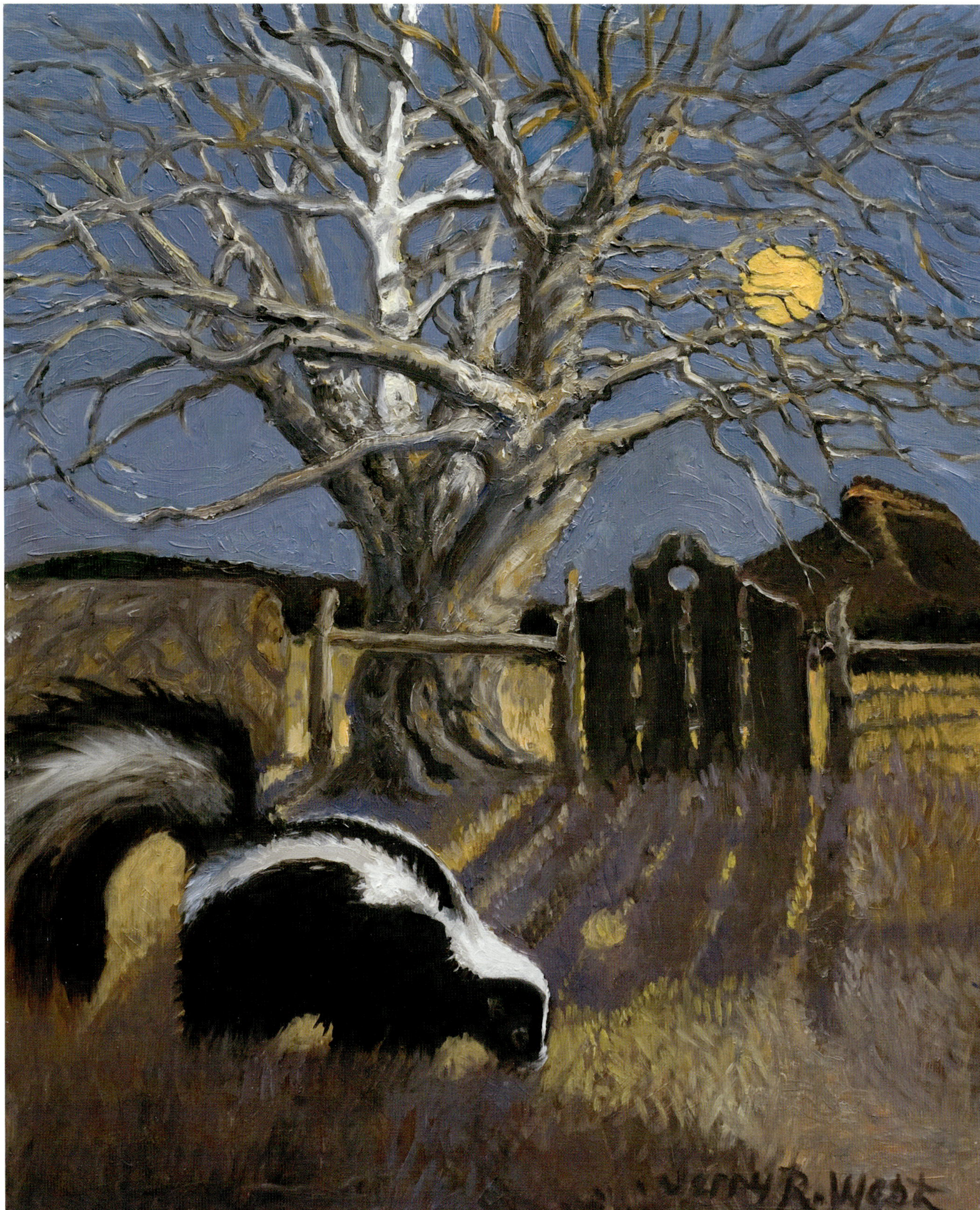

56.
Skunk in Moonlight, 2009
Oil on Masonite, 26 × 38 in.
Private collection

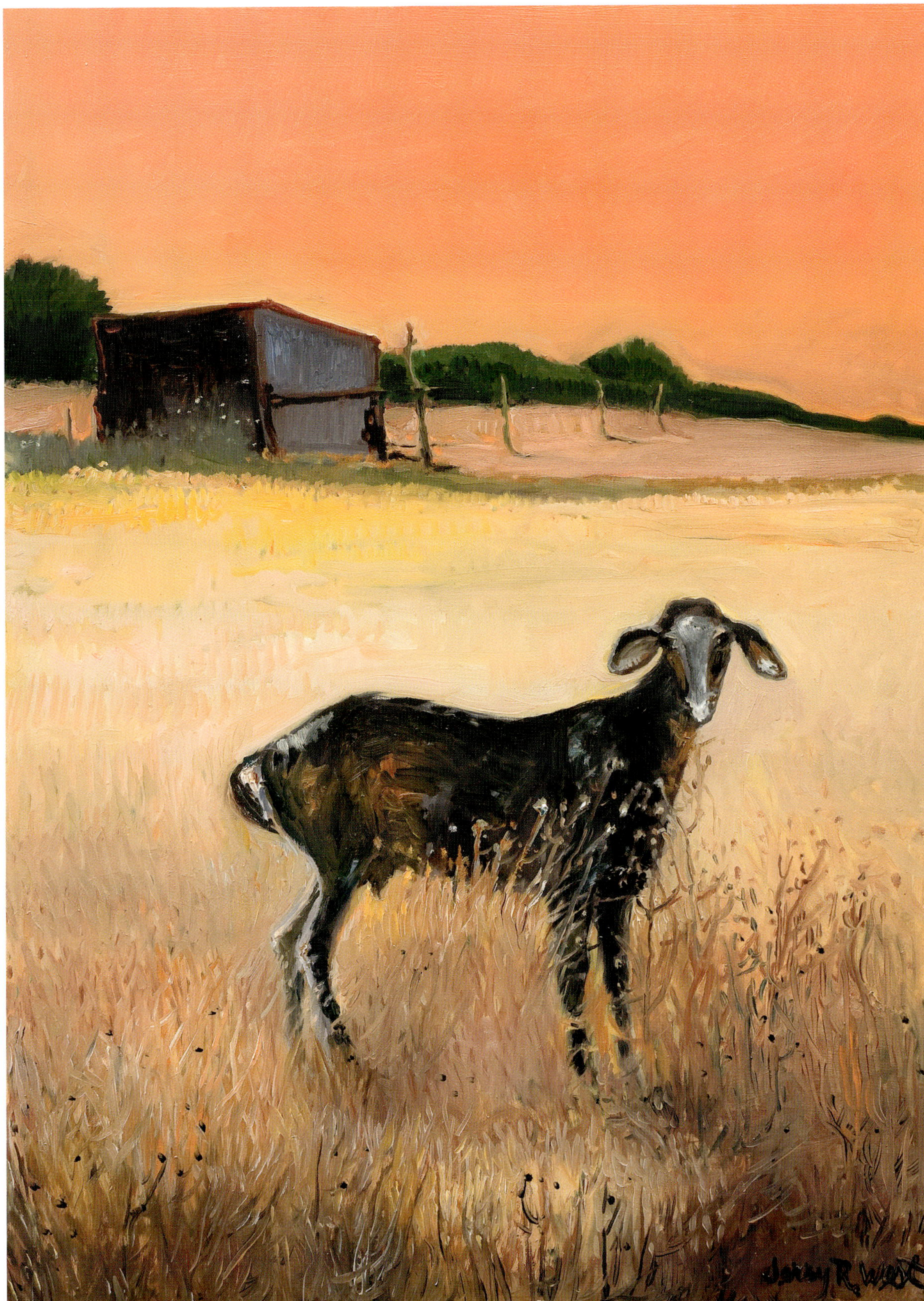

57.
The Black Goat of Bernal, 2008
Oil on Masonite, 26 × 34 in.
Collection of Caroline Adams

58.
White Tree and Snake at Gate in Moonlight, 2010
Oil on Masonite, 24 × 30 in.
Private collection

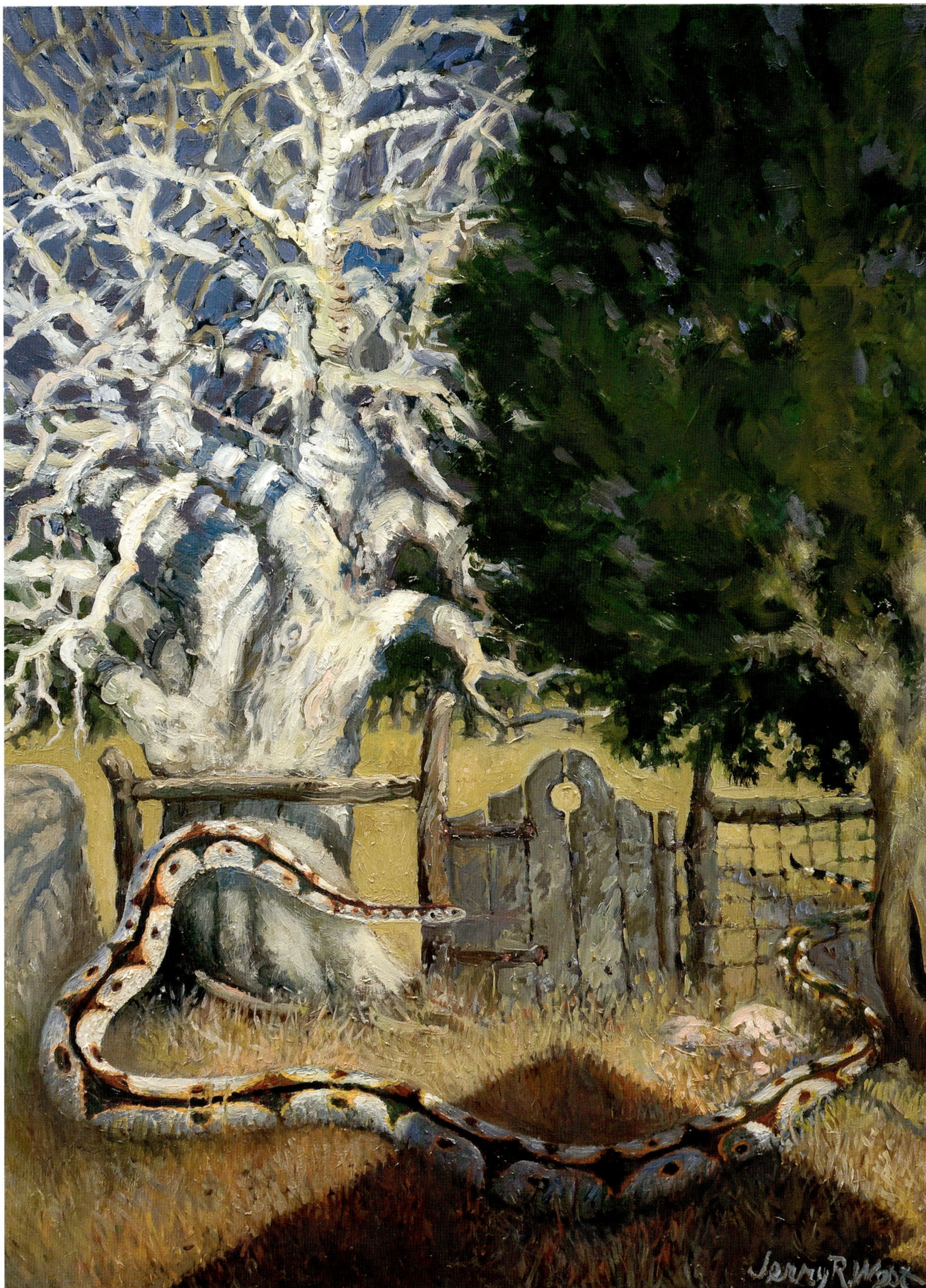

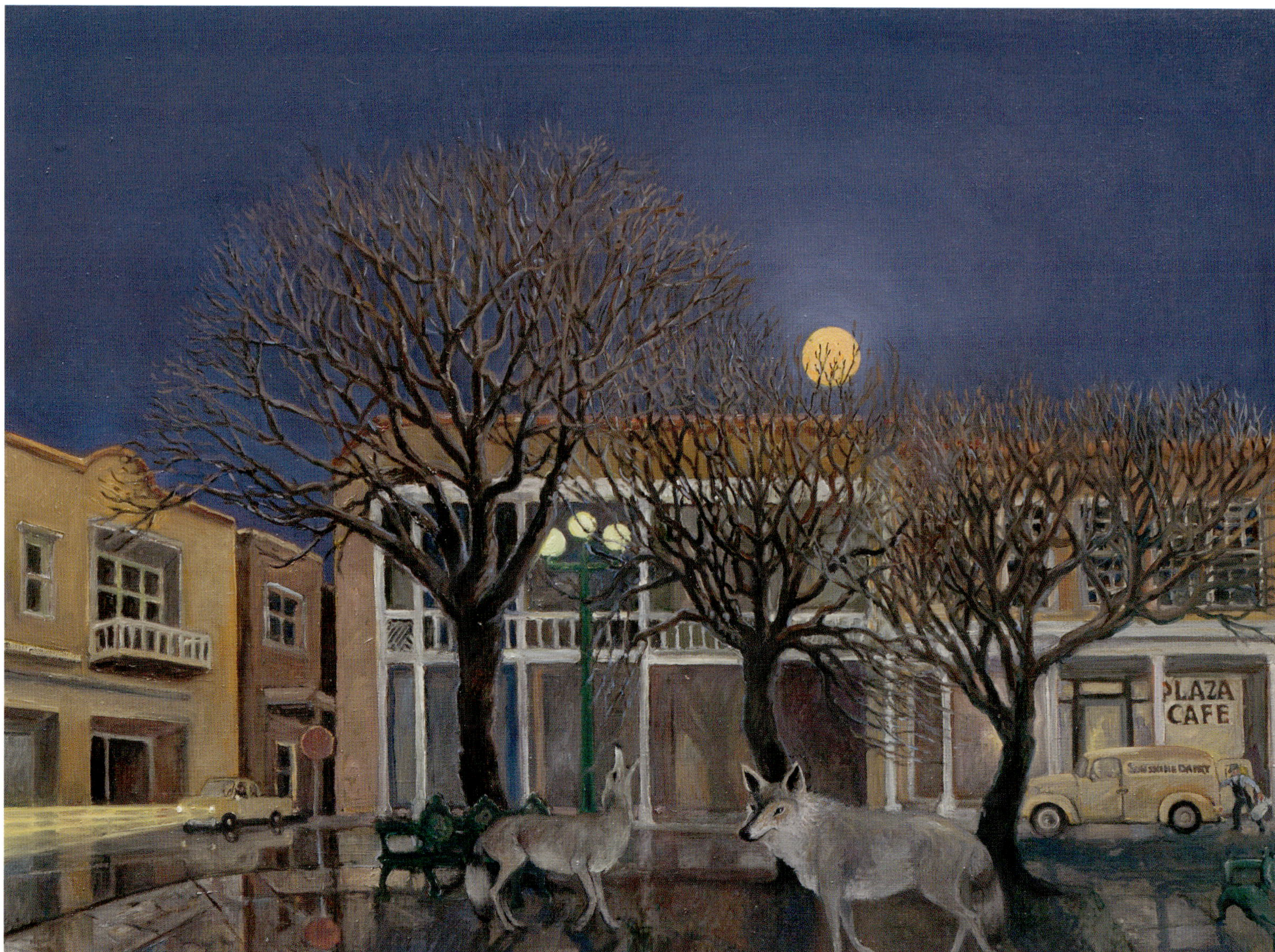

59.
Moonset over Plaza Café, 2008
Oil on linen, 42 × 32 in.
Collection of Doris Martin

VI. The Disappeared and the Reappeared

I often visited Santa Fe during the period I was living and painting in Serafina. My old hometown was going through rapid transformations, and intense bursts of energy and activity surrounded many issues. Matters as diverse and important as homelessness, poverty, domestic violence, early education, an aging infrastructure, water, and urban sprawl were being discussed and wrangled over by citizens and members of the City Council.

Where the old Santa Fe High School once sat a new ultracontemporary convention center was being built. The rail yard was rapidly being transformed into commercial spaces for a farmer's market, high-end galleries, and parkways. A new, colorful, sleek commuter train, called the Railrunner, was coming to town. The venerable Saint Francis Cathedral was covered with plastic to allow renovations to take place even during the cold of winter.

On the north side of the plaza, behind the Palace of the Governors, the oldest public adobe structure in the United States, a history museum was being built. A giant crane—the tallest object ever seen in Santa Fe—was erected for the construction. It had an arm that could reach west across Lincoln Avenue to loom over the old art museum. To the east, it could easily reach past Washington Avenue and beyond, and to the south extend past the center of the plaza. The colorful red and orange structure stood out beautifully against the ever-changing New Mexico skies and the deep blue-greens and violets of the Sangre de Cristo Mountains. It formed a lovely counterpoint to the ancient buildings and trees. All of this construction turmoil and human excitement gave me pause to think, dream, and reflect on my own past and present relationship with this old town.

In the midst of this process, a few ghosts wandered back to Santa Fe to show their pleasure, or discontent, or amusement, or perhaps just to comment on the new consciousness, surprising developments, and ever-present human folly of what is considered progress. Out of this period came these memory paintings.

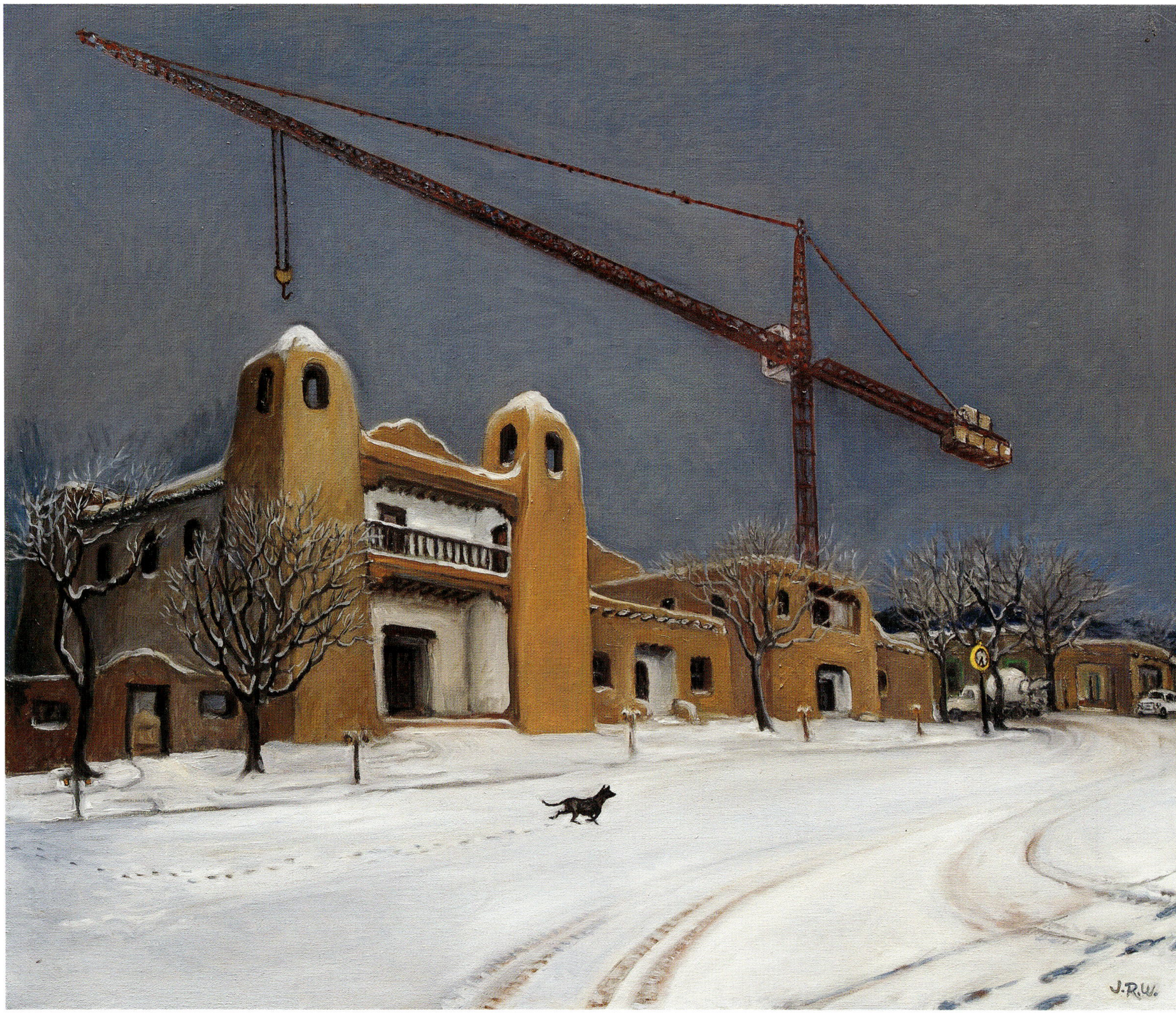

60.
The Crane, the Museum and the Black Dog, 2008
Oil on linen, 42 × 36 in.

61.
Ascension in a French Balloon, 2009
Oil on linen, 42 × 48 in.
Collection of John Eddy

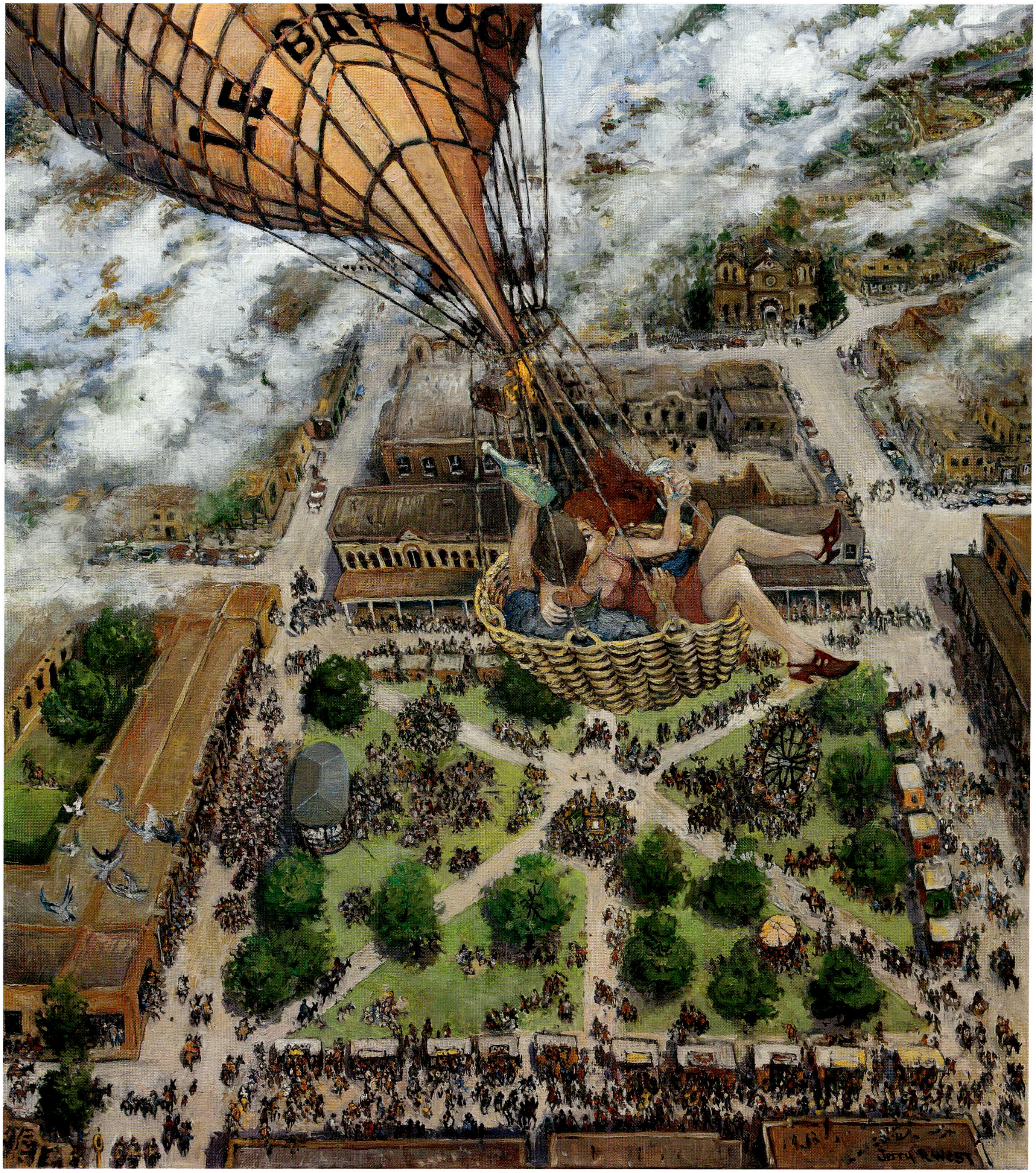

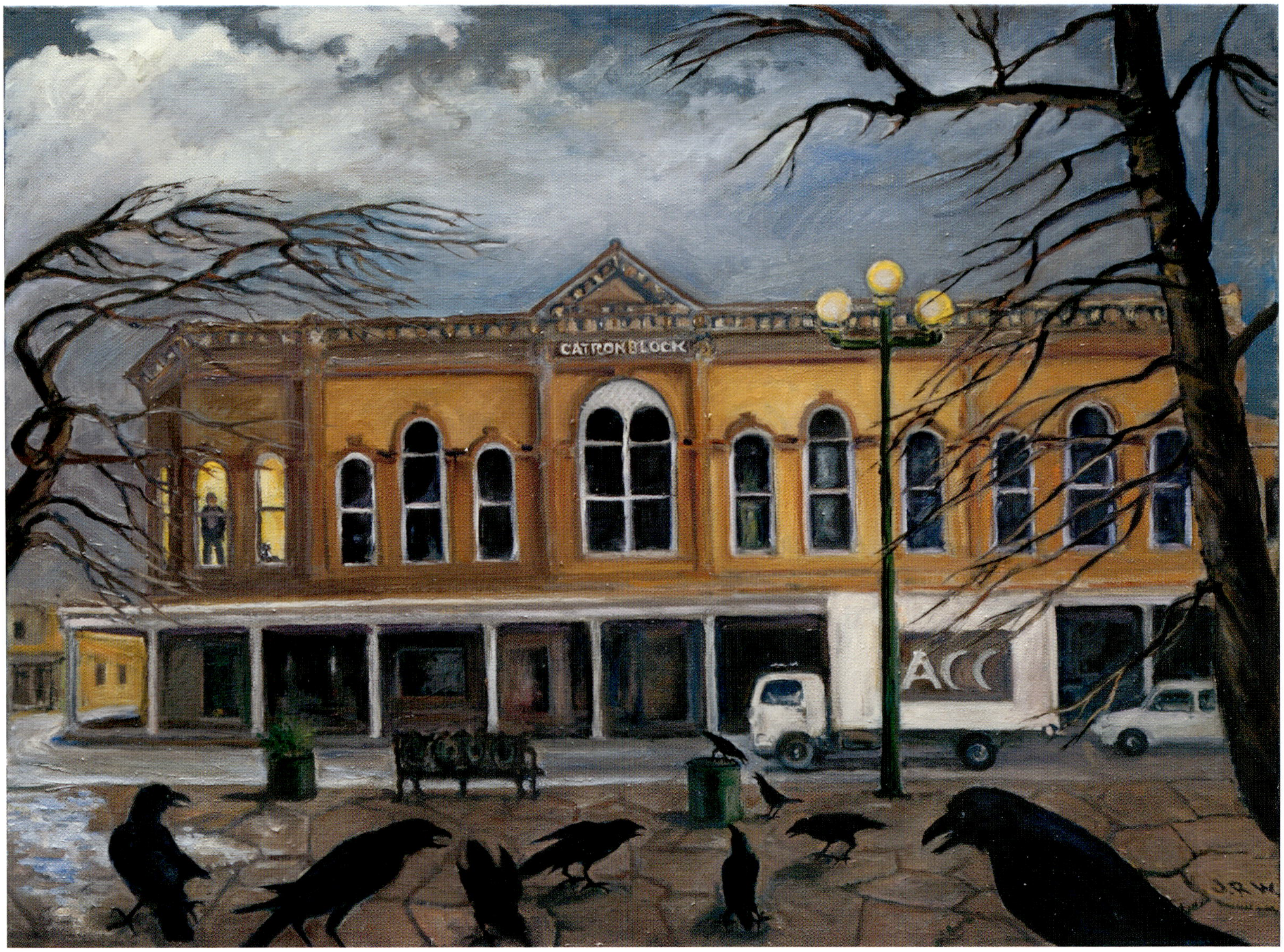

62.
Thomas Catron Returns to His Plaza Building, 2009
Oil on linen, 48 × 32 in.
Collection of Tom and June Catron

The ghost of Thomas Catron returns to Santa Fe, and to his old building, leaving behind his old colorful and adventurous past. Watching from his window, he's disturbed to find that the architecture and Santa Fe style police have managed to have a portal built on the front of his building and with some sort of "territorial flavor." The bricks on the building have been painted sort of adobe-like, but fortunately some of the decorative details of cornices have survived. Tom is excited to be back, and he perks up when he hears there's potential for oil drilling in the Galisteo Basin. He is really glad to see ravens still in Santa Fe.

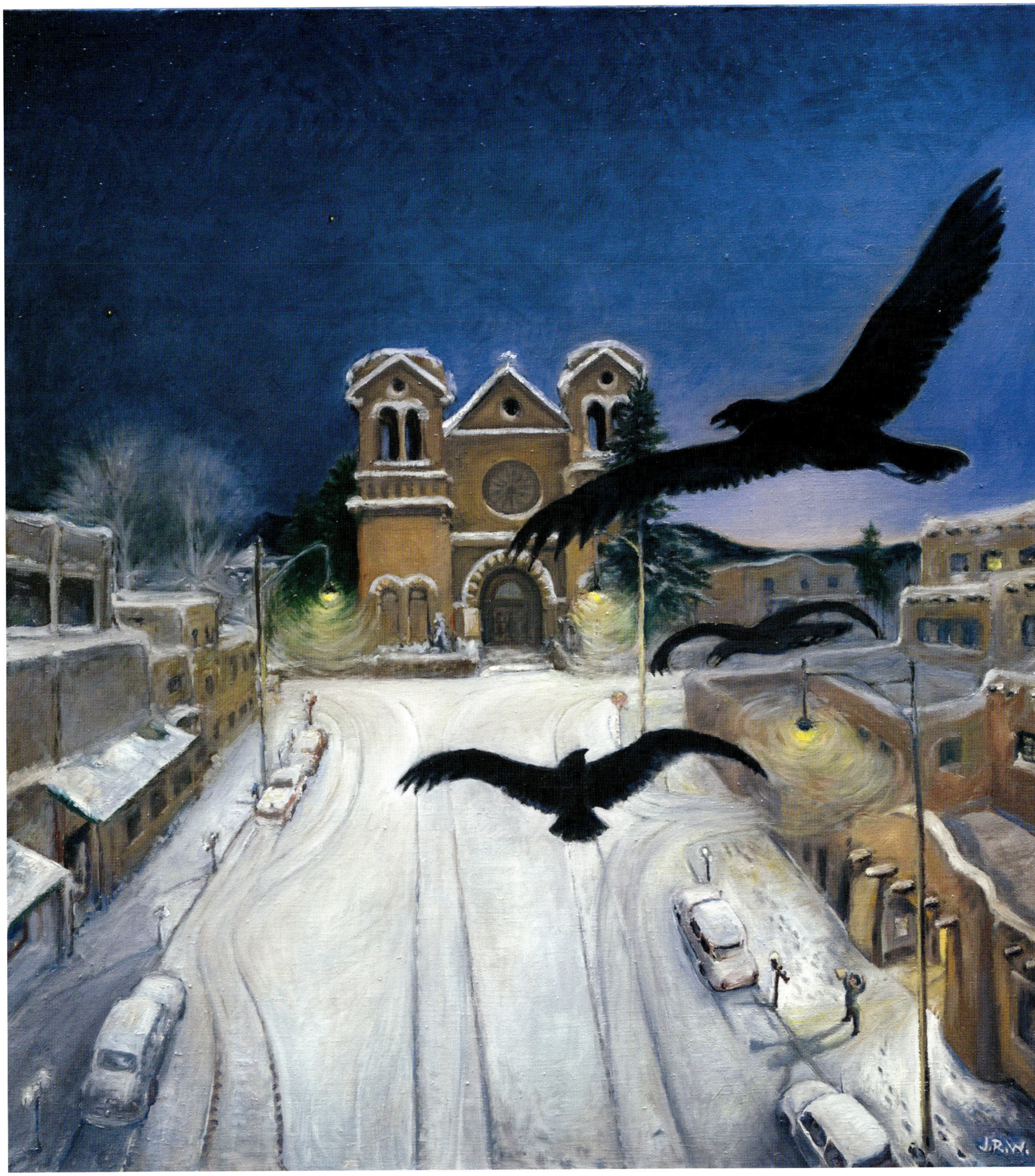

63.
Early Morning Snow, Ravens, and a Cathedral Called Saint Francis, 2009
Oil on linen, 48 × 52 in.

64.
The Ghost of Uncle Gene Returns to Fiesta and Rides into La Fonda Bar, 2009
Oil on linen, 48 × 48 in.
Collection of Meade Martin and Robin McKinney Martin

Our family moved from Canyon Road to the prairie world during the middle of the war in 1943. My Uncle Gene and his family moved out there too, shortly thereafter. Out on the prairie Uncle Gene became a more serious rancher and builder. Our families grew up together and survived the war years and postwar years in similar fashion. My brothers and I spent many days and weeks working side by side with Uncle Gene digging wells, repairing windmills, moving cows, branding calves, constructing houses and barns. Gene worked hard, loved his family, and loved his ranch and animals. He was ever the beautiful, handsome man who liked to be seen and perceived as a working guy with rough hands and scratches and blood on his hands or face. He had a great gift of making friends.He loved bars and, yes, even fights that also went with them. He loved country dances and could keep a party going strong until dawn. The myth is that Gene would ride twenty or more miles to Santa Fe Fiestas for parties, parades, and good times. It was claimed that Gene once rode his horse into a bar. So in this painting I honor Gene, his undaunted spirit, his gift for laughter, his ability to tell stories, and for his great and unshakeable gusto for life.

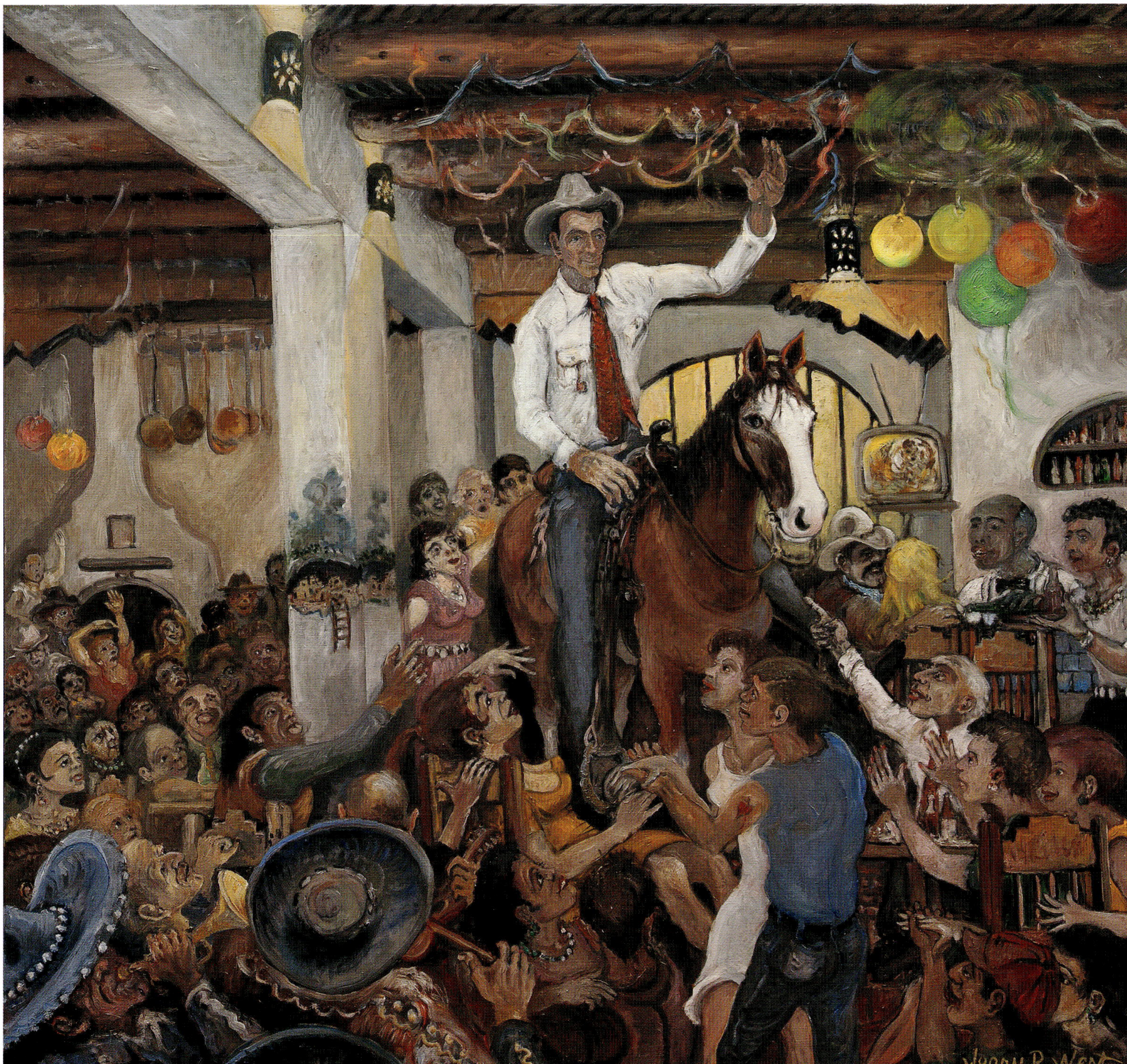
Jerry R. West

65.

Georgia O'Keeffe Pays a Visit to the Plaza Bar, 2009

Oil on linen, 36 × 48 in.

Collection of Linda Durham

There was a moment back in the 1980s when Georgia O'Keeffe was being recycled into even greater prominence. There was talk that some serious patrons were investing huge sums of money toward creating a museum in Santa Fe exclusively for Miss O'Keeffe and her work, and she was the star of a documentary about her life on PBS. I walked into the Plaza Bar, a good hideout for the art crowd, the night of the broadcast. The booths were filled with people snuggled together, smoking, drinking, and talking. No one in the dingy barroom paid the least bit of attention to O'Keeffe on TV except for myself and another guy. I invented a lot in this painting. I put my friend and great artist Ted Rose in the painting with his wife Polly. Ted and Polly had met in that bar years before. By the time I made the painting, Ted had died. The blind artist being led by a seeing-eye dog I invented as a metaphor for the artists, who are supposed to be the ones who "see" and really attempt to dig deep into the human psyche. Far too often we fall short of that mark.

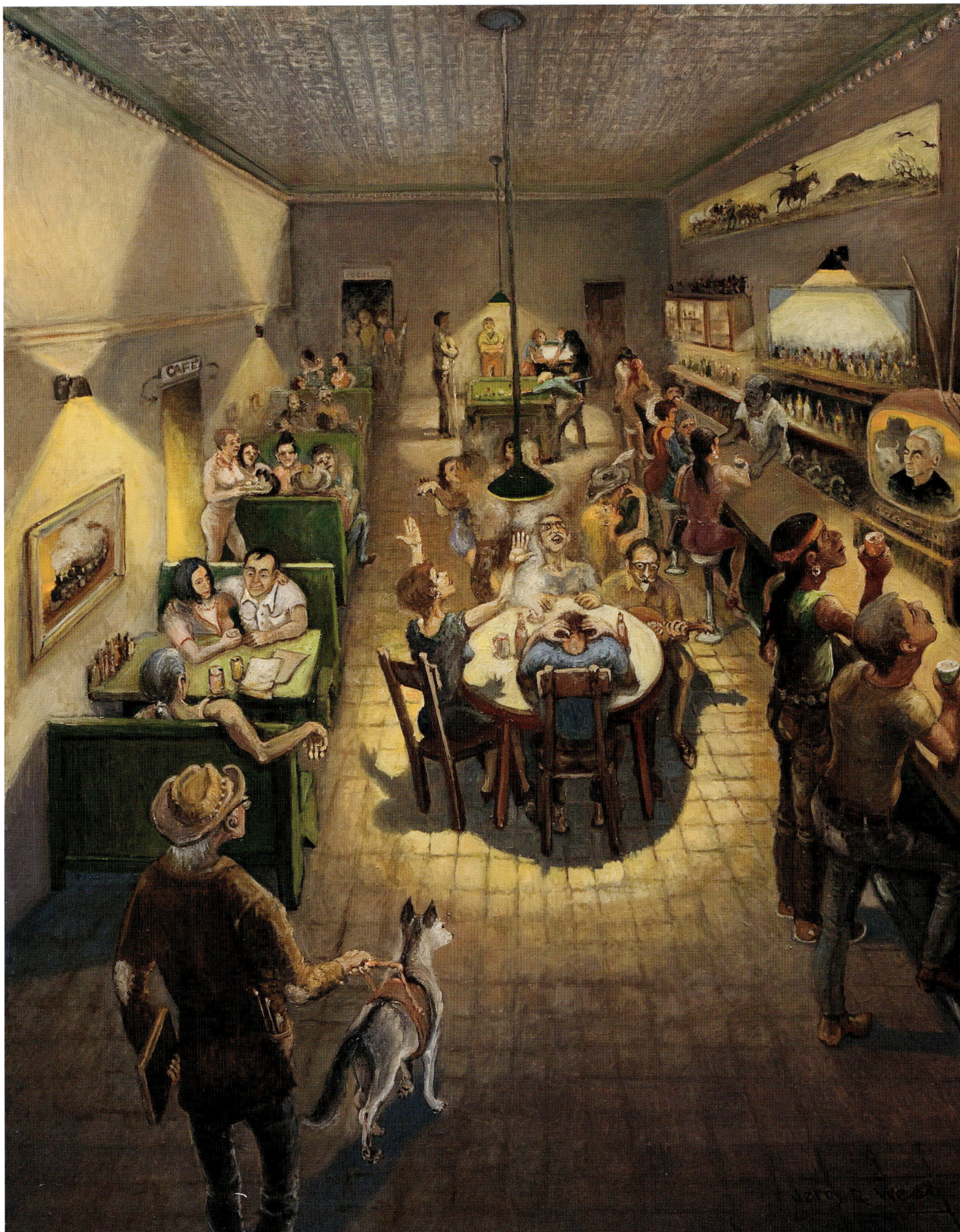
CAFE

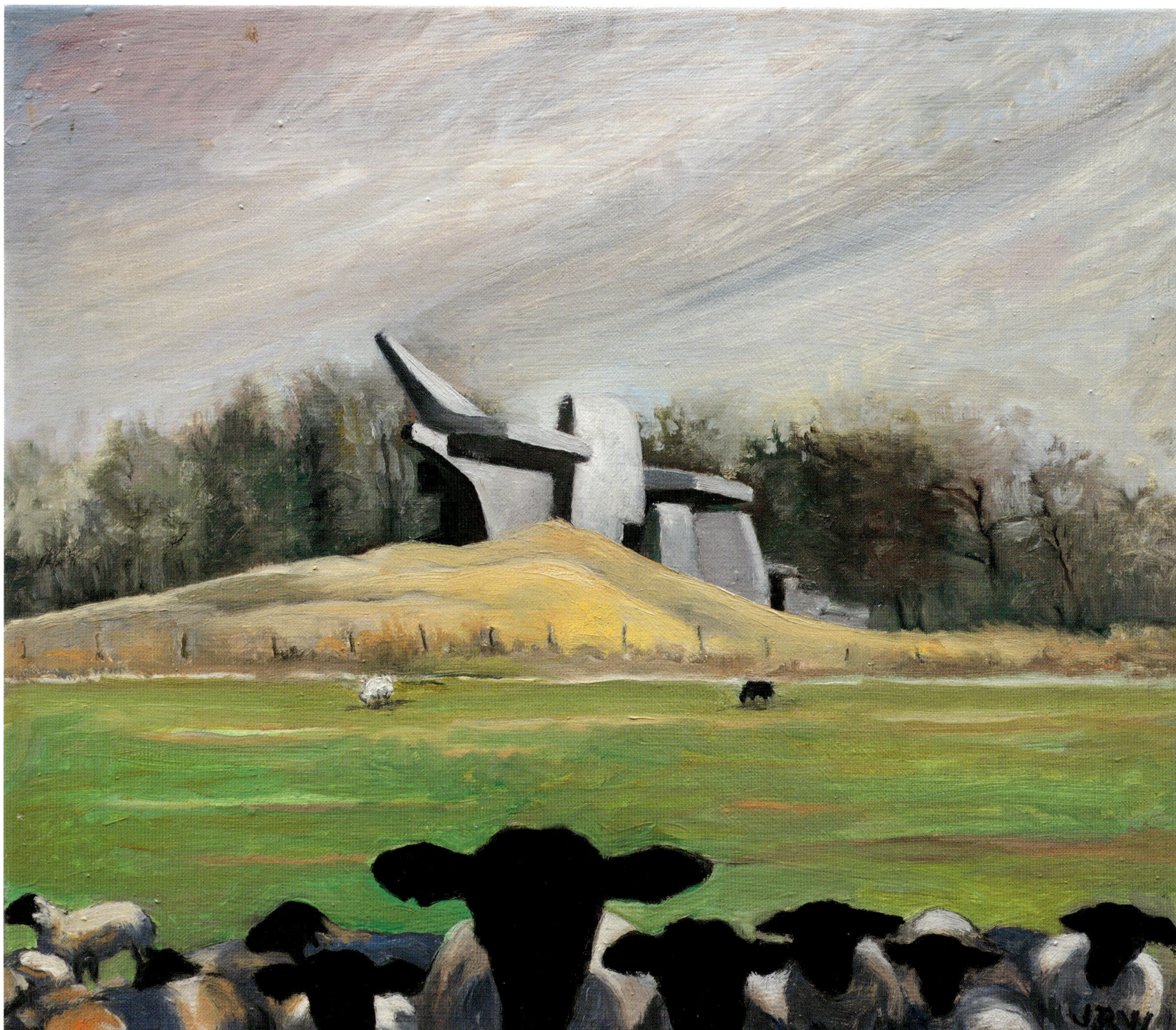

66.
Blackface Sheep at the Henge of Roswell, 2012
Oil on linen, 24 × 18 in.
Collection of Donald and Sally Anderson

VII. A Trip to Roswell, New Mexico

One day early in 2011, while I was painting and wintering in the landscape of Serafina, I received a letter from Donald Anderson and Stephen Fleming, the founder and executive director, respectively, of the Roswell, New Mexico, Artist-in-Residence Program. A special category in residency had been created for the upcoming 2012 year in celebration of the centennial of New Mexico statehood. They wanted an older, lifetime resident of New Mexico to fill the position of "centennial artist." I was honored to accept and told them I would join them in January.

In April 2011, I invited friends to my last opening in the Serafina studio and then returned to Santa Fe to begin preparations to spend a year painting in Roswell. I worked the rest of that summer and fall building a couple of small houses and finishing up a few projects at my Santa Fe studio.

Having never been in a residency lasting a full year, and never before having the luxury to set aside other work to paint every day for a year, I was a little apprehensive. In anticipation I visited Roswell often to explore and discover the town. One day I met Arturo Gonzales. He and his wife, Lucy, ran a café called Mi Casita. Arturo was interested in Mexican revolutionary history, and we both shared a love for Mexican artists such as Rivera, José Posada, and Orozco. I talked him into letting me paint a mural along one wall in his café that would portray some of the places and people he admired, including his family. We made a "trade deal," and from that time on for three days and nights a month from June to November, I made the trip from Santa Fe to Roswell to paint the mural. I would set up a scaffold, move tables and chairs, put down tarps, and paint hard and fast. The customers always seemed to enjoy the process as much as I did.

By the time I officially started the residency on January 1, I felt I was getting a feel for the town of Roswell. I'd met lots of people from many parts of town with many different perspectives and professions. I had talked to farmers, ranchers, mechanics, oil-drillers, teachers, doctors, politicians, military personnel, and local boxers, and I had begun seriously painting. Shortly after I arrived, Arturo, his family, and I had a party with an official unveiling of the mural in his café. It was an amazing cross-cultural happening, complete with paper decorations, a Mexican band, food, speeches, and dancing. It was an exciting way to start my residency and to celebrate a sense of community. I continued through the year painting, sketching, photographing, hiking, and exploring. I interviewed and painted many people in Roswell: my fellow artists in residence and locals, including well drillers, ranchers, and boxers. In November my final show was scheduled at the Roswell Museum and Art Center, and it was time to account for what I had accomplished. My art was in many ways a meditation on objects, animals, people and their environment, stories, and histories. My paintings were psychological, allegorical landscapes. I called my painting year "A Trip to Roswell, New Mexico."

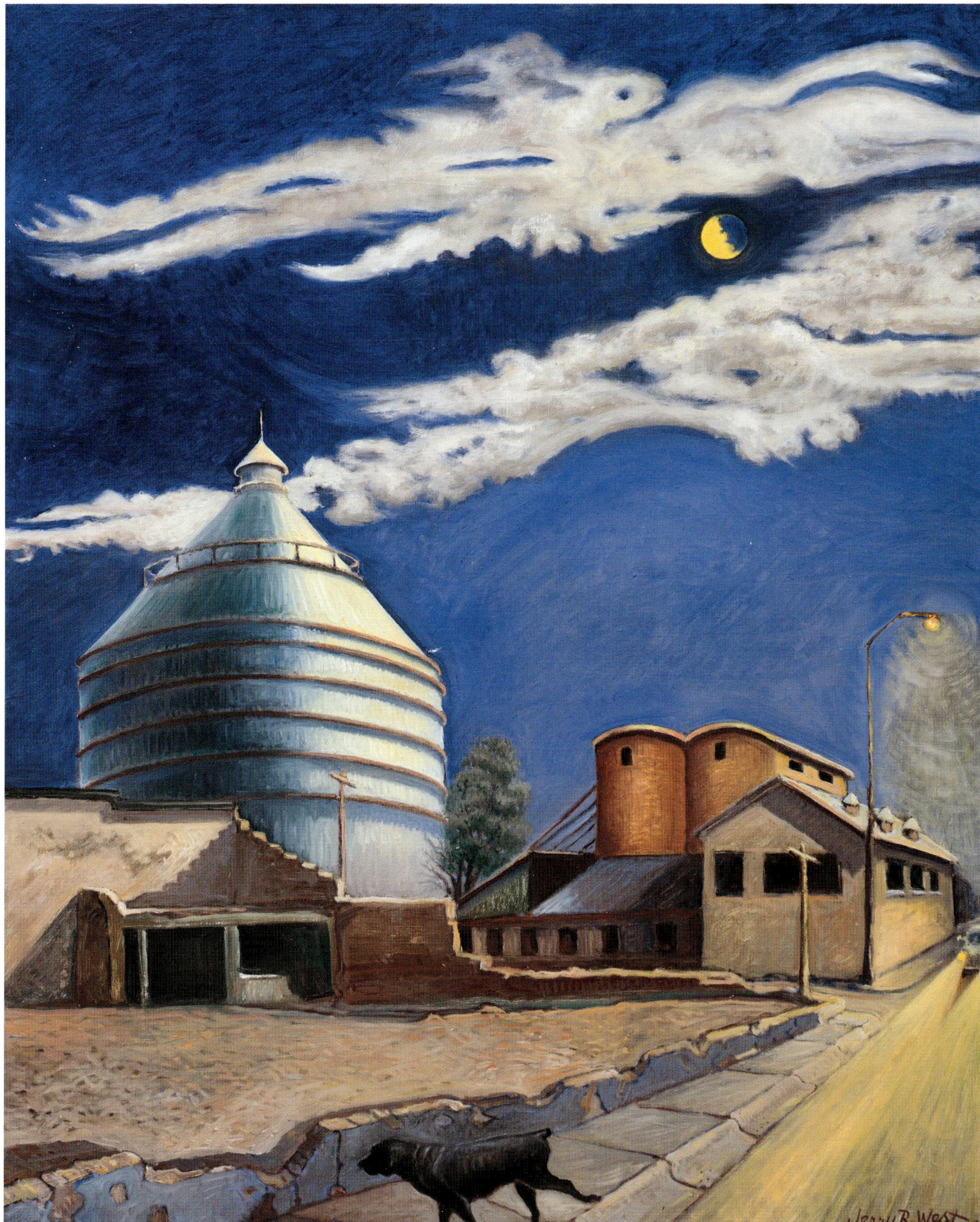

67.
Cotton Warehouse with Black Dog and Broken Moon, 2012
Oil on linen, 38 × 48 in.
Anderson Museum of Contemporary Art

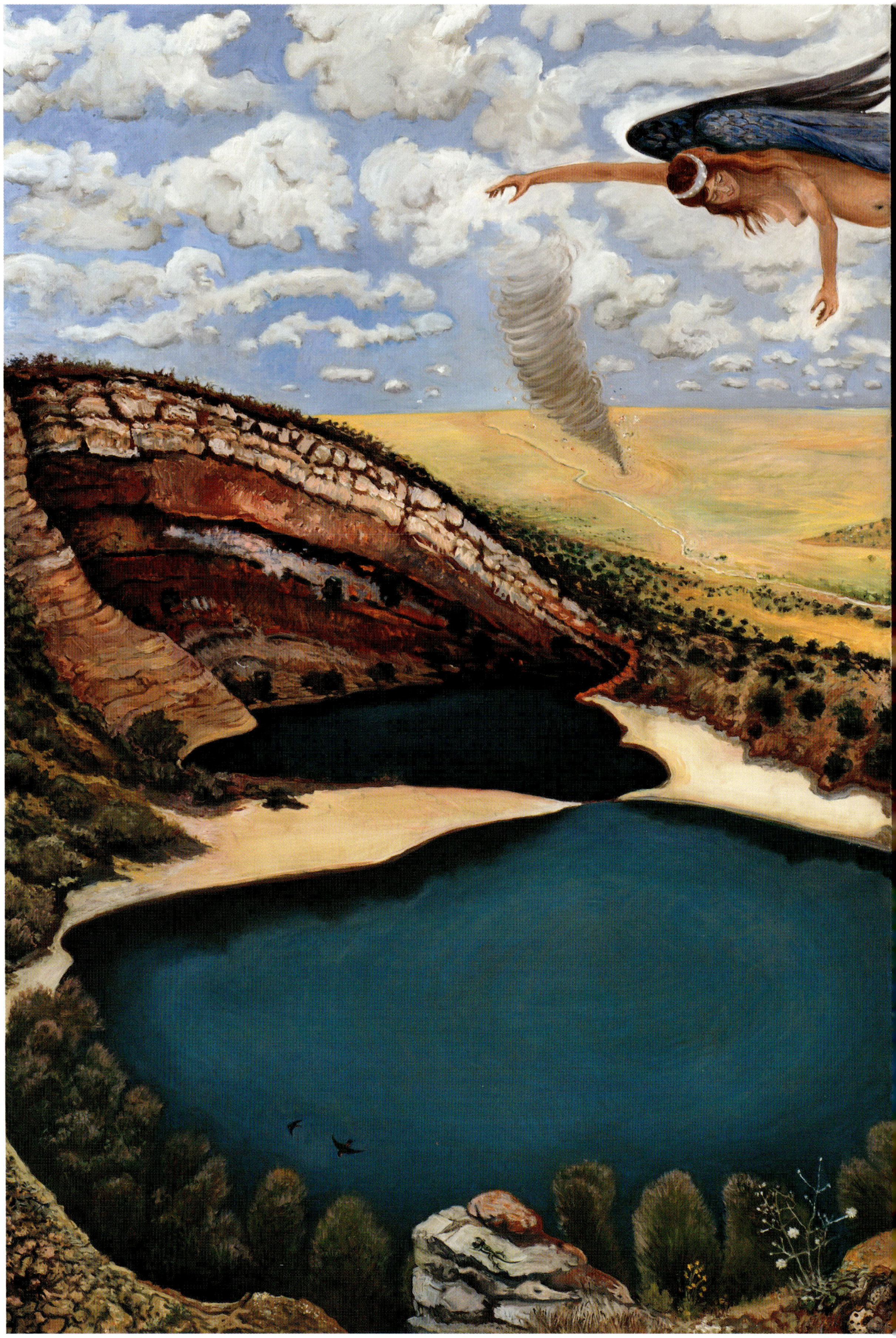

68.
Artist in Search of Tranquility, 2012
Oil on linen, 96 × 72 in.
Collection of Meridel Rubenstein

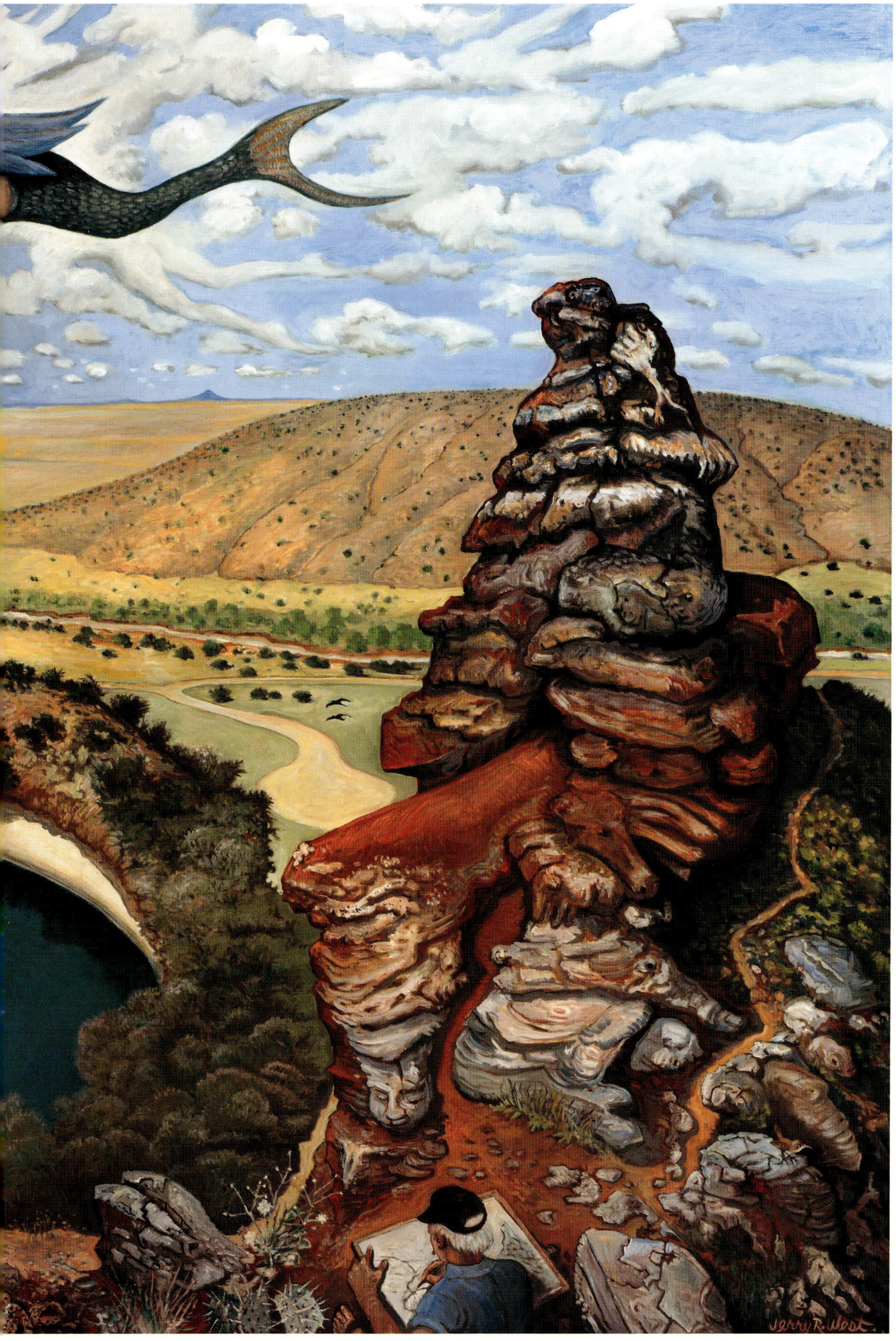
Jerry R. West

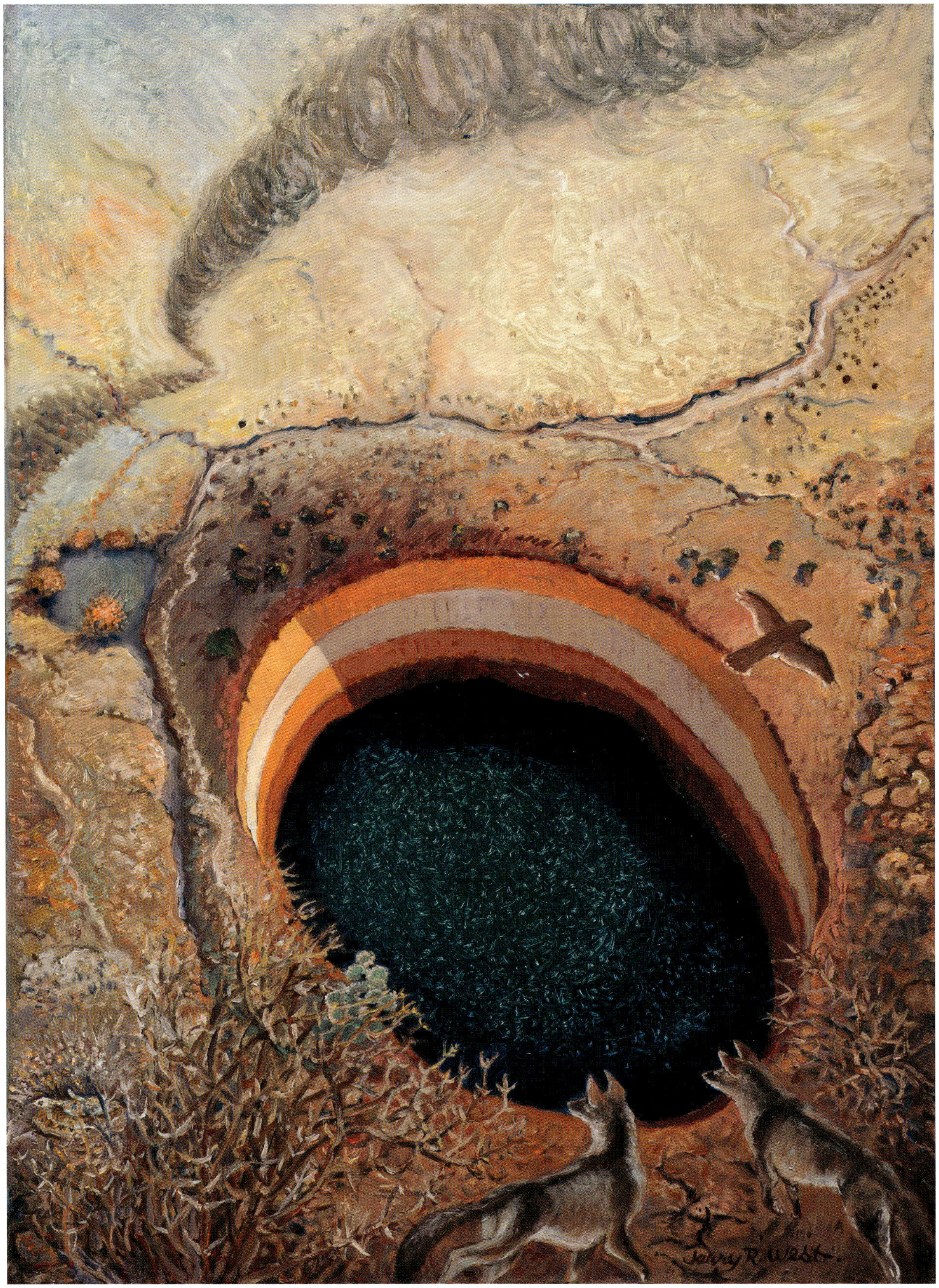

69.
Inkwell Sinkhole with Coyotes, Rattlesnake and Distant Dust Devil, 2012
Oil on linen, 24 × 30 in.
Collection of Sally Parsons

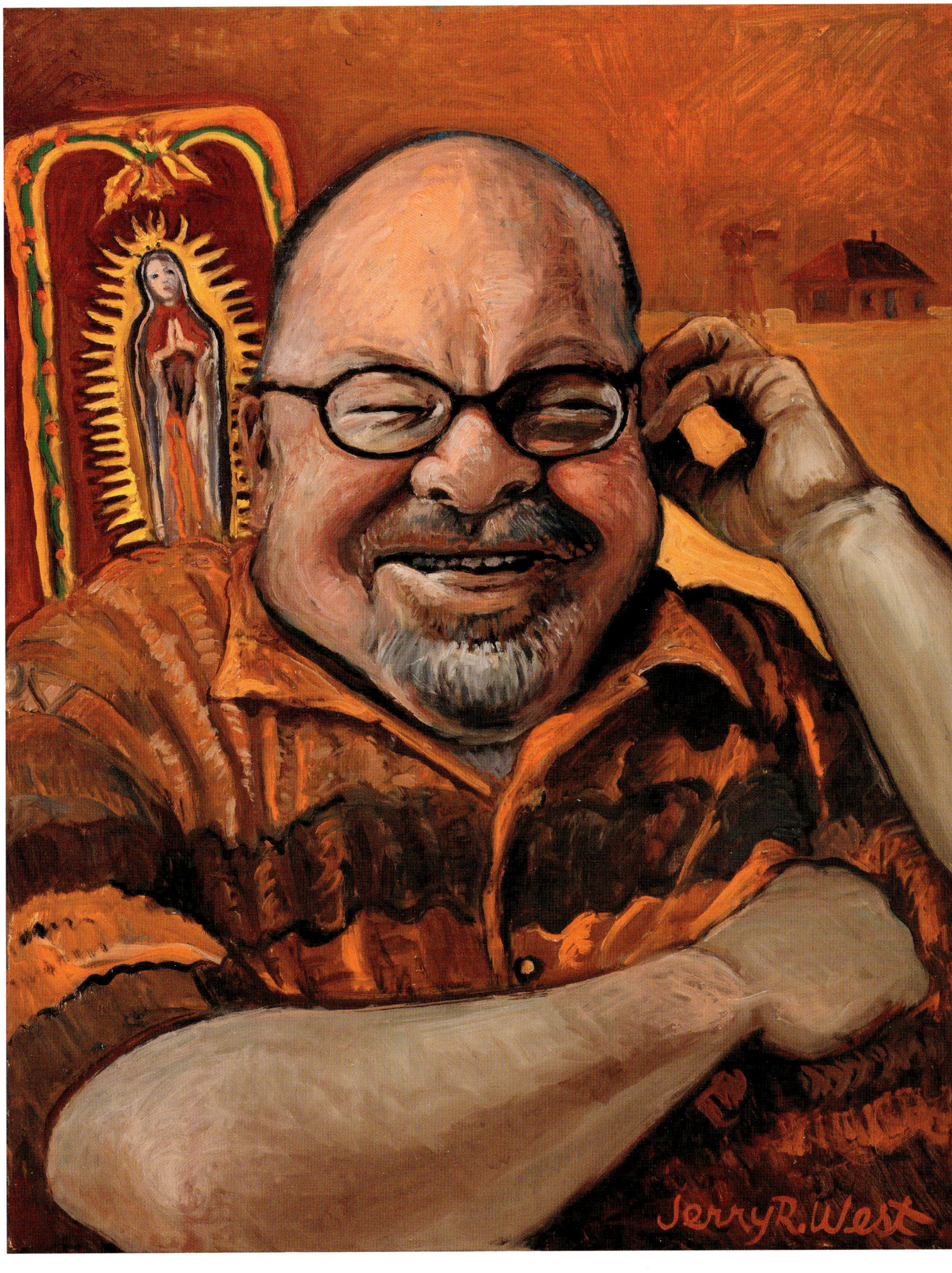

70.
Brinkman Randle, 2012
Oil on Masonite, 18 × 24 in.
Collection of Sharbani Das Dupta

71.
Mysterious Exodus from Roswell Farm, 2012
Oil on linen, 40 × 42 in.
Collection of Ann and Phelps Anderson

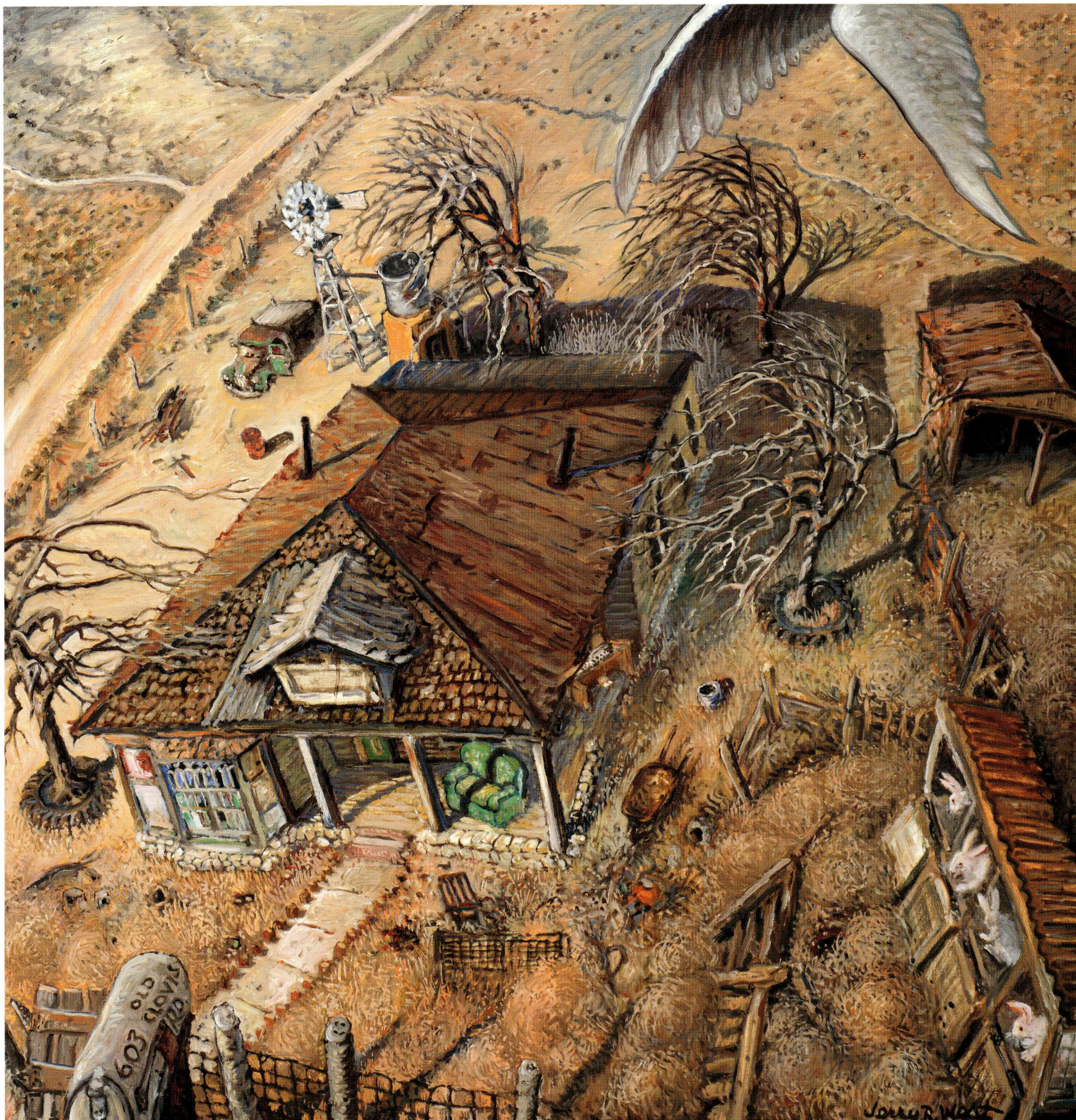
603 OLD CLOVIS RD.
Jerry R. West

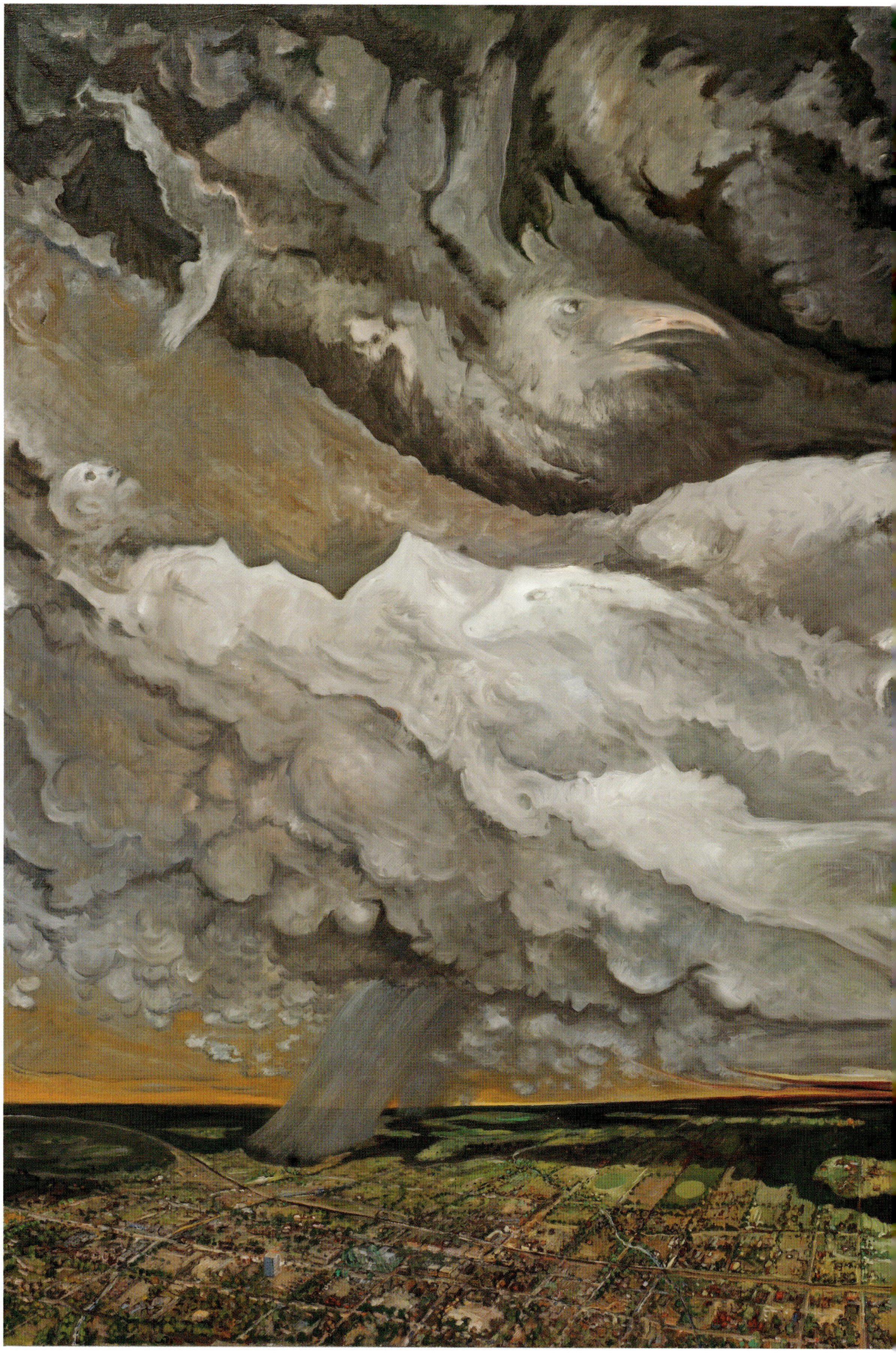

72.
Cosmic Storm Approaching Roswell, 2012
Oil on linen, 96 × 72 in.

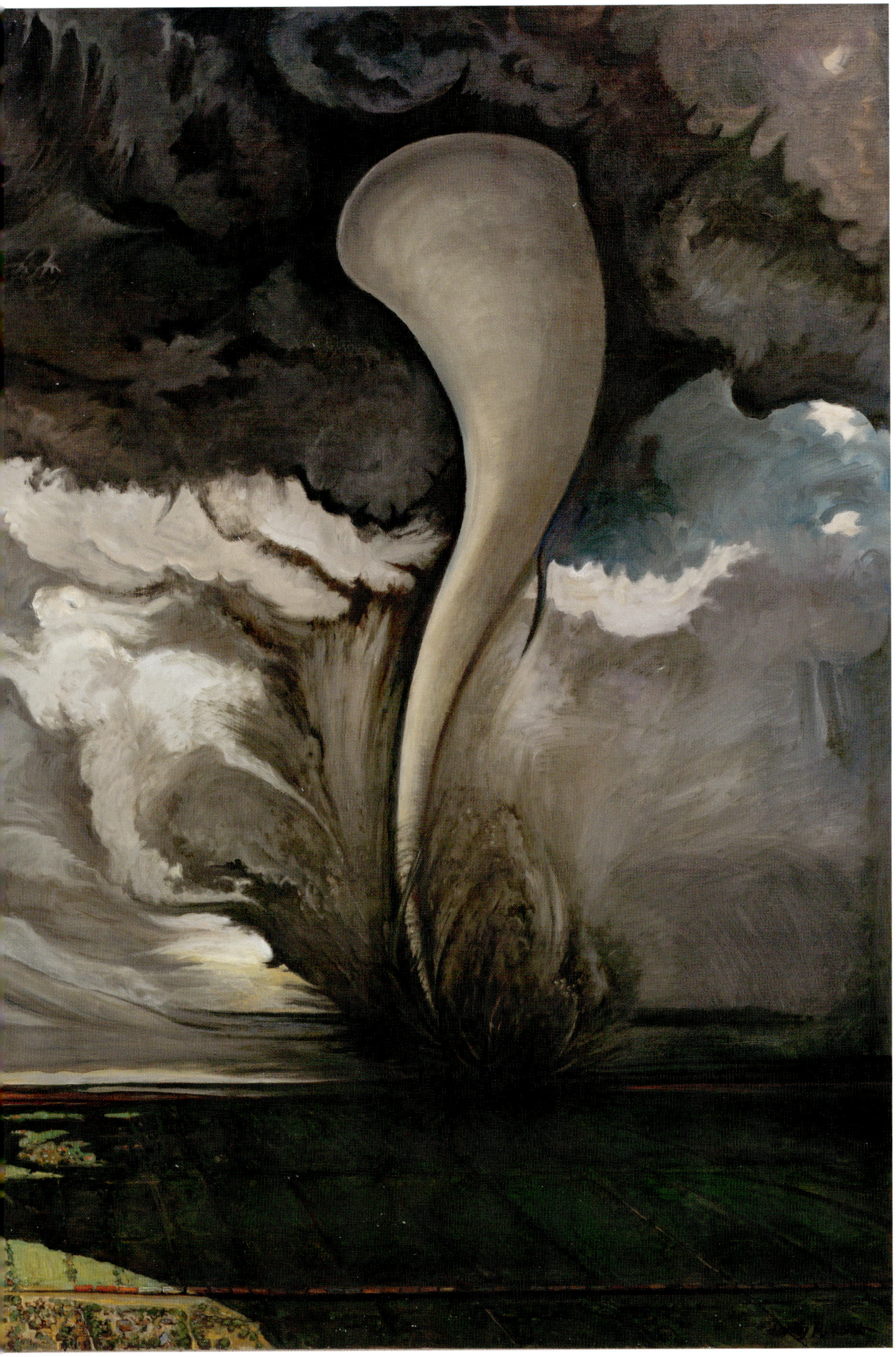

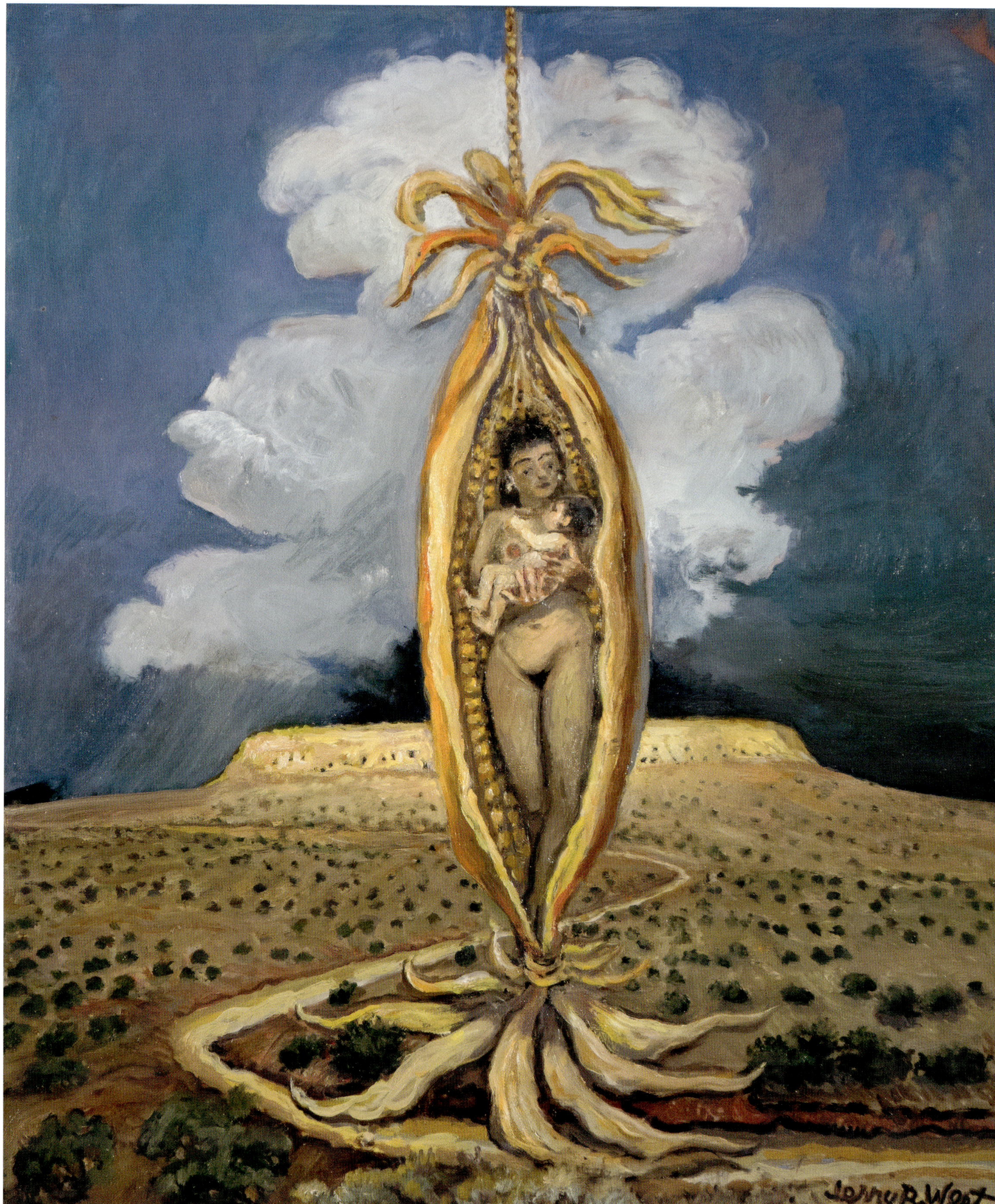
Jerry R. West

VIII. Another Return

I returned to the prairie south of Santa Fe in late May 2013, and I reinhabited my old studio at #6 Loma Oriente, near the old family homestead. I started making paintings of the world around me, including fires in the Jemez Mountains, inspired by recent years' intense fires in the area. I reintroduced myself to the high-desert region by visiting the Hopi world and Navajo country and Taos, as I have always seen these visits as being an intrinsic part of my return.

Toward the end of the year I showed my larger Roswell work along with some newer pieces at James Hart's gallery, Phil Space, in Santa Fe. The show was supported with the screening of a short documentary about my work filmed by John Eddy. During the winter holidays I held an open house at my prairie studio with a show of my drawings, etchings, and recent paintings.

I found myself eager to begin a new adventure, returning to the countryside with a sketchbook and again getting back to the process of painting.

73.
Corn Woman with Child, 2013
Acrylic on Masonite, 18 × 24 in.
Collection of John Eddy
Photograph by John Eddy

74.
Cerro Pelon and Lone Coyote, 2013
Oil on linen, 48 × 48 in.
Collection of Arthur Brooks

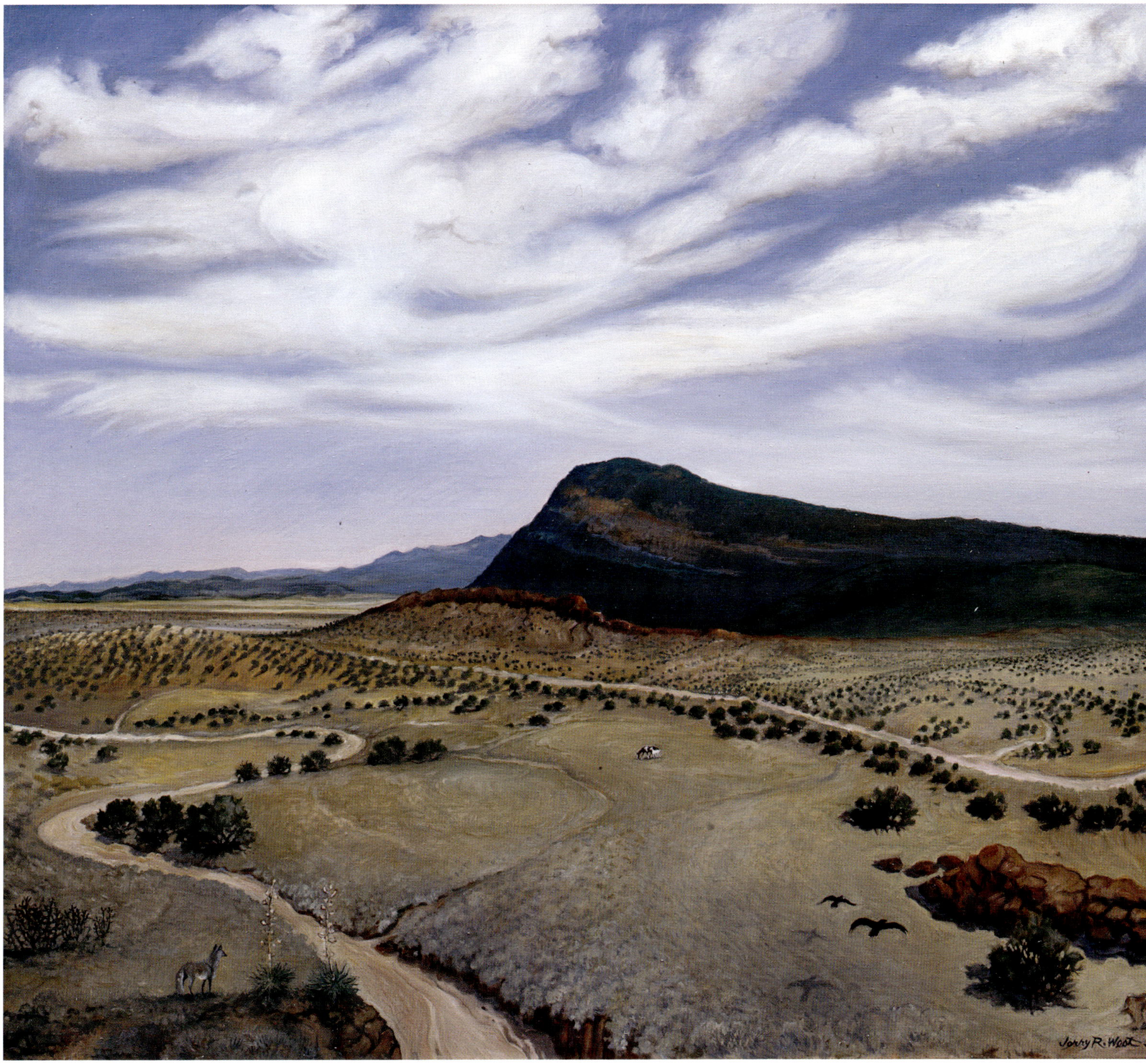

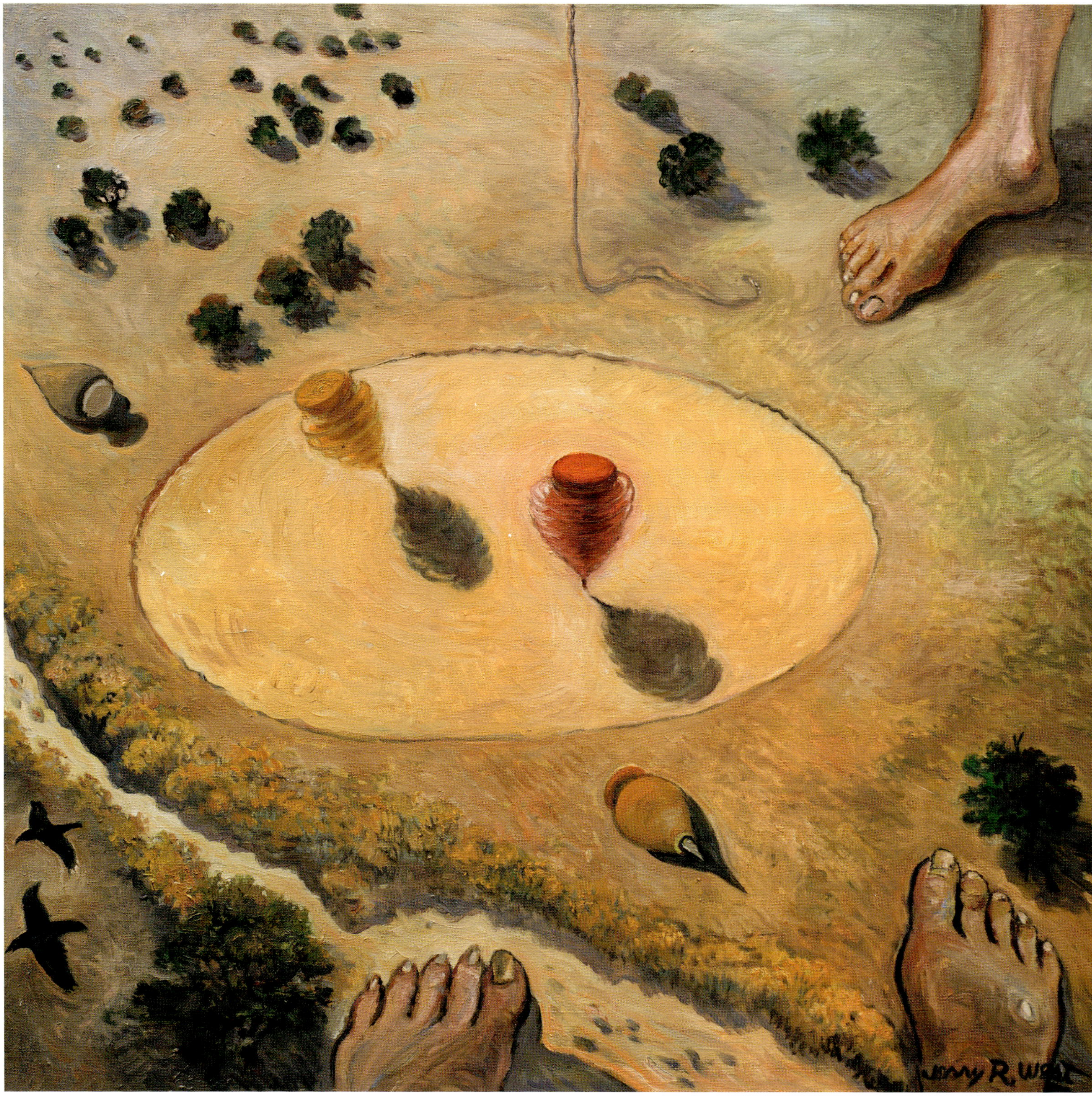

75.
Playground of the Gods, the Battle of the Tops, 2013
Oil on linen, 32 × 32 in.

76.
Playground of the Gods, the Gamble for Marbles, 2013
Oil on linen, 24 × 34 in.

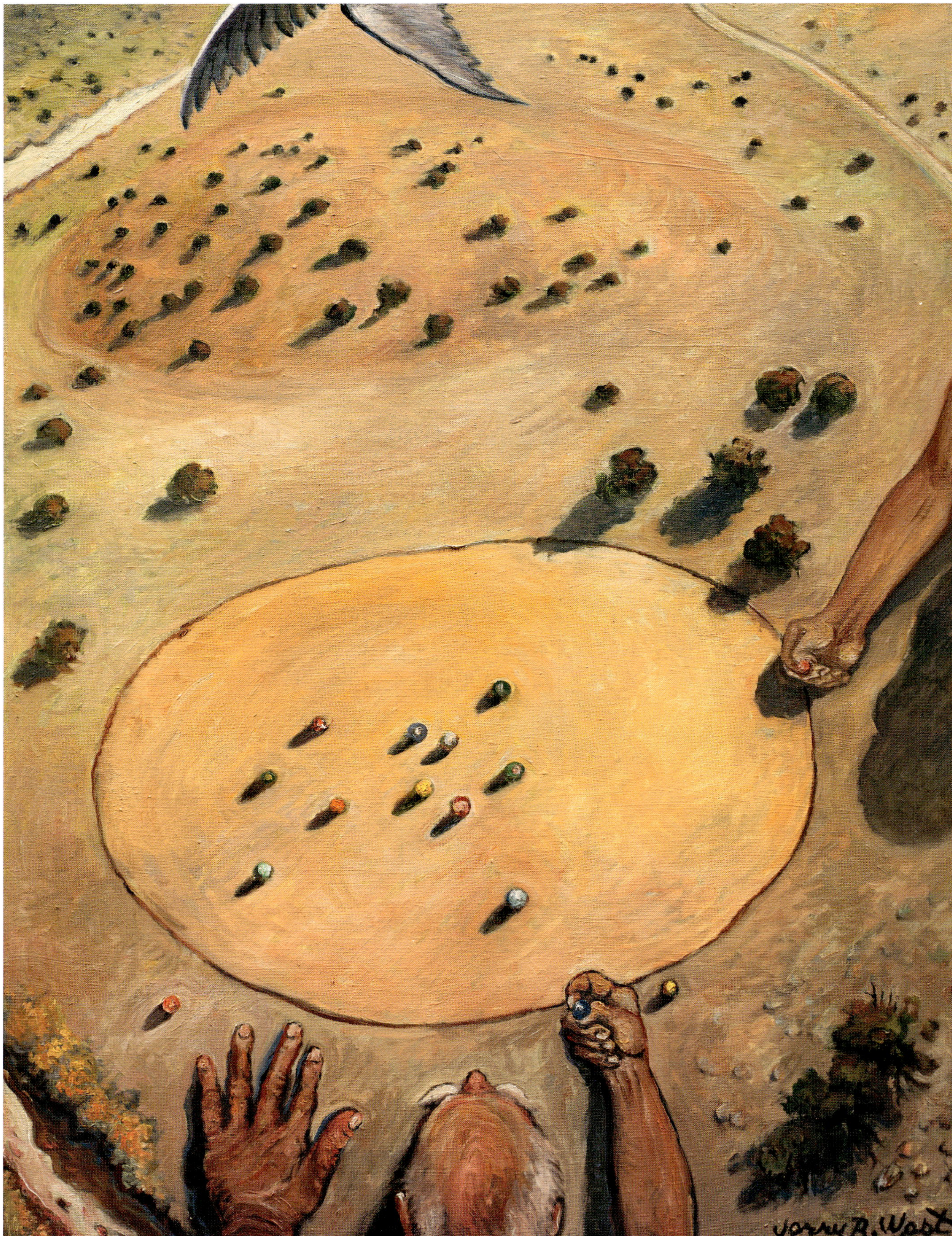
Jerry R. West

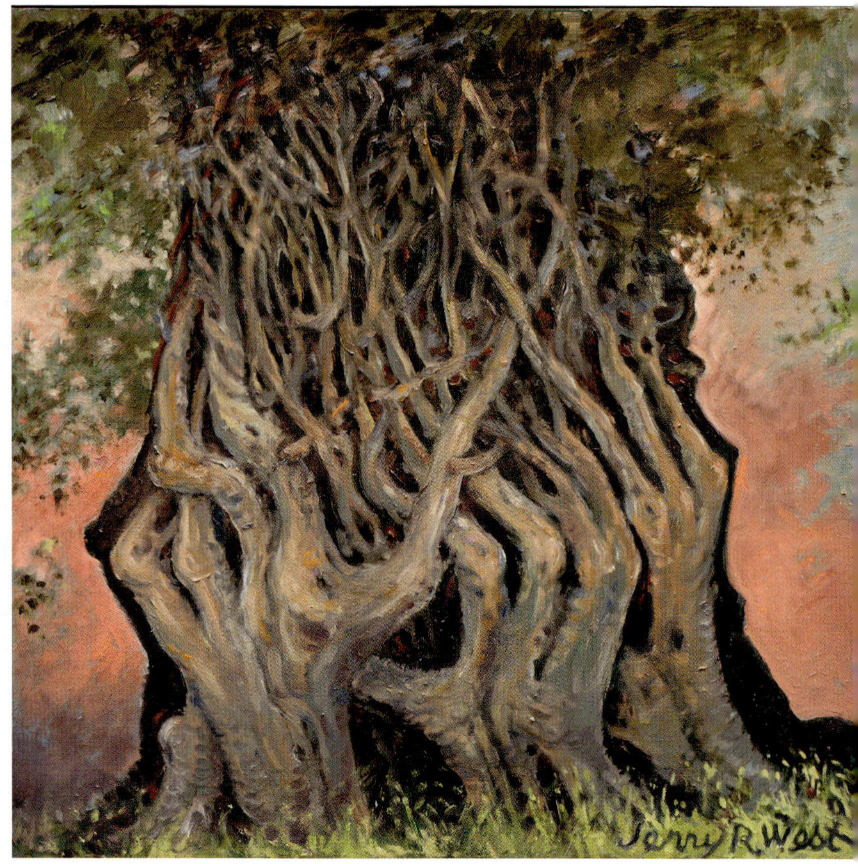

77.
Italian Olives in Singapore, triptych, 2013
Oil on Masonite, 54 × 18 in.
Private collection

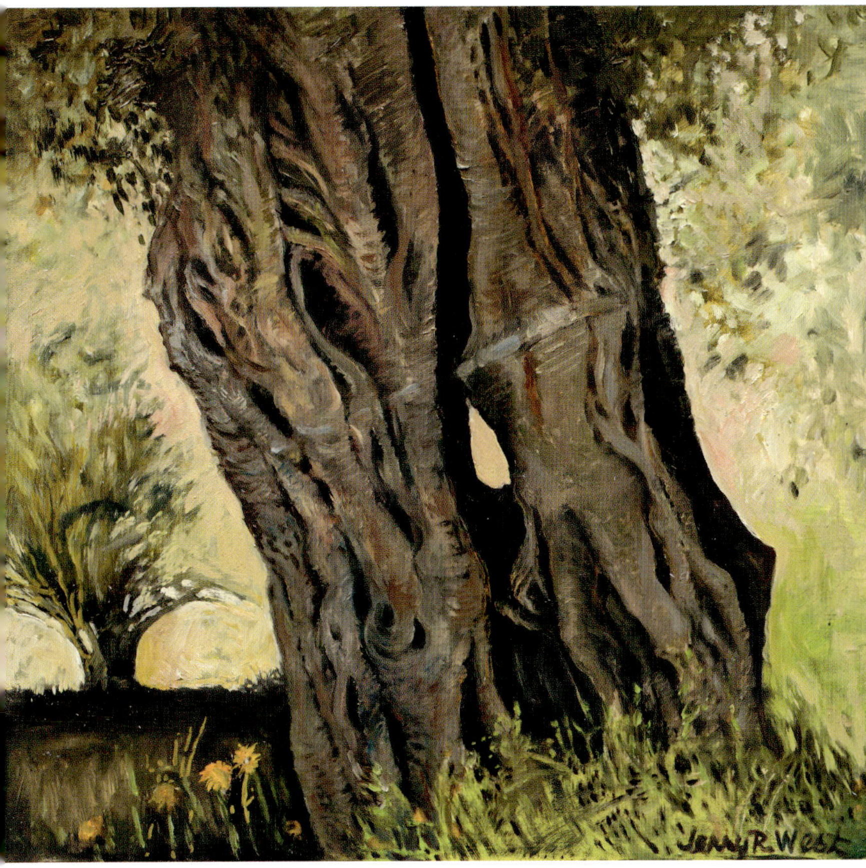
Jerry R. West

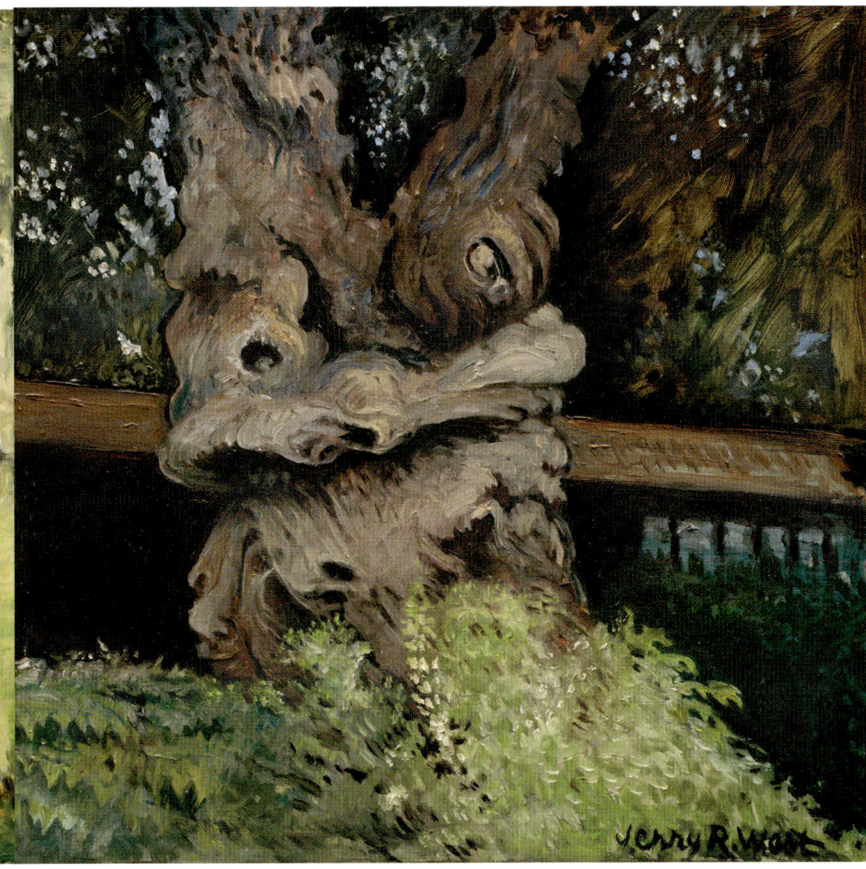
Jerry R. West

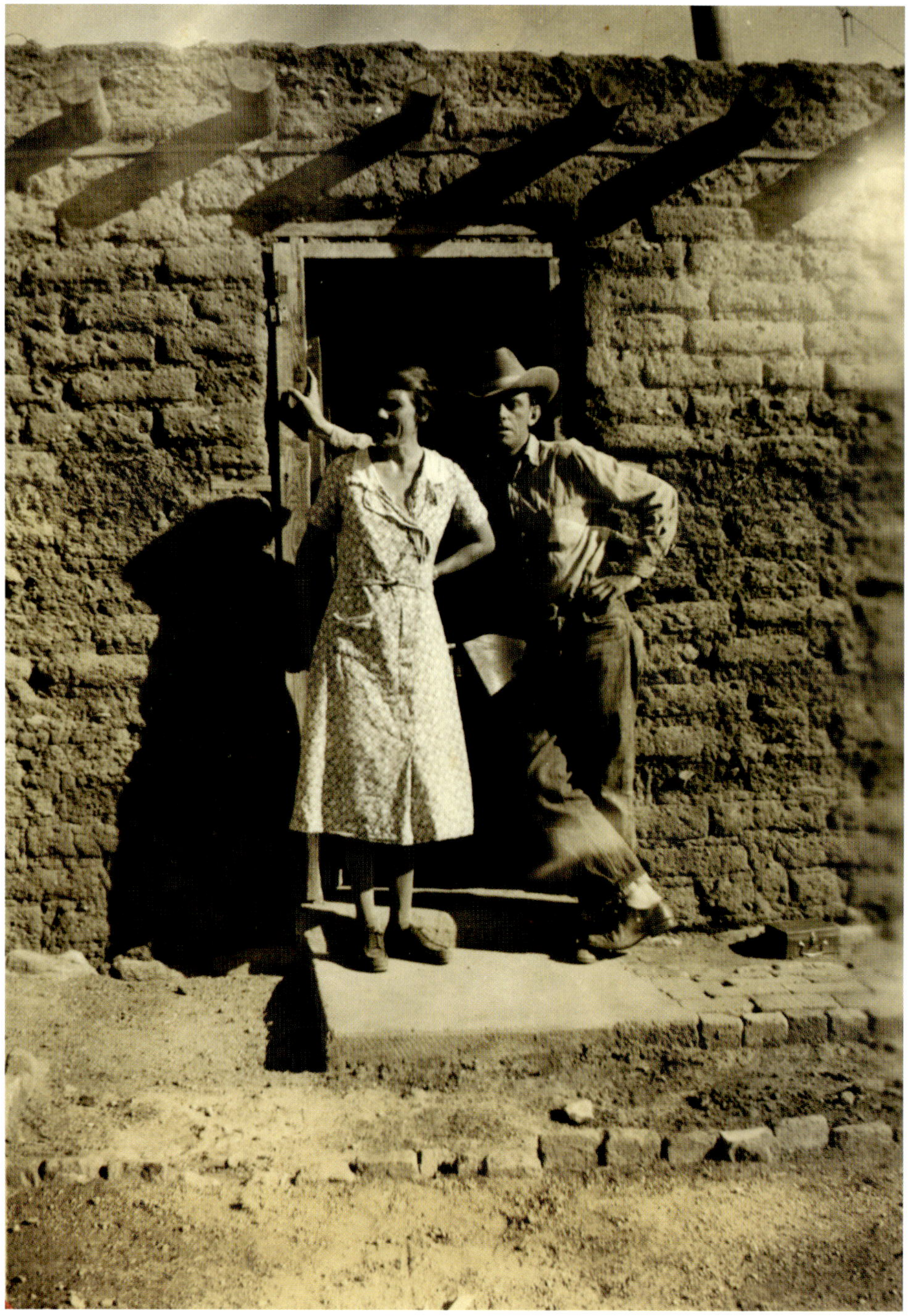

Mildred and Hal West in front of Hal's first printmaking studio, 1936, photographer unknown.

IX. The Artist As Printmaker

Printmaking has been a huge part of my image-making world. Some of my earliest and most engaging memories are of my father, Hal West, carving wood and linoleum blocks for making prints. His studio and printing area were set up in a corner of the living room of our small adobe house when I was a young child. He used this studio from 1936 to 1941.

I can remember him sitting hunched over a small table, where he would first draw on a block before meticulously carving out the image, leaving the areas of high relief that would receive the ink. With a brayer, he would spread the ink on a flat glass pallet. The odors of the ink were intoxicating, as were the strange little clicking and crackling sounds made by the leather brayer as it picked up the sticky ink. Next he carefully laid the ink on the high areas of the carved block. On clean white paper, he placed the inked block, directly under the press. Then, after applying pressure, he raised the press bar and removed the block from the paper that retained the printed image. Hal would hold the print up between thumb and forefinger and show it to me with a big grin. What magic!

Years later, when I decided to study art at Highlands I enrolled in Elmer Schooley's Printmaking 101. I suspect that somewhere in my brain I was still carrying part of that childhood thrill of watching my father make block prints.

I admired Schooley's generosity and teaching method, and he shared his respect for the history of the ancient art of etching. I enjoyed the interactive spirit of cooperation that I found with my fellow students. I loved the excitement, the high level of energy, and the all-night work sessions in the studio. I was intrigued by the equipment: the presses, the simple, ancient hand tools, and the unique chemistry of printmaking. I left Highlands knowing that printmaking was to be a big part of my future as an artist.

For several years following graduate school I returned often to Highlands, where I was welcome to continue to use the facilities. Later I worked with a friend and fellow graduate, John Hogan, making prints in his studio in El Paso. I made lithographs, serigraphs, and etchings. My travels to New York led me to the printmaking studio of

Bob Blackburn. There I met fellow printmaker Cathy Caraccio, and I returned in the late 1990s to print in her studio.

I taught art at both Santa Fe High School and the Santa Fe Preparatory School, and in California at the University of California, Santa Cruz, where I taught etching and painting, and also made my first reductive woodblock prints.

Eventually, I obtained my own etching press, and for years have made many large, multicolored etchings out of my own studio. I still continue to move between the two great disciplines of painting and printmaking.

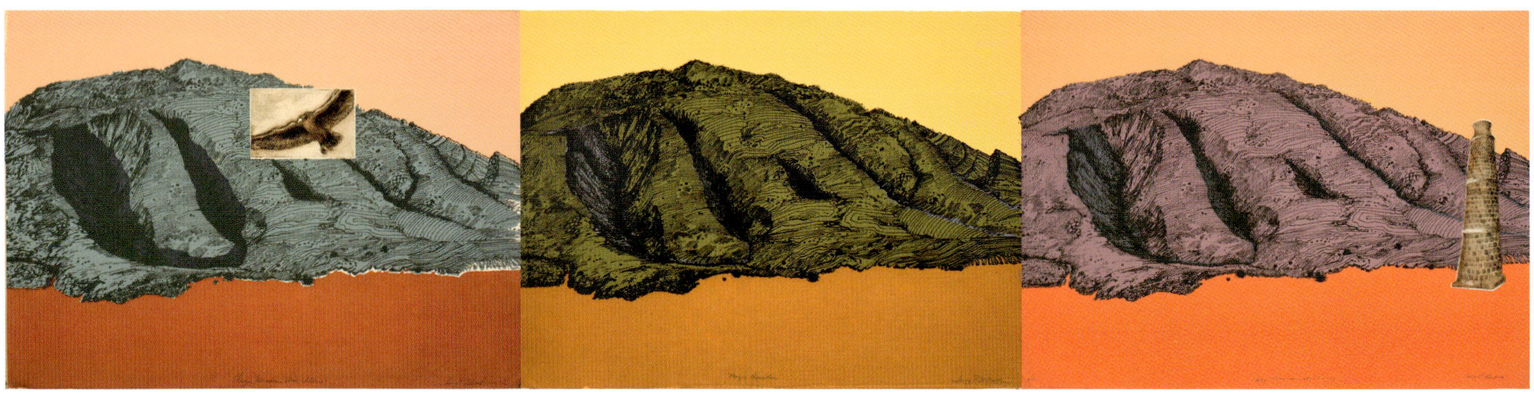

78.
Magic Mountain, 1972
Serigraph print with etching, triptych,
72 × 24 in.
Edition of 10

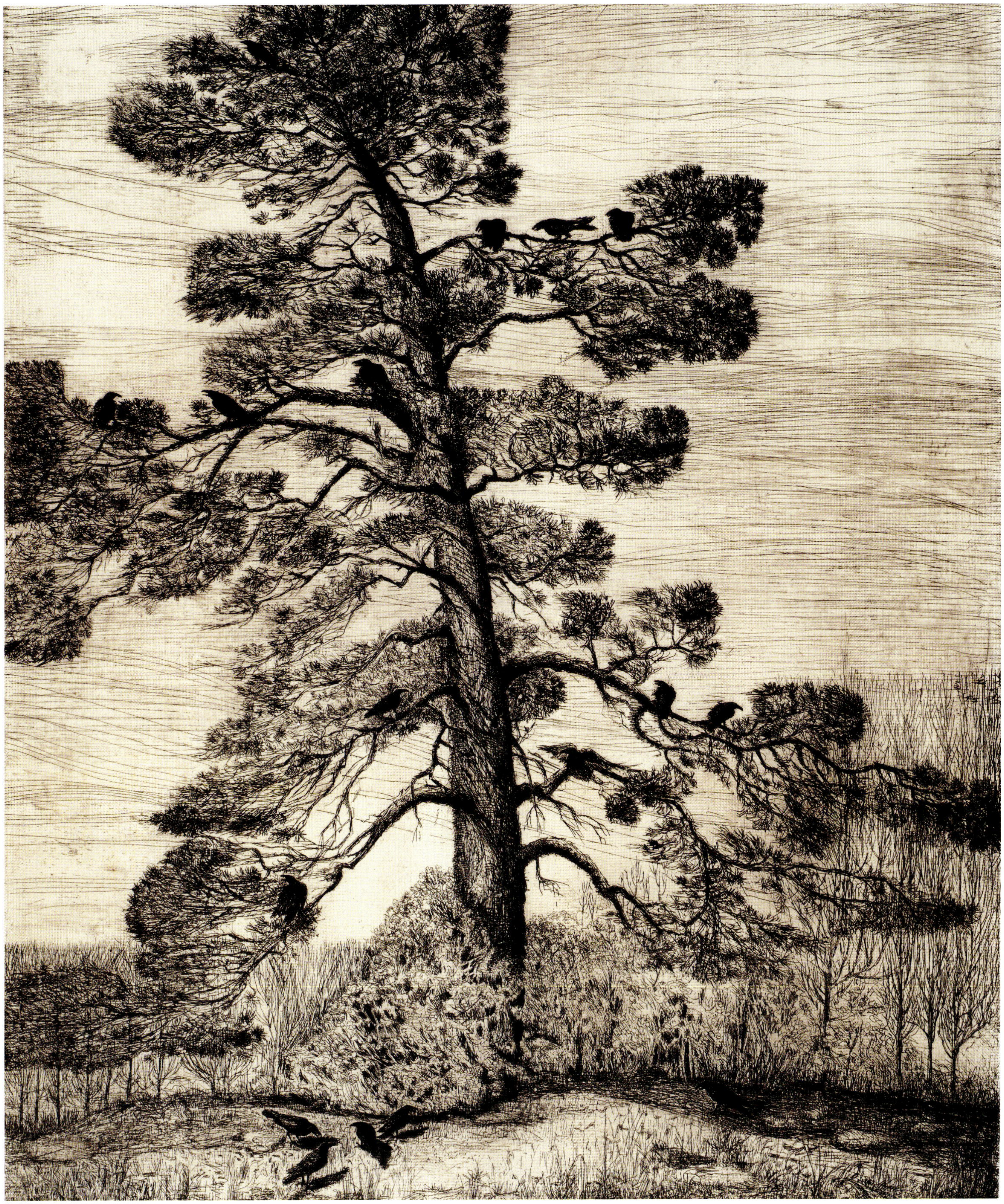

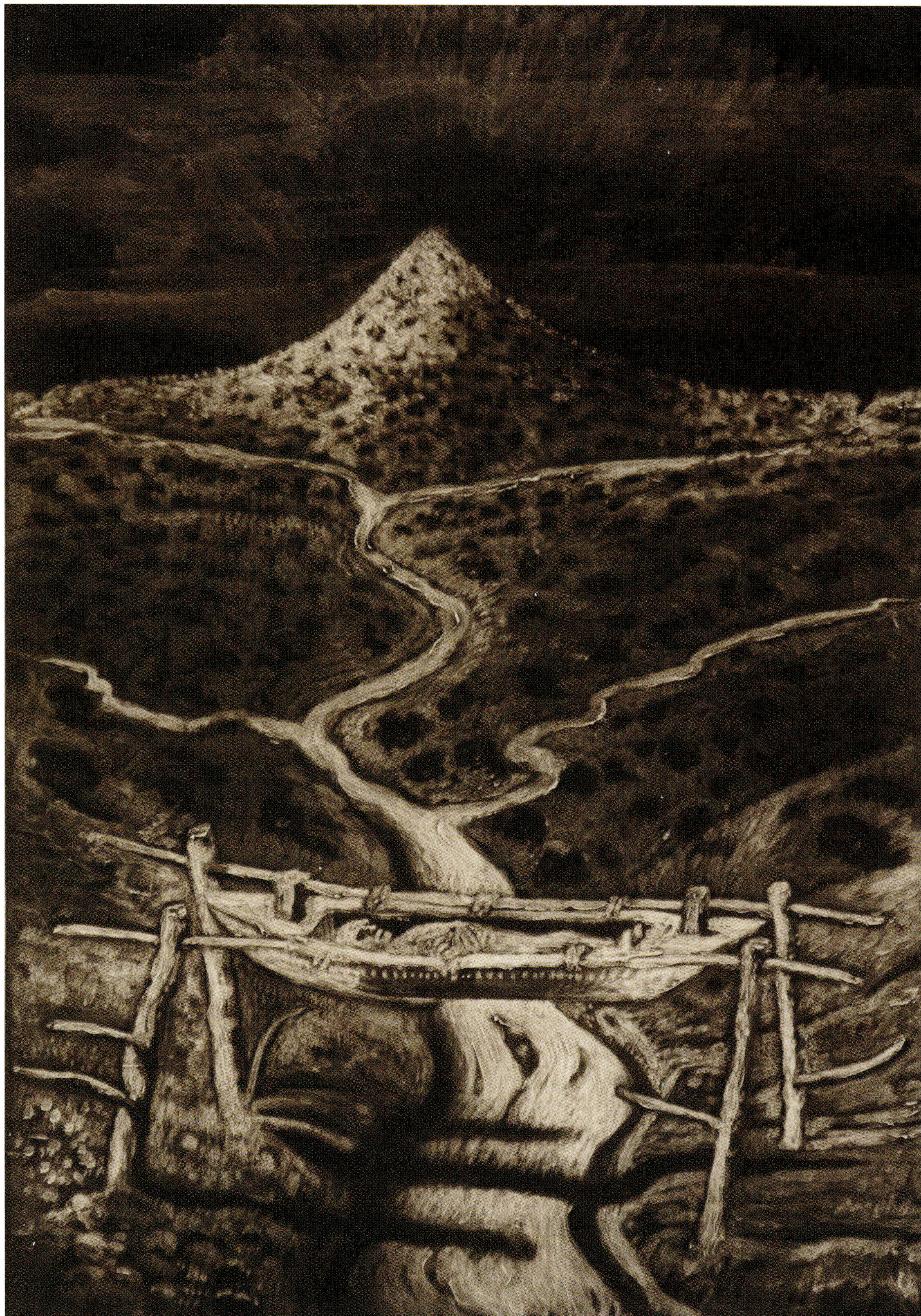

83.
Boat Coffin for Matriarch, 1990
Silk screen aquatint, 15 × 21 in.
Edition of 10
Photograph by John Eddy

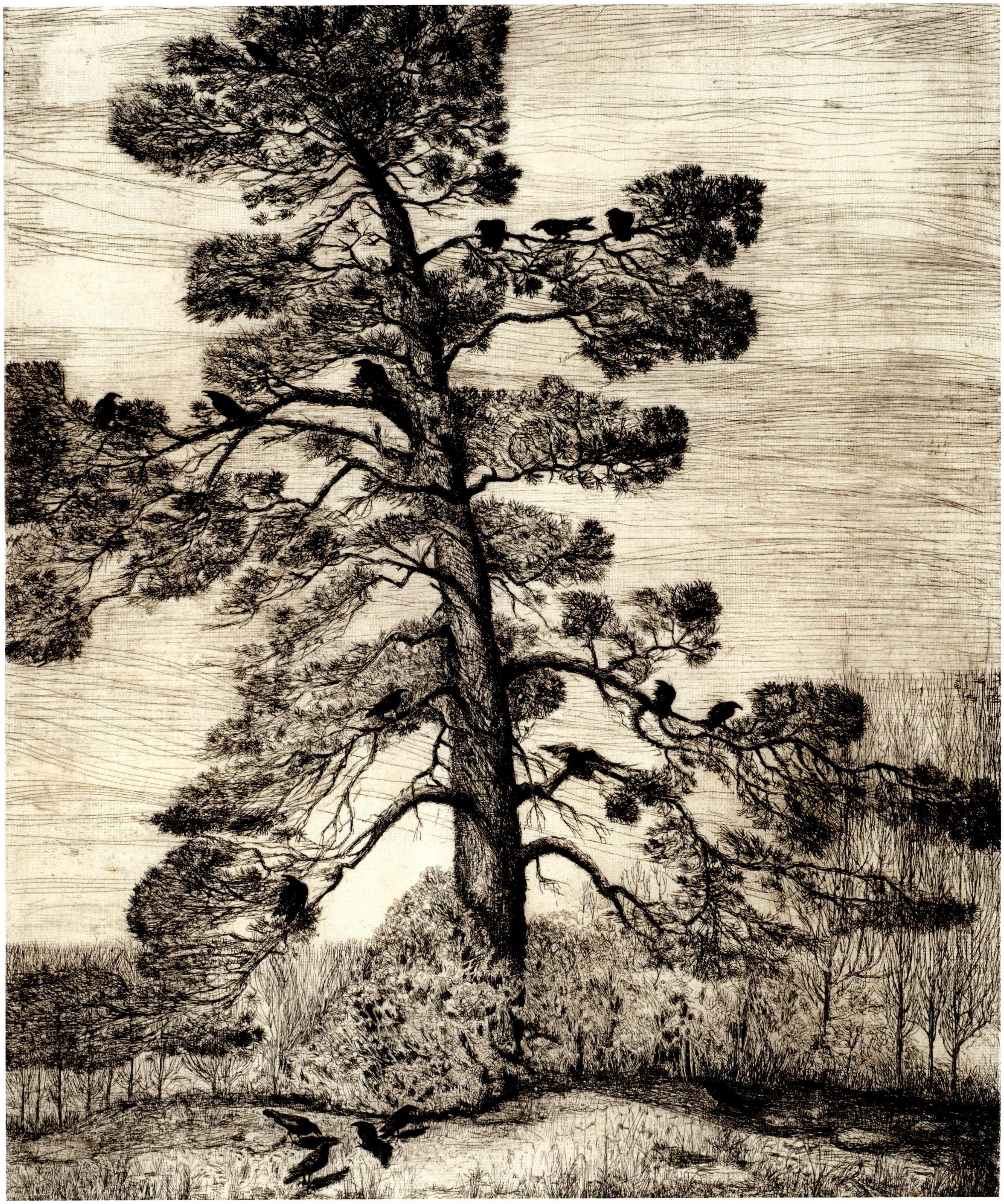

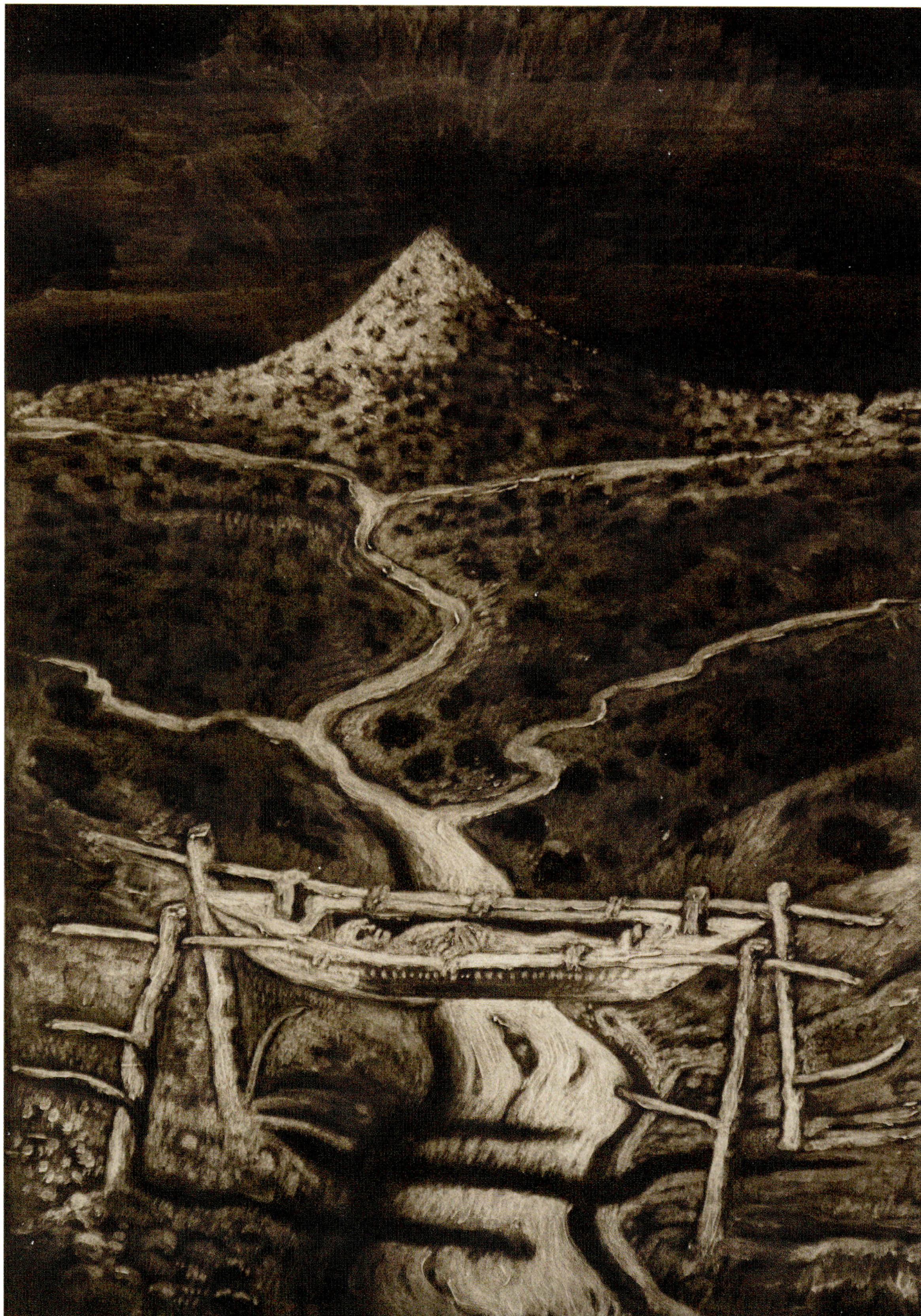

83.
Boat Coffin for Matriarch, 1990
Silk screen aquatint, 15 × 21 in.
Edition of 10
Photograph by John Eddy

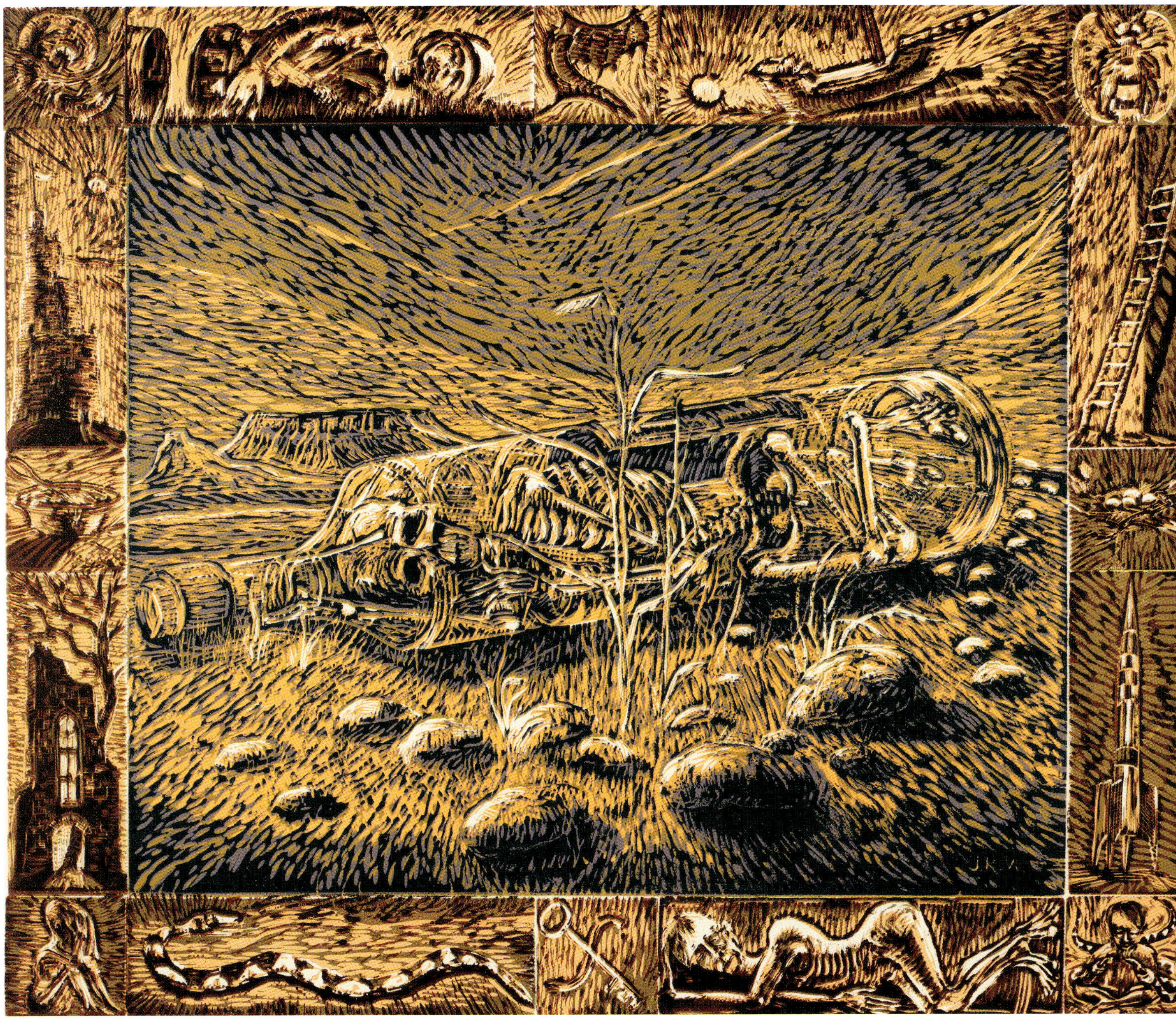

84.
Death in a Bottle, 1990
Reductive woodcut print, 30 × 22 in.
Edition of 8

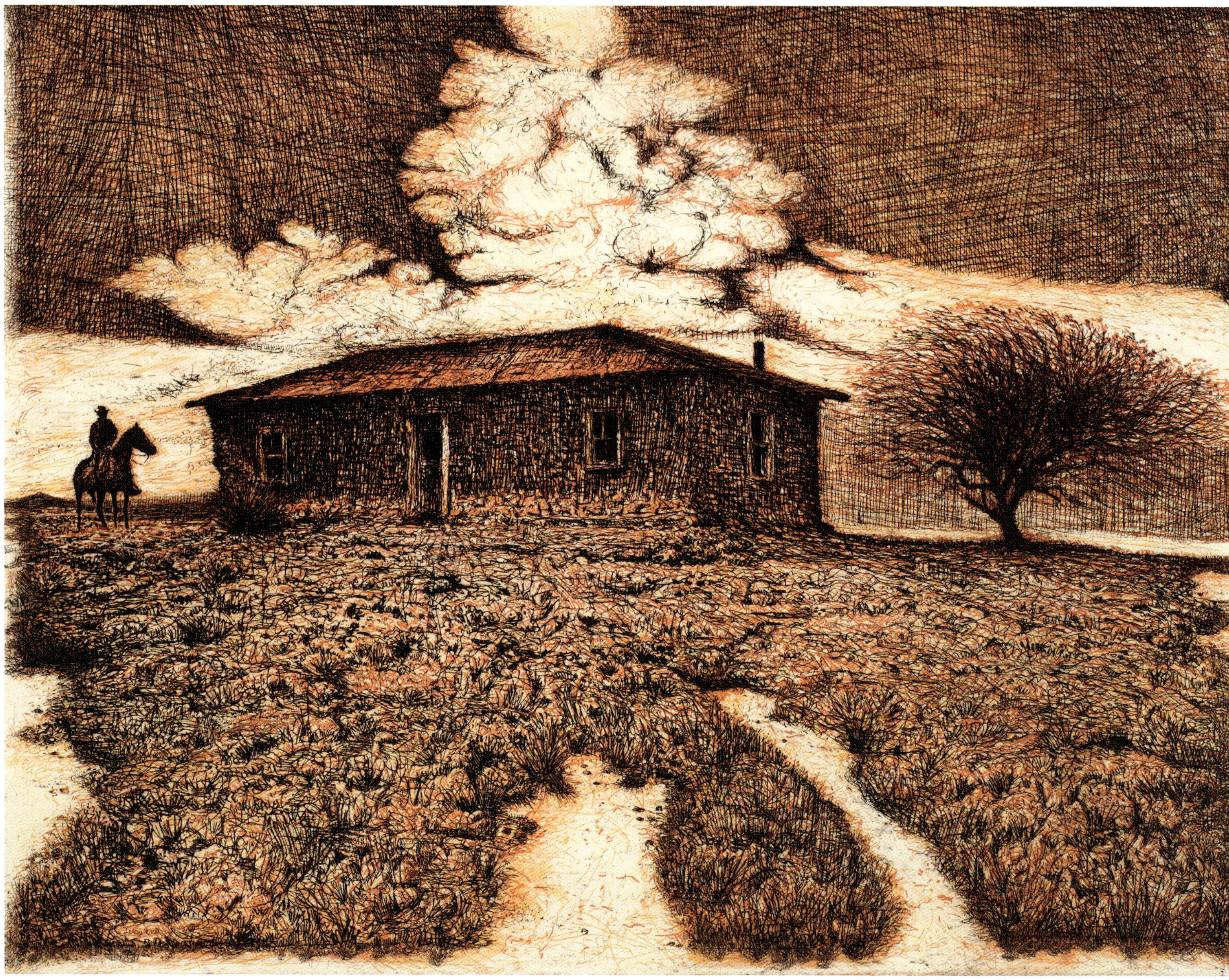

85.
Merle Morrow, 1974
Three-plate color etching, 18 × 15 in.
Edition of 10

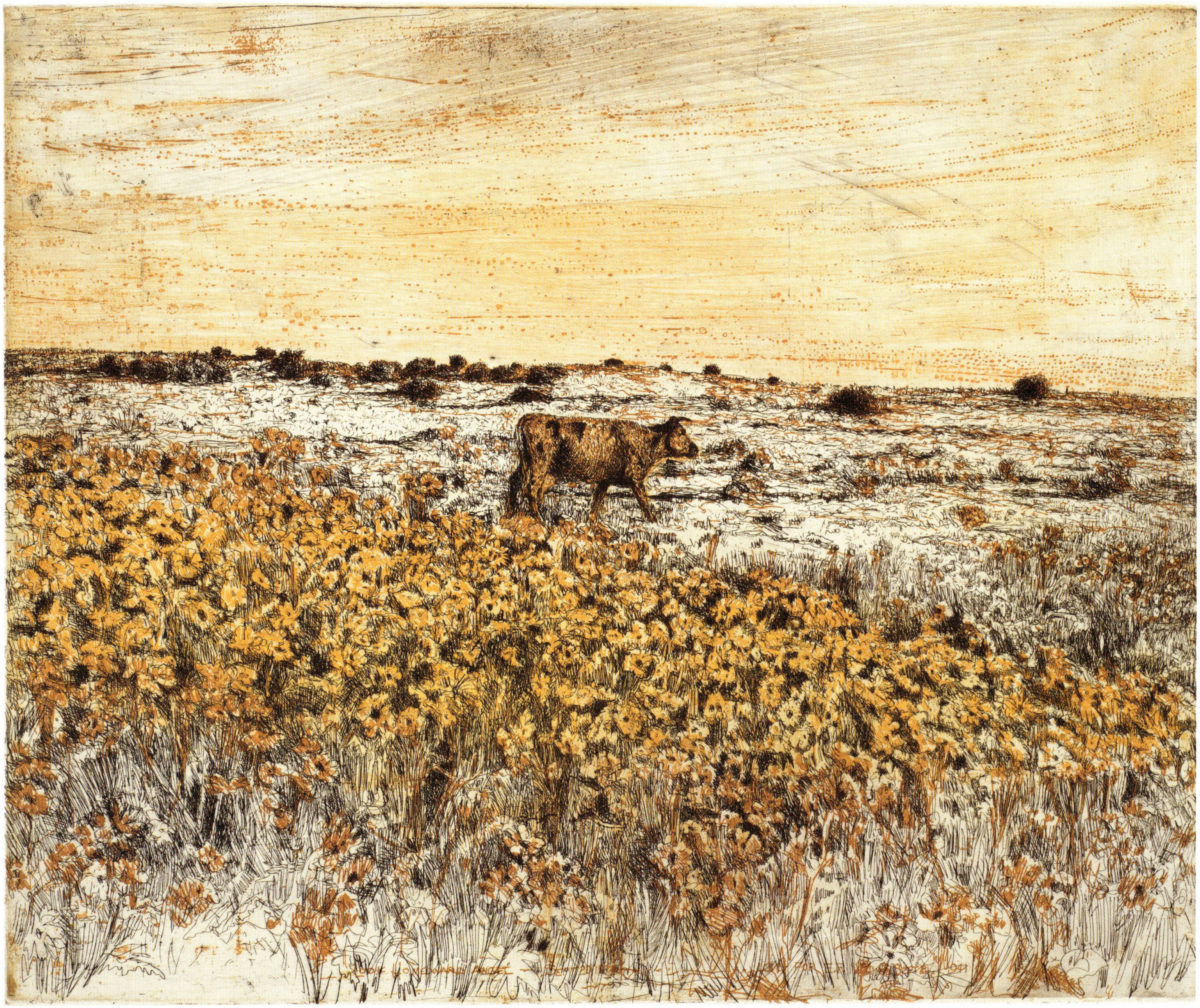

86.
Look Homeward Angel, 1974
Three-plate color etching, 24 × 20 in.
Edition of 24

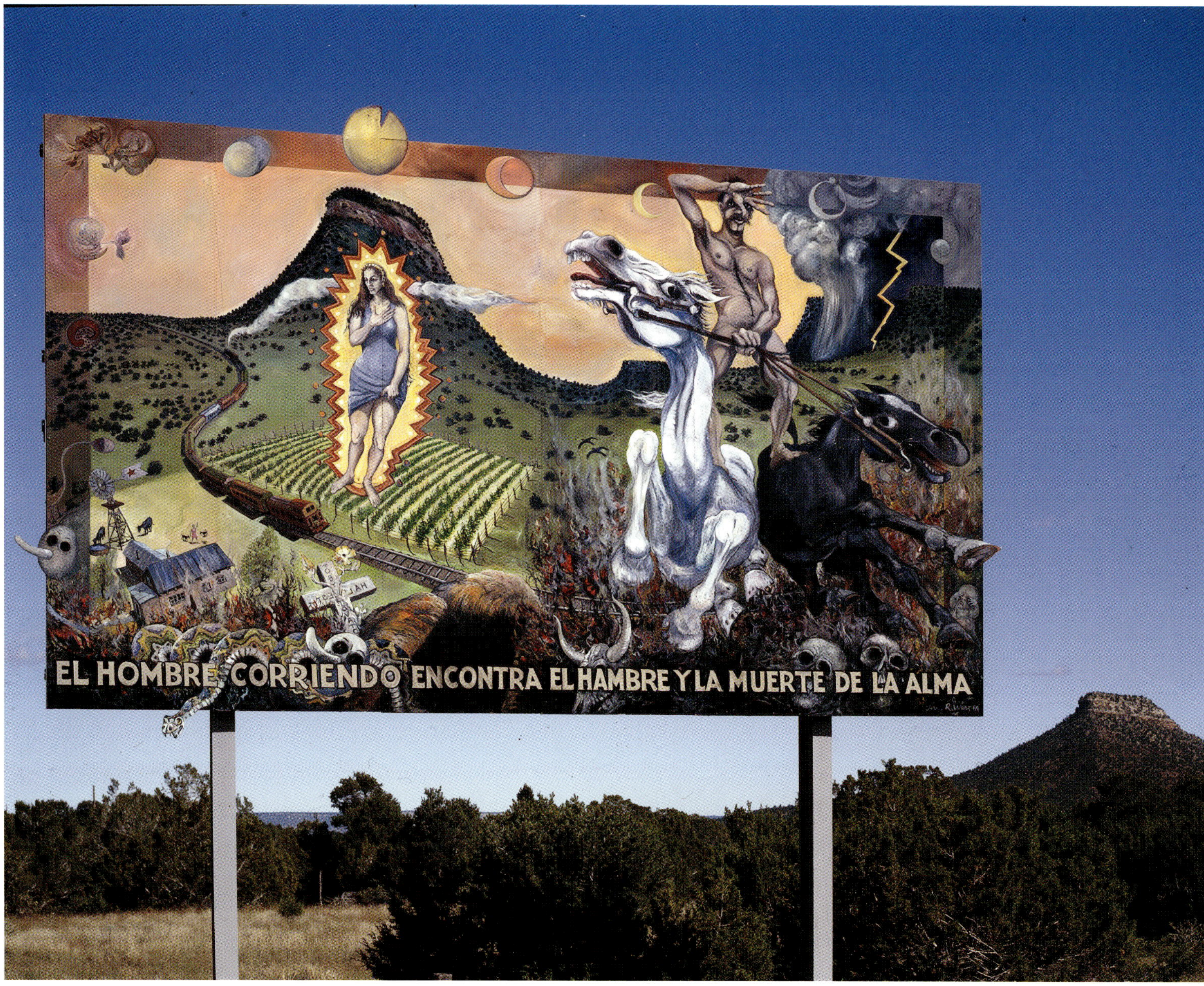

Billboard with Starvation Peak, 1983.
Photograph by Robert Reck

(following spread)
Archie (in hat) and Jerry with finished billboard in the Roundhouse studio, 1983.
Photograph by Robert Reck

X. Art in Public Places

As a child growing up in Santa Fe, I was proud to see murals painted by my dad hung in the old Cash and Carry grocery store near the plaza. Public murals had become increasingly popular throughout the United States in the days of the WPA during the Depression, in part due to the influence of the great Mexican muralists.

In elementary school, I was encouraged to make chalkboard murals for my classroom. For my family and some friends, I painted images on doors, cabinets, and outhouses—some of my very early public art. Much later, while my young family and I visited my wife's parents in South Dakota in 1962, I was invited to paint a series of mural panels that were placed in Babe's Bar that was run by my father-in-law and where I was working washing dishes and serving beer each day until about noon. The panels I painted that summer remained for many years until finally the bar closed. Much to my amusement, more than fifty years later some photographs of them have surfaced on the Internet.

In 1970 my sculptor friend Charley Southard and I were commissioned by a local bank in Santa Fe to make a combined work incorporating his sculpture and my paintings. This body of work was eventually split up, and my paintings are now in the hands of a different bank.

What really encouraged me to do larger canvases, giant billboards, and extensive murals was a group student project at the high school in Quemado, New Mexico, where Meridel Rubenstein and I had a dual artist-in-residence grant to work with the Quemado students for about a month. The project combined paintings, photographs, and oral history. Altogether, we produced one giant mural about sixty feet long.

In 1983 I got my chance to do another large work when Ray Graham commissioned me to paint an art billboard, twenty-five feet across and sixteen feet tall, in Bernal, near Las Vegas, alongside the right-of-way of the A.T. & S.F. Railroad. This project raised a fair amount of controversy. Although it was a site-specific piece, it also spoke for the then-current wars in Central America and the Iran-Contra Affair. It was also a dreamscape about the mythology of Starvation Peak. Ultimately, a lot of good came out of it, because a lively dialogue ensued around the concept of art in public spaces, bringing diverse people together.

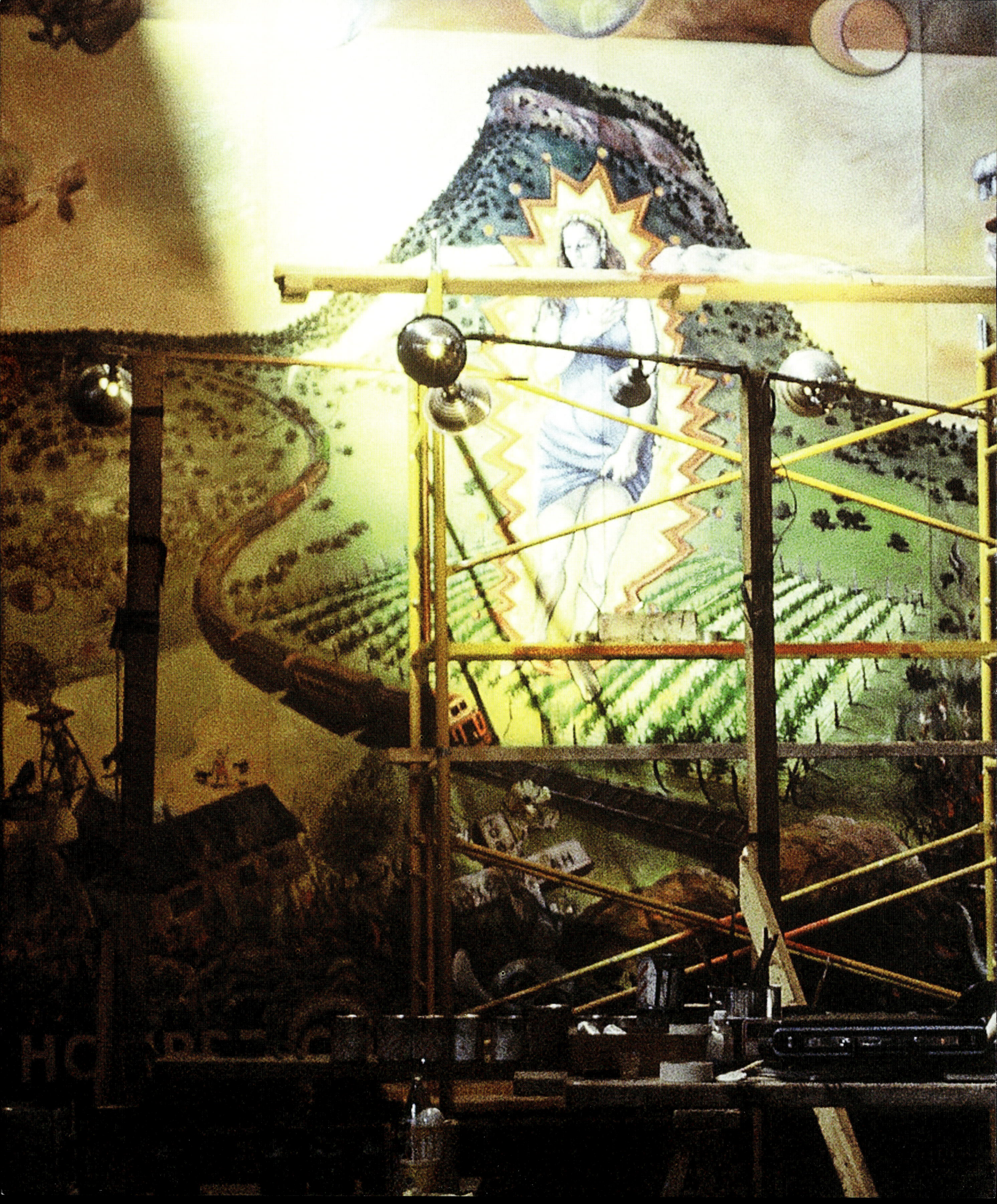

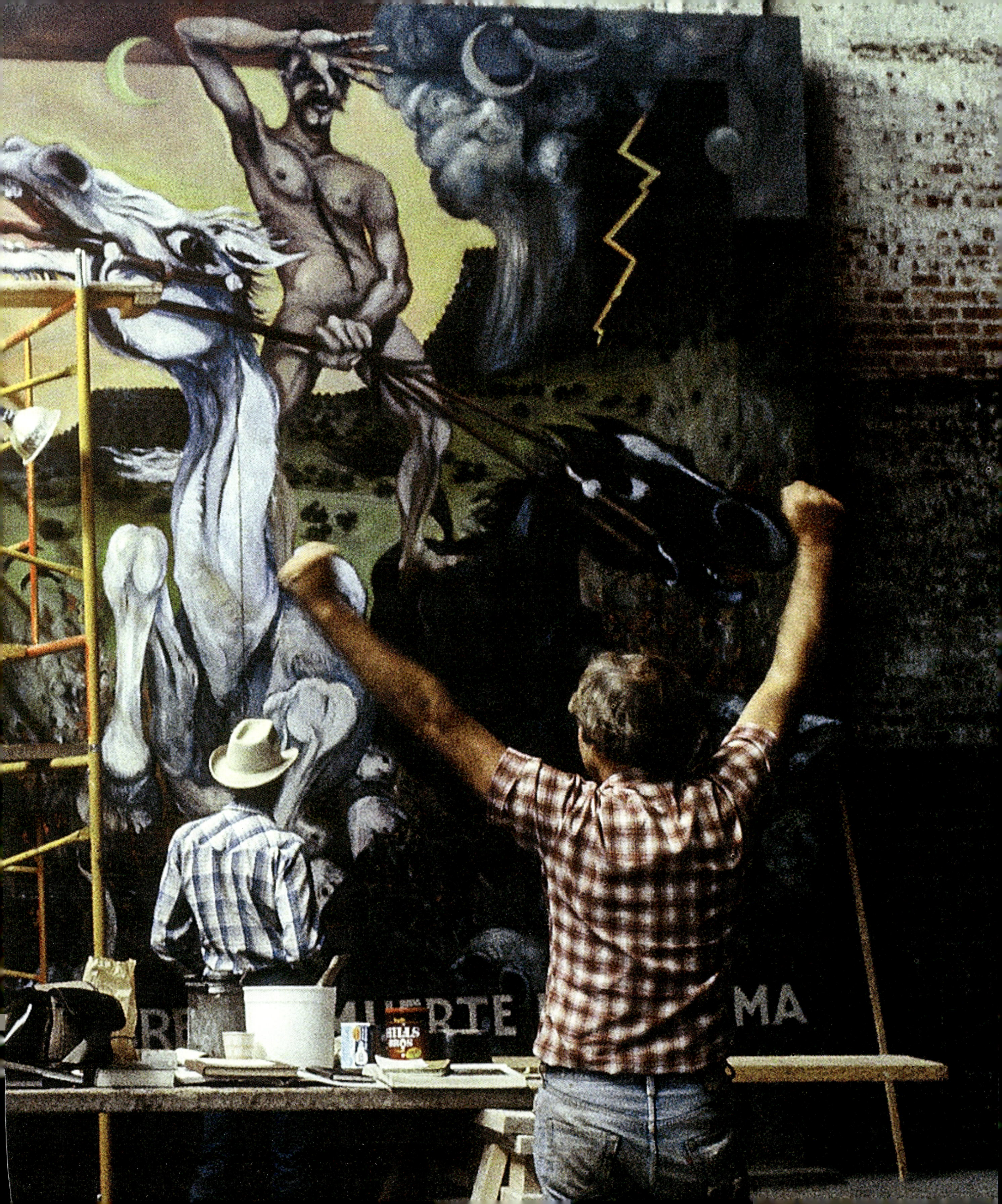
HILLS BROS

In the 1940s, the Southern Pacific Railway began divesting its peripheral holdings, among these the majestic, half-circle train repair station on the outskirts of Las Vegas, New Mexico, known as the Railroad Roundhouse. This enormous complex had thirty sections, each forty by ninety feet, with forty-foot-high cast concrete ceilings. Acquired by longtime residents John Octherbeck and family, it variously housed flocks of pigeons and fleets of diesel trucks and currently warehouses farm seed milled nearby. For twenty-two years beginning in 1983 it was also where Jerry West had his painting studio.

Jerry had been commissioned by Ray Graham to paint an art mural on a large billboard situated by the train tracks near Serafina, about twenty miles west of Las Vegas. A very big enclosed space was needed to paint it. Jerry had known Octherbeck for a long time and worked out a deal where Jerry traded paintings for his rent. The unpainted billboard was attached to one of the brick walls in the roundhouse.

Jerry would drive down from Santa Fe, park his truck inside the roundhouse, and paint, taking about four months to complete the project. He liked working in isolation, and he liked the crudeness of the place. Later he set about transforming a part of the roundhouse into a painting space for himself. He framed up the walls and enclosed the space with a double layer of heavy plastic to help control the dust and make it more comfortable. He carpeted the modest twenty by thirty-foot interior, set aside a small area for a bed and a telephone, and cut a small window in the back wall to bring in fresh air. There was electricity for the light necessary for painting in the smaller space he had created within the cavernous building. He liked living primitively and still remembers how special it was to paint and work in that place.

And so the years passed productively. Jerry hosted at least three memorable openings in that magical space, including the first that presented the finished billboard. After more than two decades the time in the roundhouse came to an end due to a combination of events. The diesel trucks were stored near Jerry's painting area, and every morning the drivers would run the engines for half an hour to warm them up; the fumes came into where he was painting. There was also a lot of dust blowing around in there. With the fumes, the dust, and the cold one winter, Jerry got pneumonia. Later, after recuperating, Jerry returned one day to his studio and discovered that a huge chunk of cast concrete had broken off the ceiling and fallen right on the spot where he had always stood to paint. It was like an omen. He thought he'd better think about painting somewhere else. It seemed like the right time to end this happy adventure.

—Dana Newmann

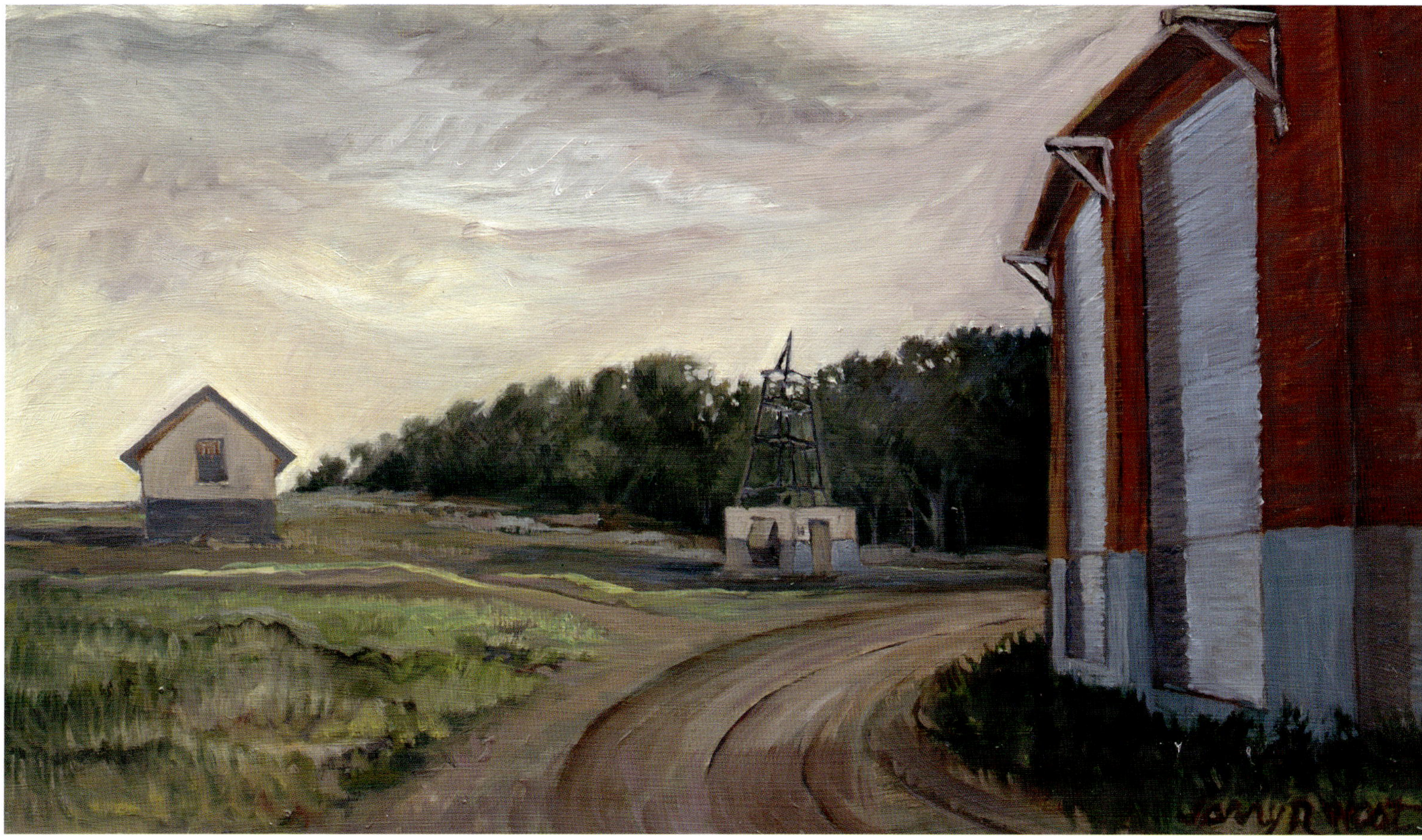

87.
Roundhouse Studio at Dusk, 1986
Oil on Masonite, 30 × 18 in.

After the billboard, I worked on many murals and cooperative endeavors. I helped create works at senior centers in Santa Fe, Chimayó, Santa Cruz, and El Rancho. I worked with young people and students in Springer in northern New Mexico and in Cuba on the Navajo Reservation. At the Youth Diagnostic and Development Center in Albuquerque I collaborated with the poet John Brandi combining poetry, writing, and visual arts for a sixty-foot-long mural that included each student's visual image of his or her inner self.

Through artist-in-residency programs, I have also been commissioned to work with prison inmates to paint murals at the New Mexico State Penitentiary and with inmates at the San Francisco County Prison in California. The mural at the New Mexico State Penitentiary encircled the exercise area and was composed of dream images by each inmate. At the bottom of the mural was a colored ribbon of poetry running throughout that was created by a Navajo inmate, with the images above appearing to float off up to the sky, carrying the hopes and messages of the prisoners to the outside world.

In the 1980s, the Santa Fe City Council decided to officially participate in public art, which many cities around the country were exploring at the time. Santa Fe had many examples of informal public art around town, but the city wanted to formalize the process and it formed an arts commission, drew up a mission statement, and allocated monies. A director was appointed. One of the first projects planned was a mural for City Hall. A prospectus and guidelines were written specifying goals for the mural, which included giving attention to Santa Fe's multicultural background and to the historic site of the present City Hall.

However, when the new director appointed an artist to do the mural without consulting the committee, the city attorney and council countered that a big city project must be put out to bid. A jury was selected, notification for bids went out to the public, and a deadline was set. I nearly missed hearing about the competition, but someone stopped me on the street one day and told me about it. I became one of about fifty artists who submitted slides and a written proposal with a maquette to the jury committee.

I'd had a strange dream some weeks before, involving my beloved old high school janitor Amarante Tapia, a hardworking and manic sweeper who was also a natural jester and storyteller. Our high school was in the old Catron Building, the exact location of the present City Hall. In my dream, Amarante swept out the building then continued out to the sidewalk. As he steadily swept towards the plaza, students lined up behind him, forming a procession. It struck me that this powerful dream was a metaphor I could use for the mural: a clownlike janitor sweeping up the collective past of Santa Fe's multicultural history.

Several weeks passed before I read with some disappointment in the *Santa Fe New Mexican* that three finalists had been chosen and I was not one of them. When I went in a week later to pick up my slides, the nice woman at the desk hesitated a little and said, "Mr. West, I think you should wait—I think a mistake has been made." It turned out that the members of the jury had also read the notice in the paper, and the results printed did not reflect their vote. The director heading the arts commission had substituted his own selection in place of the jury's winner, which had been me.

When the director was confronted, he reluctantly added me back into the running. Now there were four of us vying for the commission, going through the long, laborious process with slide presentations to committees.

At each presentation, I kept winning the first-place vote. When the commission finally voted overwhelmingly in my favor, the various opponents unfortunately became more vocal. The main offense was that I was not of Hispanic descent: "Only a native Hispanic" should paint a painting in City Hall, said the critics. (If this kind of logic were really followed, only a Native American should have been entitled to compete.) In addition, a petition was circulated that no working-class janitor should lead a parade in the mural. Some said, "If anyone should lead it, it should be a Hispanic doctor or lawyer but never a lowly janitor; that's a demeaning and not-so-subtle put-down."

Finally, after six months and my threat of a legal suit for breach of contract by the city, the council moved on the issue and approved the jury's original vote.

I began the mural by plastering the wall and putting down several coats of gesso, then at last began to paint. The painting took more than half a year. Many people stopped to watch me work and to ask questions. The commission required that I give at least four talks and slide shows during the process, which I did with pleasure. I also conducted interviews, talking with each person who had opposed my painting the mural. This was healing for all.

With the mural completed I made a presentation in the City Council chambers, which was full to overflowing with citizens. Debbie Jaramillo, City Councilor, the first and most vocal opponent, stood up in the back of the room and delivered a dramatic speech, a public confession and an apology. She said that my painting was a great mural, and that the whole process was the most unifying event that year for the City of Santa Fe.

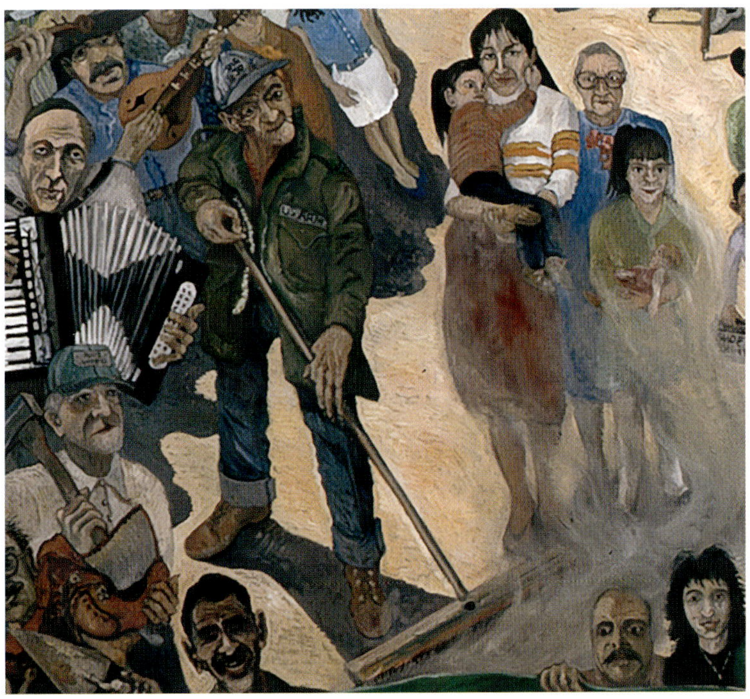

Amarante Tapia sweeping, Santa Fe City Hall Mural (detail), 1989.

88.
Recuerdos y Sueños de Santa Fé, 1989
Oil on gessoed plaster, 14 × 18 ft.
Collection of City of Santa Fe, NM

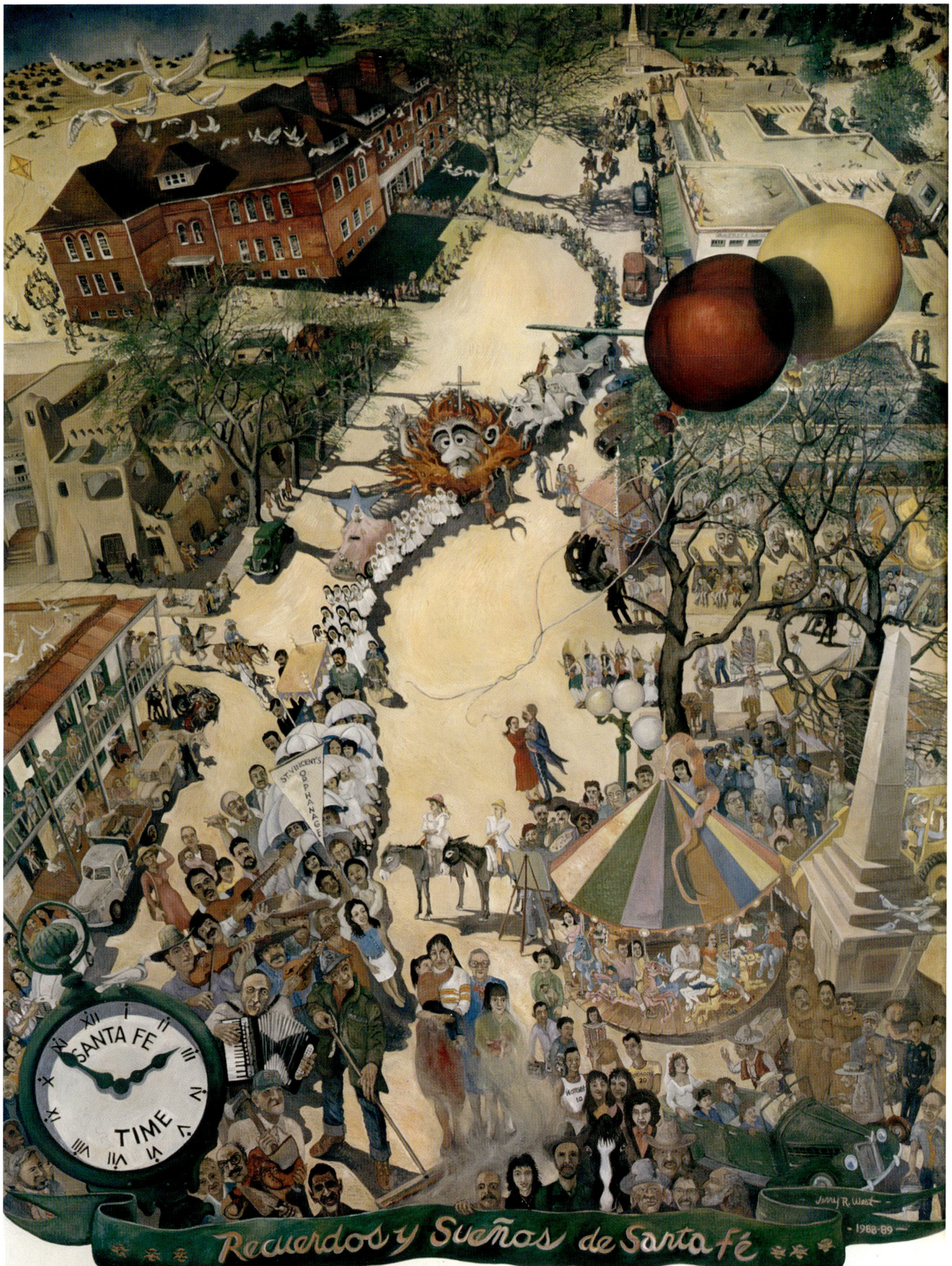
SANTA FE
TIME
ST. VINCENT'S ORPHANAGE
Recuerdos y Sueños de Santa Fé
Jerry R. West
1988-89

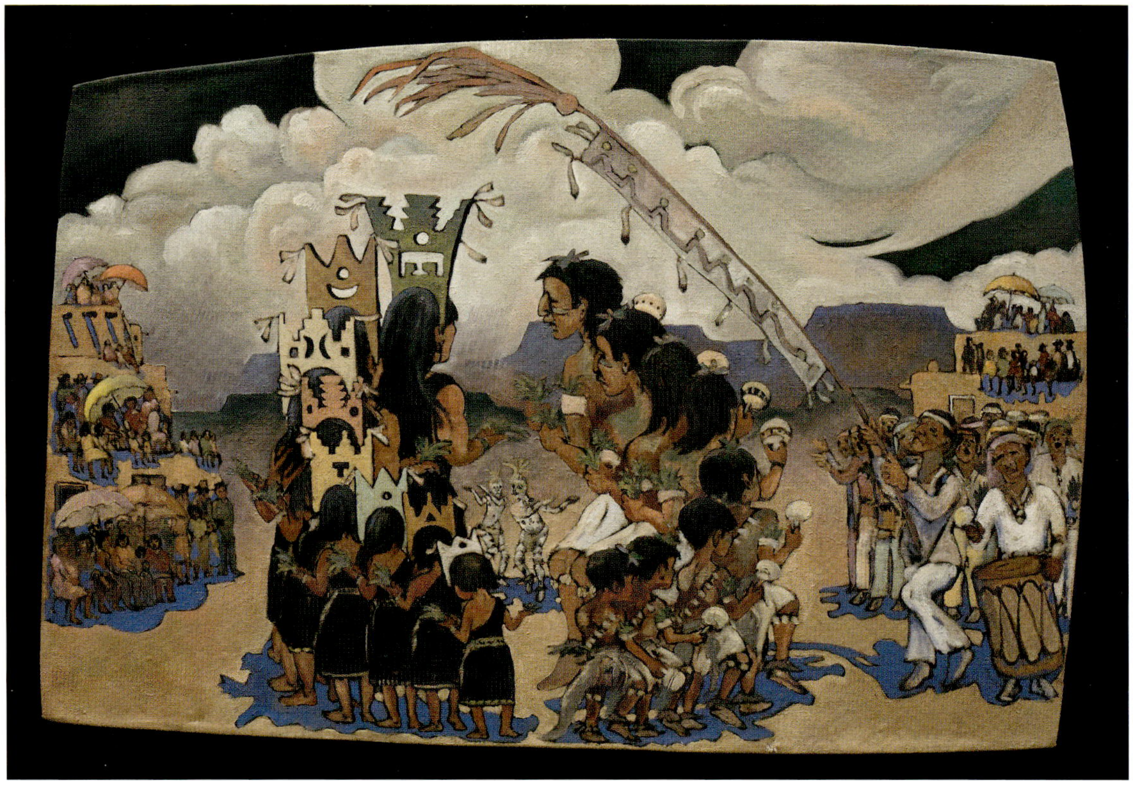

89.
Pueblo Ceremonial, 1974
Oil on Masonite, 40 × 26 in.
Collection of Wells Fargo Company

90.
Fiesta, Santa Fe Plaza, 1974
Oil on Masonite, 50 × 28 in.
Collection of Wells Fargo Company

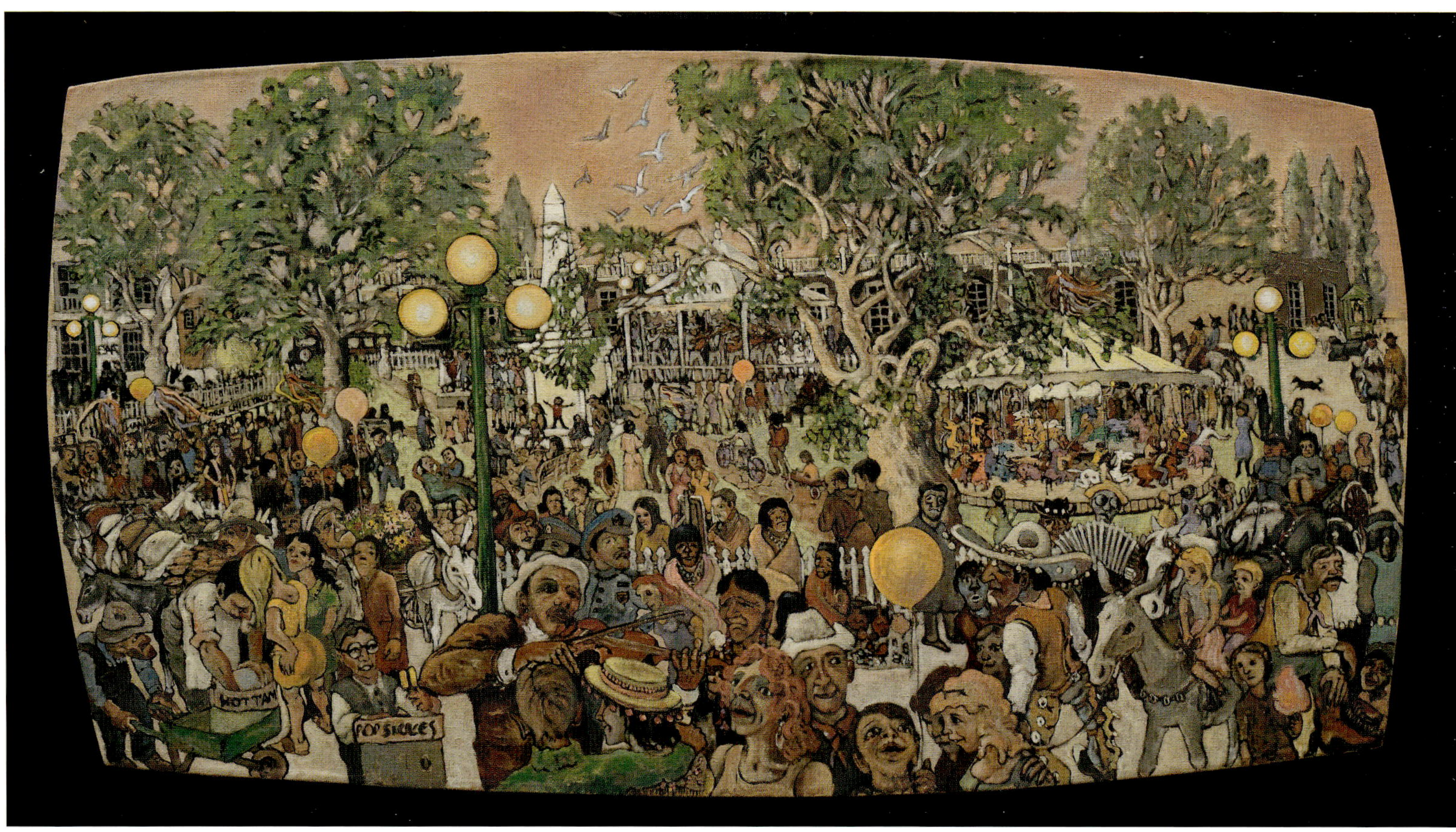

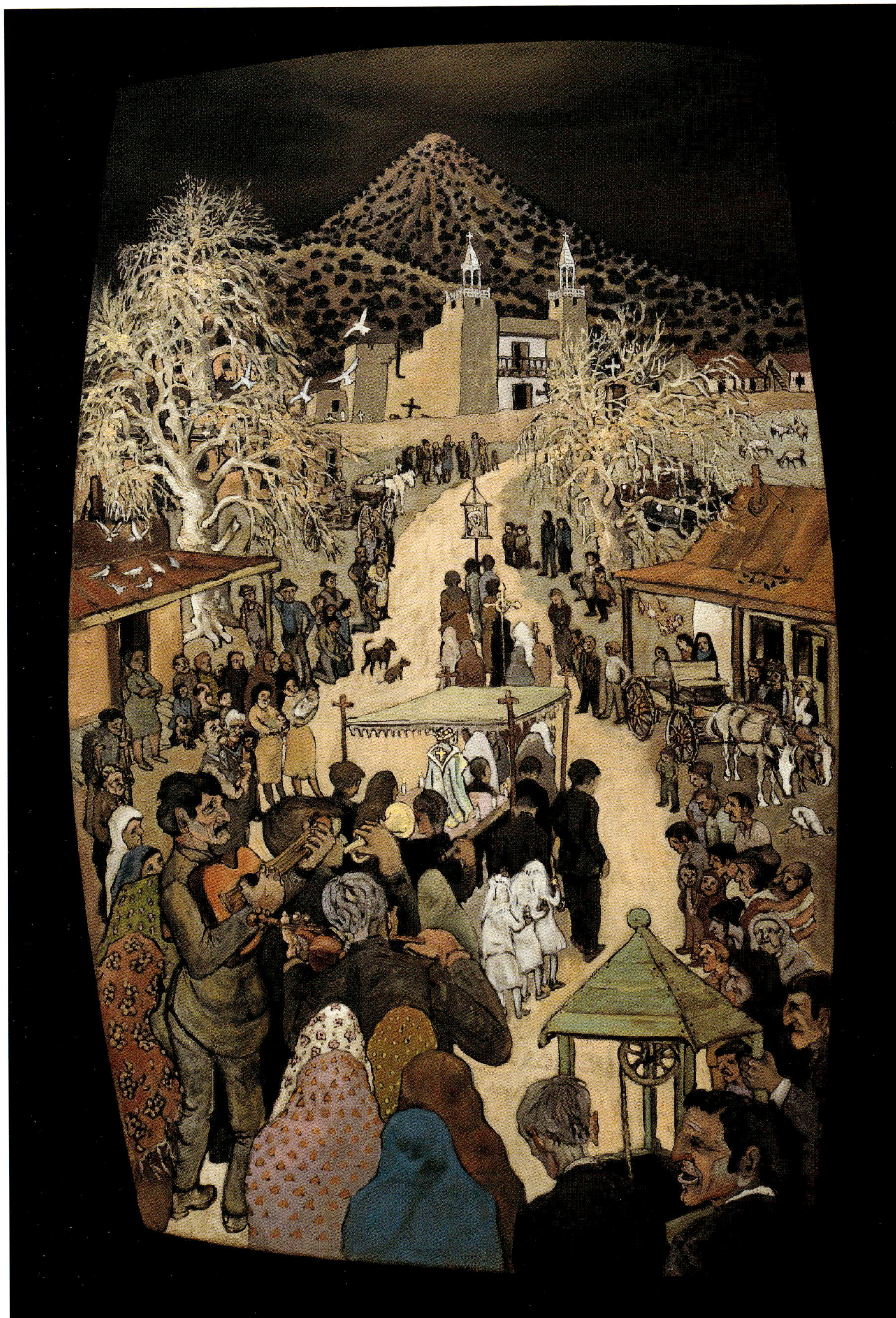

91.
Trampas Procession, 1974
Oil on Masonite, 30 × 48 in.
Collection of Wells Fargo Company

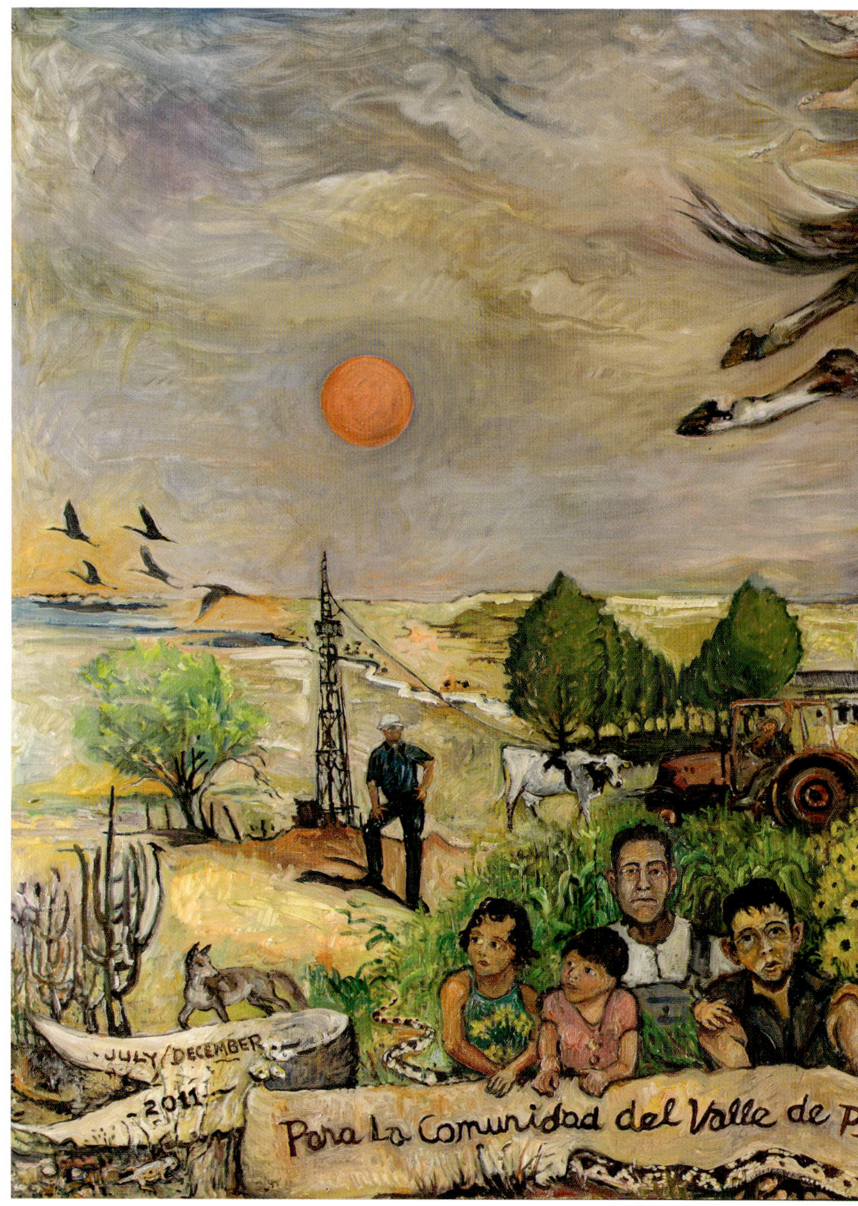

92.
Mi Casita, 2011
Oil on Masonite, 12 × 5 ft.
Collection of Lucy and Arturo Gonzales

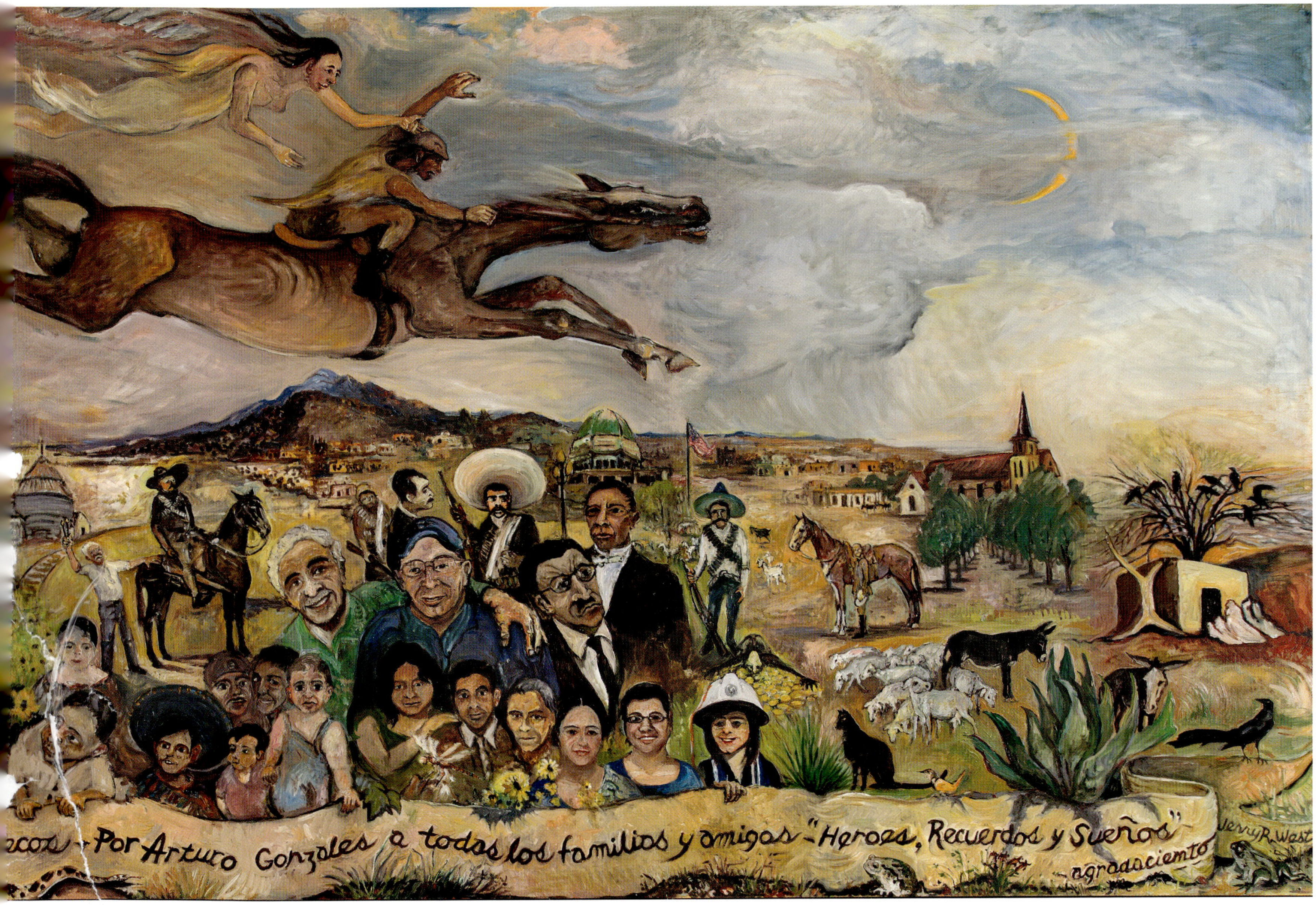
ecos – Por Arturo Gonzales a todas los familias y amigas "Heroes, Recuerdos y Sueños"
agradaciento
Jerry R. West

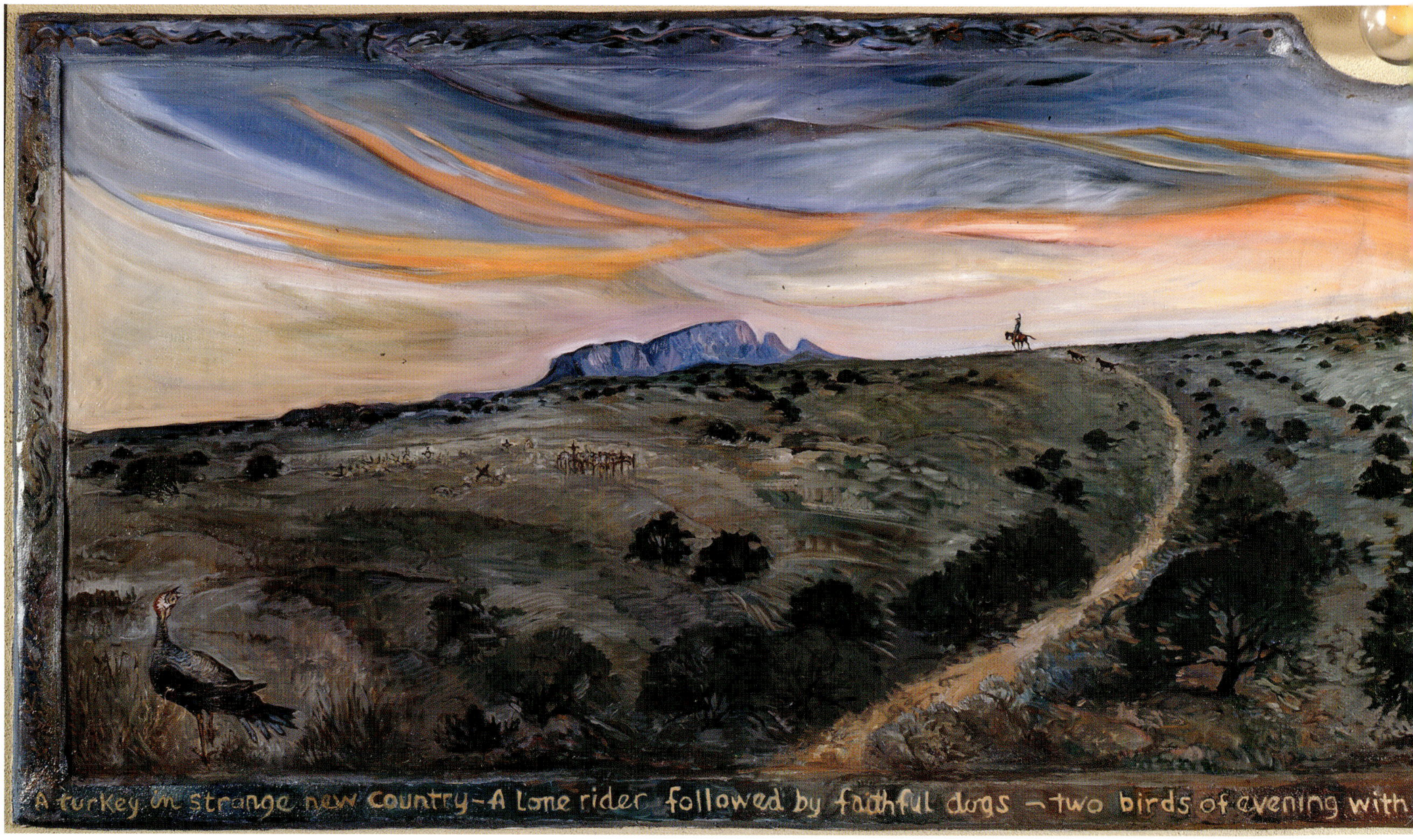

93.
In a Strange New Country, 2006
Oil on gessoed plaster, 12 × 4 ft.
Collection of Cynthia and Mark Holloway

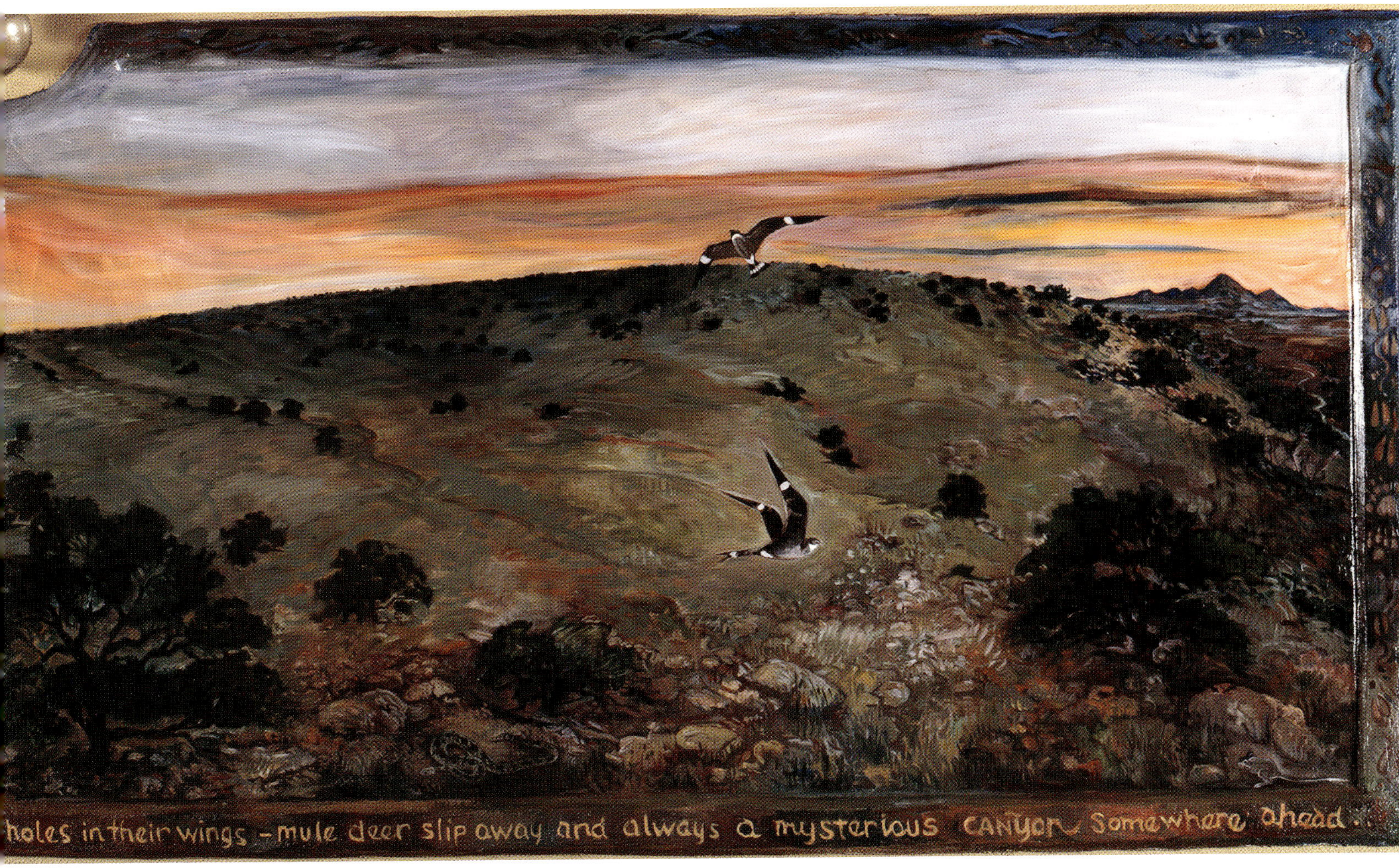
holes in their wings – mule deer slip away and always a mysterious CANYON somewhere ahead . .

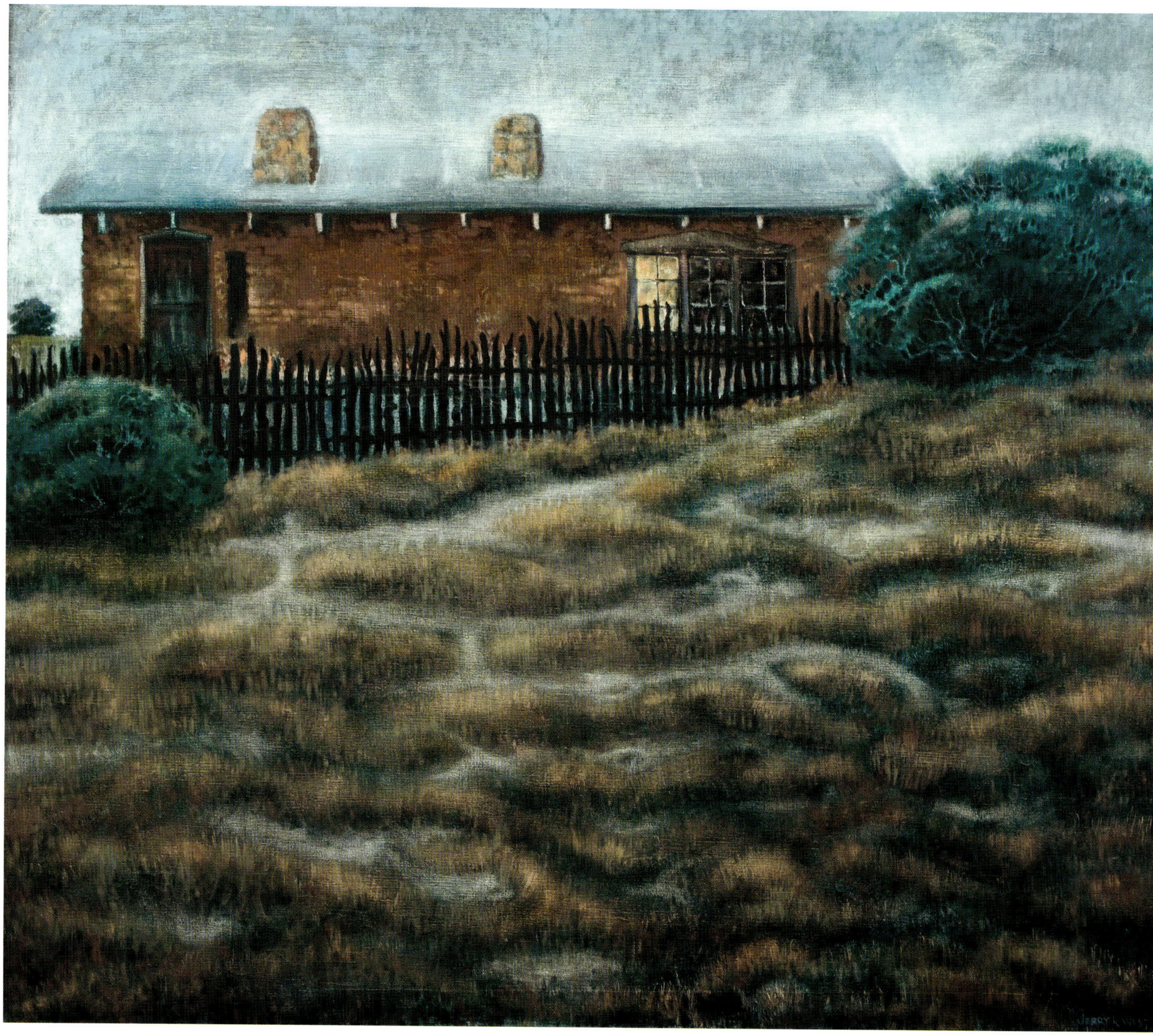

94.
First House, 1970
Oil on linen, 52 × 48 in.
Collection of Valli West-Davis
Photograph by José Valle Rivera

The Building Impulse

One of the first building projects I organized myself, as a grown man, was the design and construction of the house built with my wife, Sharon, and our children in the 1960s on the prairie south of Santa Fe near the family homestead. With the help of my brothers I made all the adobes for the project. I dug the footings, laid the adobes, hauled old beams from abandoned mines in the Cerrillos area and then carved them, built a rock fireplace, used found objects such as old pickets that had been cast aside, and plastered the house inside and out. One day while working we heard that President John F. Kennedy had been shot. The house was completed on weekends over several years. We lived there for about four years before we got electricity and a well for water. It was a special time, a magical time, building and living that way: it was a labor of love.

In the first four or five years of my life our dad would take me and my siblings on jaunts into the hills to cut firewood. Along with his serious woodcutting, Hal would take time to help us build a brush hut from the leftover bows of juniper trees. These constructions became our own little houses and sanctuaries where we could play and let our imaginations roam. I think of these childhood events as the beginnings of inspiration for all of the building and construction that I have done in the many years since.

Growing up in the 1940s there was never a shortage of jobs to be done. Our dad was not himself a great worker in those years, probably because of his poor health, but what he did do so well was to carefully and patiently instruct each of his sons in how to do tasks efficiently and with integrity: how to use a shovel or a posthole digger, for example, or a wheelbarrow; how to twist wire correctly; how to hammer or use a chisel or a saw. He would usually give only one clear lesson, and from then on we would be on our own to perfect the task. Hal instructed us to move with intention and dignity and to carry through any task with care and respect. During those years we derived a great deal of enjoyment from the actual act of working together.

I loved the idea of working on the ranch projects that needed to get done: building a chicken house or a pigpen or the calf house and corrals for horses. My enthusiasm for building may have come from the fact that we were far from the city, far away from other young friends and the involvement in organized sports. But we did like the work, with or without pay—working with the family, or for our Uncle Gene West or neighbors, including repairing windmills and digging ditches and wells. In high school, my brother Jack and I were doing all kinds of jobs, many to try and make some money and many just for the experience. One year Jack started The Santa Fe Adobe Company. Since that year was a good year for rain it turned out not so good for making adobes. Both my younger brothers, Archie and Philip, worked with me building projects, too. We came to know and love Flavio Gonzales, a craftsman who really taught us how to lay adobe with the traditional skills.

When I was a sophomore at Santa Fe High School, one of the Cinco Pintores, an artist named Josef Bakos, was teaching art classes part time there. He took notice of me in class, and then outside of class he made a special effort to teach me to plaster and work with him on the adobe house he was maintaining for himself up on Camino del Monte Sol. We worked together on various building projects, and I became his assistant in his painting studio as well. He was in his mid-nineties when we finally reroofed his studio.

By 1970, Charley Southard, a fellow graduate student and sculptor, and I worked together in Alamogordo, New Mexico, on a studio complex for artists, and then back in Santa Fe we continued to build one-of-a-kind custom homes. We would build a house between the months of May and January, and then do our own artwork from January to May. In 1980 we arranged to get insurance and a license and formed a little company called the Blue Raven Construction Works, and continued to build some beautiful homes. The company thrived for about twenty years; however, after about seven years I decided to concentrate on my own artwork.

Looking back, I can think of many houses I've built or remodeled, always with help, of course. I've contributed to many studios for fellow painters and artists, and multiple projects for family and friends. There is something very gratifying about constructing a building, and that includes the pleasure of chopping a *nicho* into a wall, plastering the sensual shape around a window, carving a corbel or a beam, and the simple satisfaction of making one's own adobes.

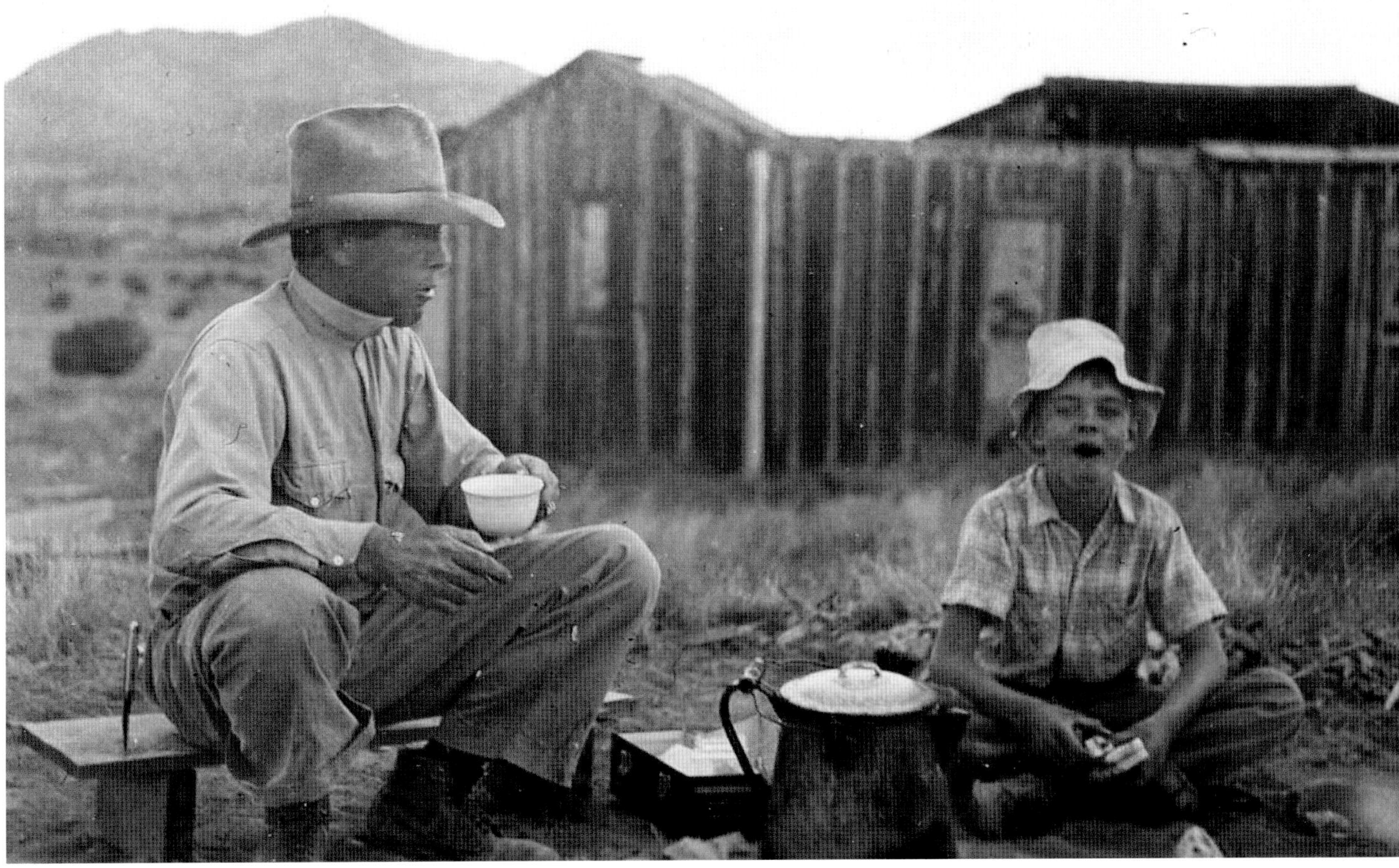

Hal and Jerry, 1944.
Photograph by Robin Brooke.

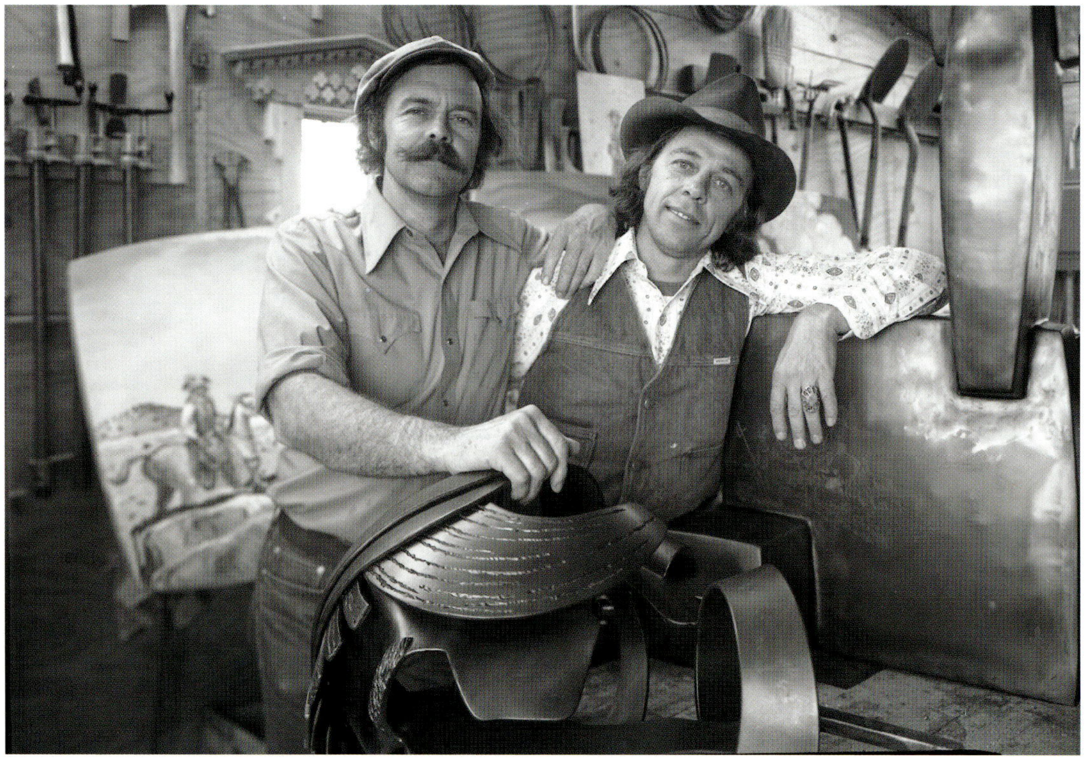

Jerry and Charley Southard, 1978. Photograph by Meridel Rubenstein.

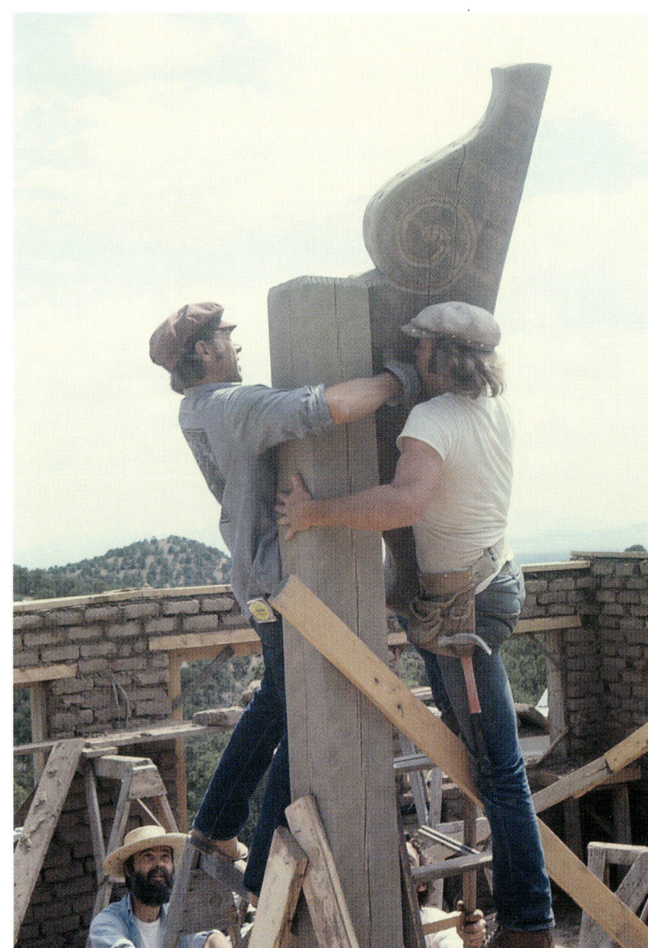

From left, John Hogan, Charley Southard, and Jerry setting a corbel, 1975, photographer unknown.

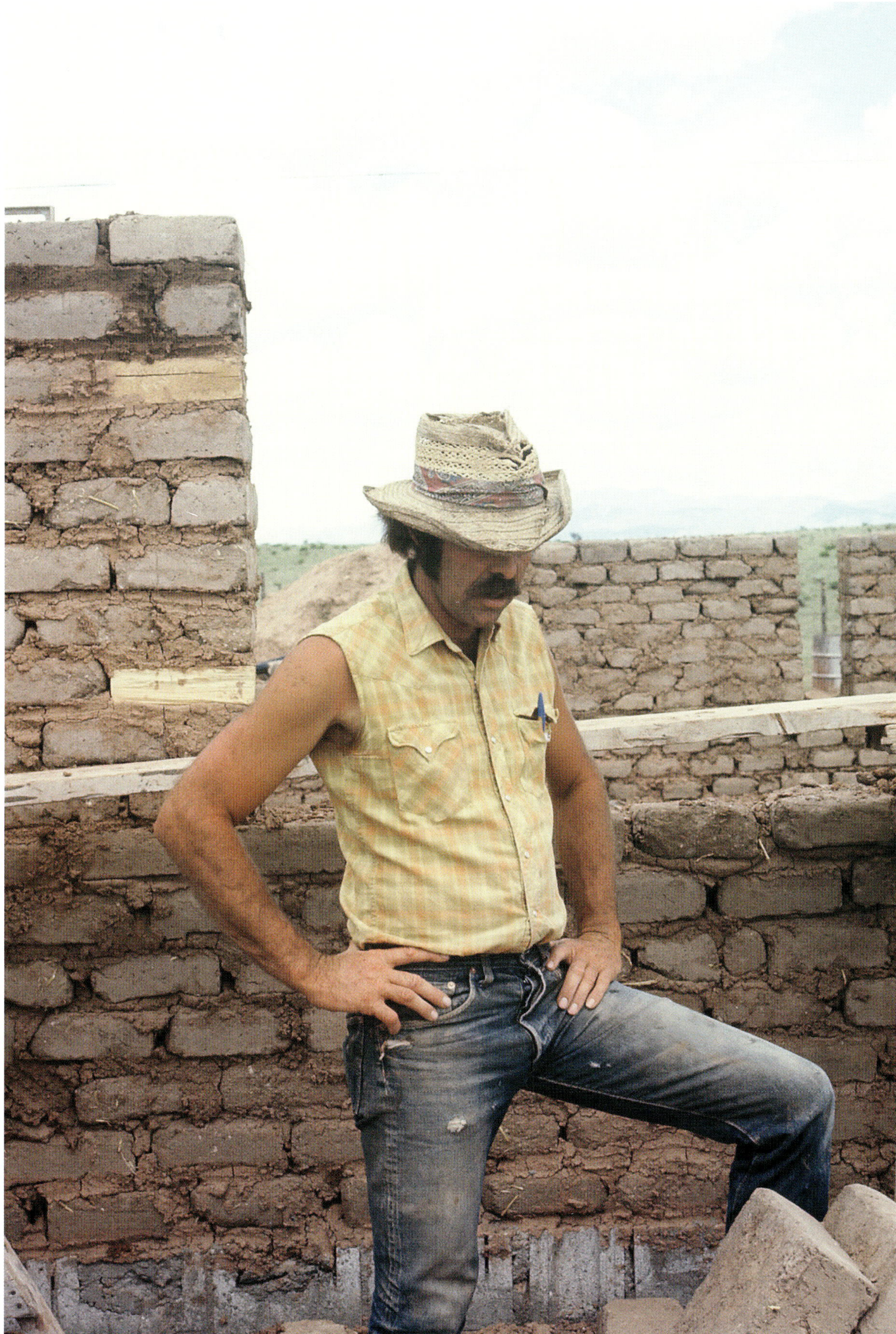

Jerry on site, 1972, photographer unknown.

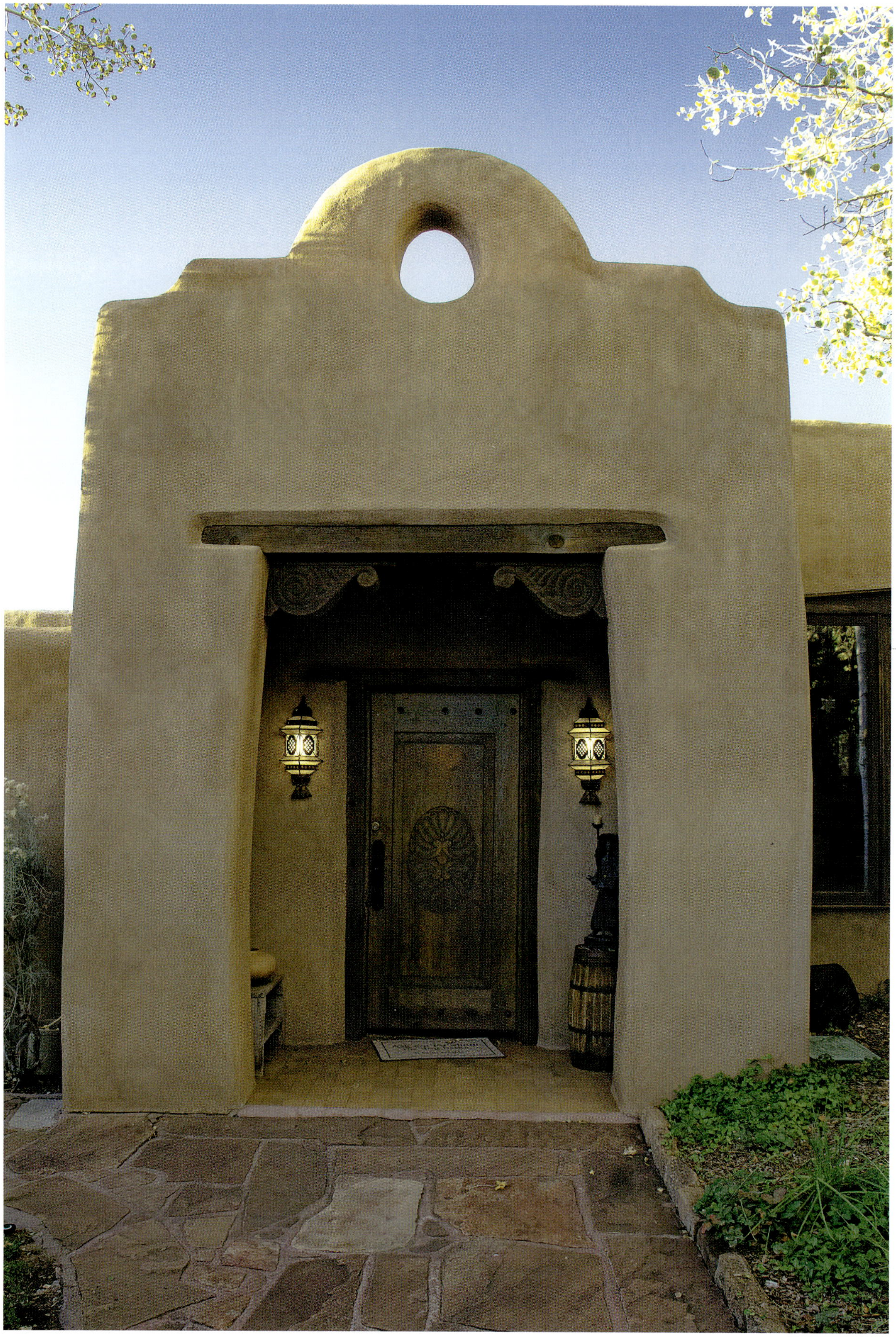

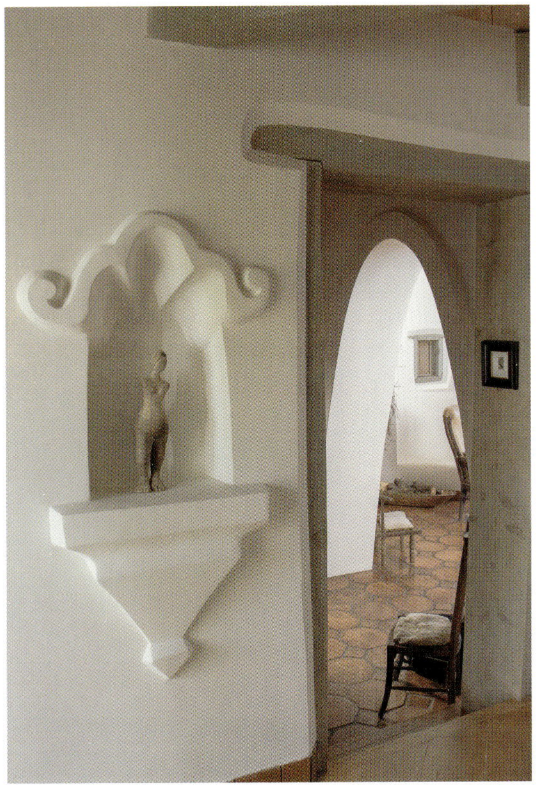

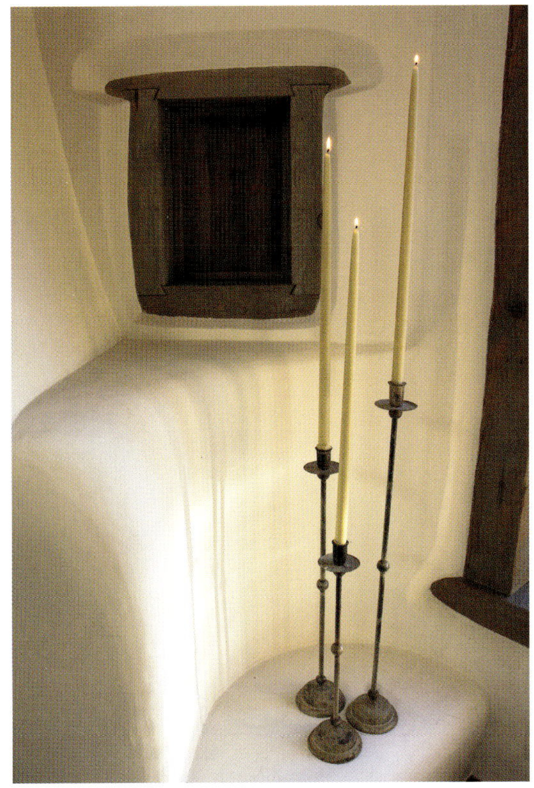

Design details from a private residence, mid-1970s. Photographs by John Eddy.

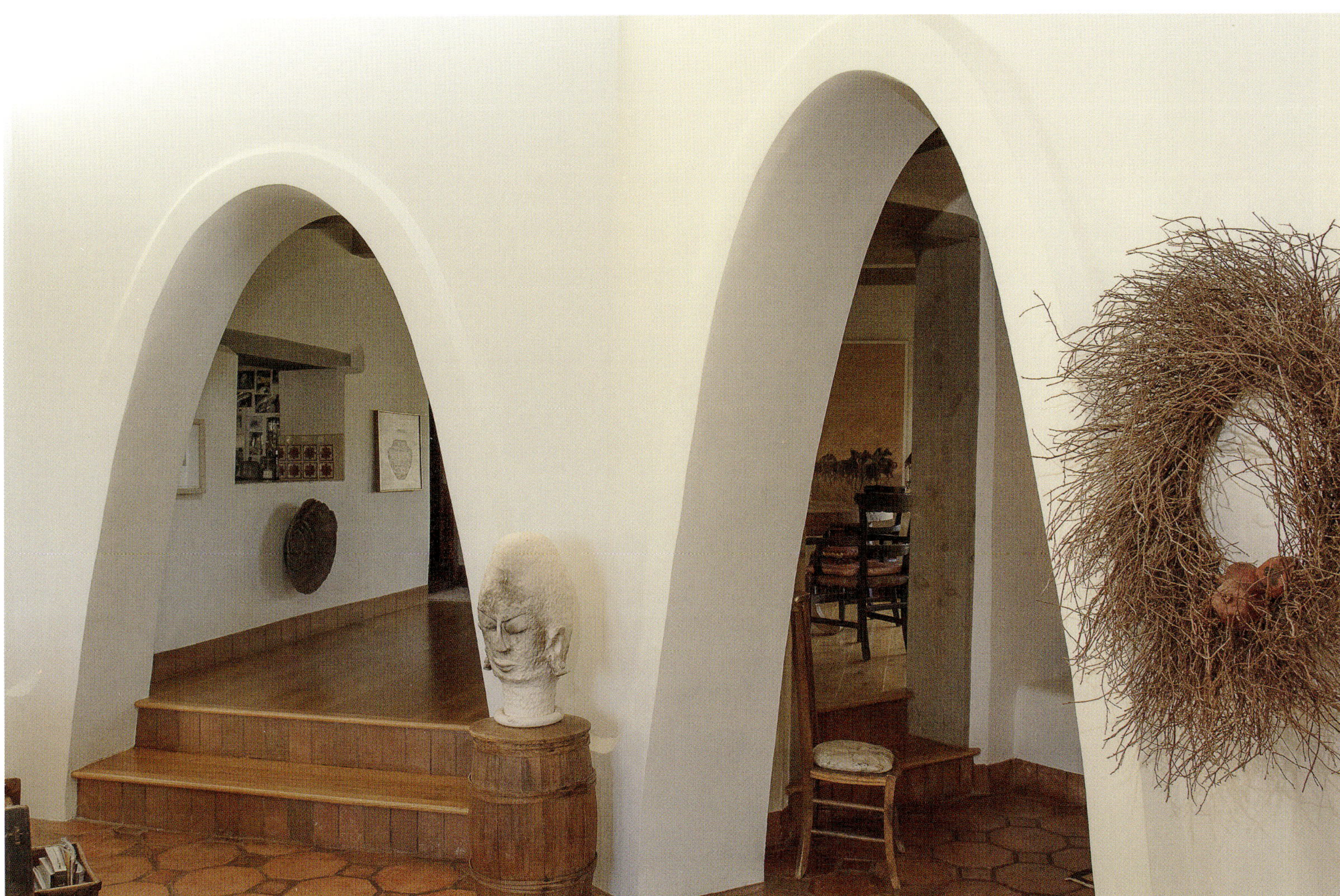

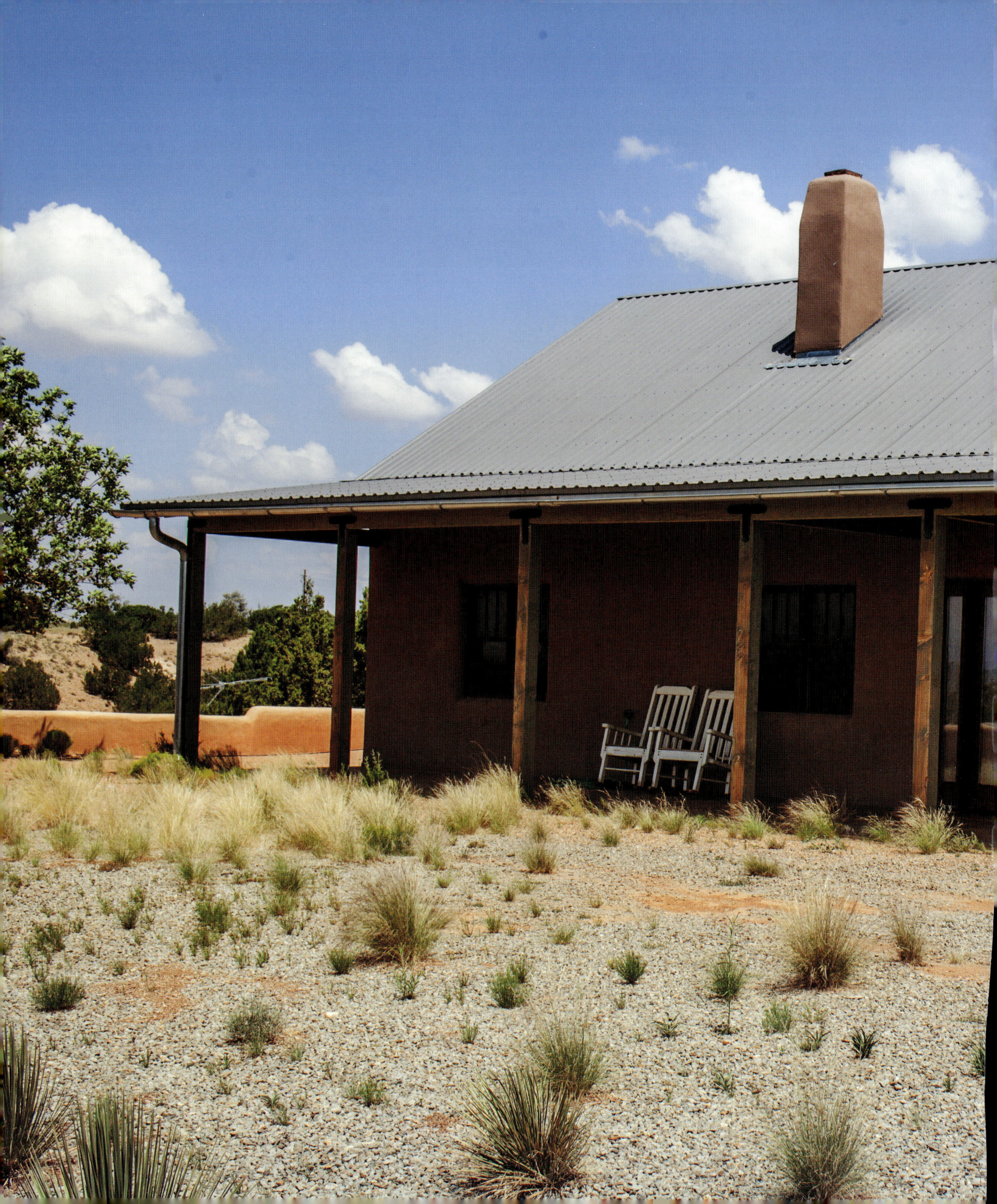

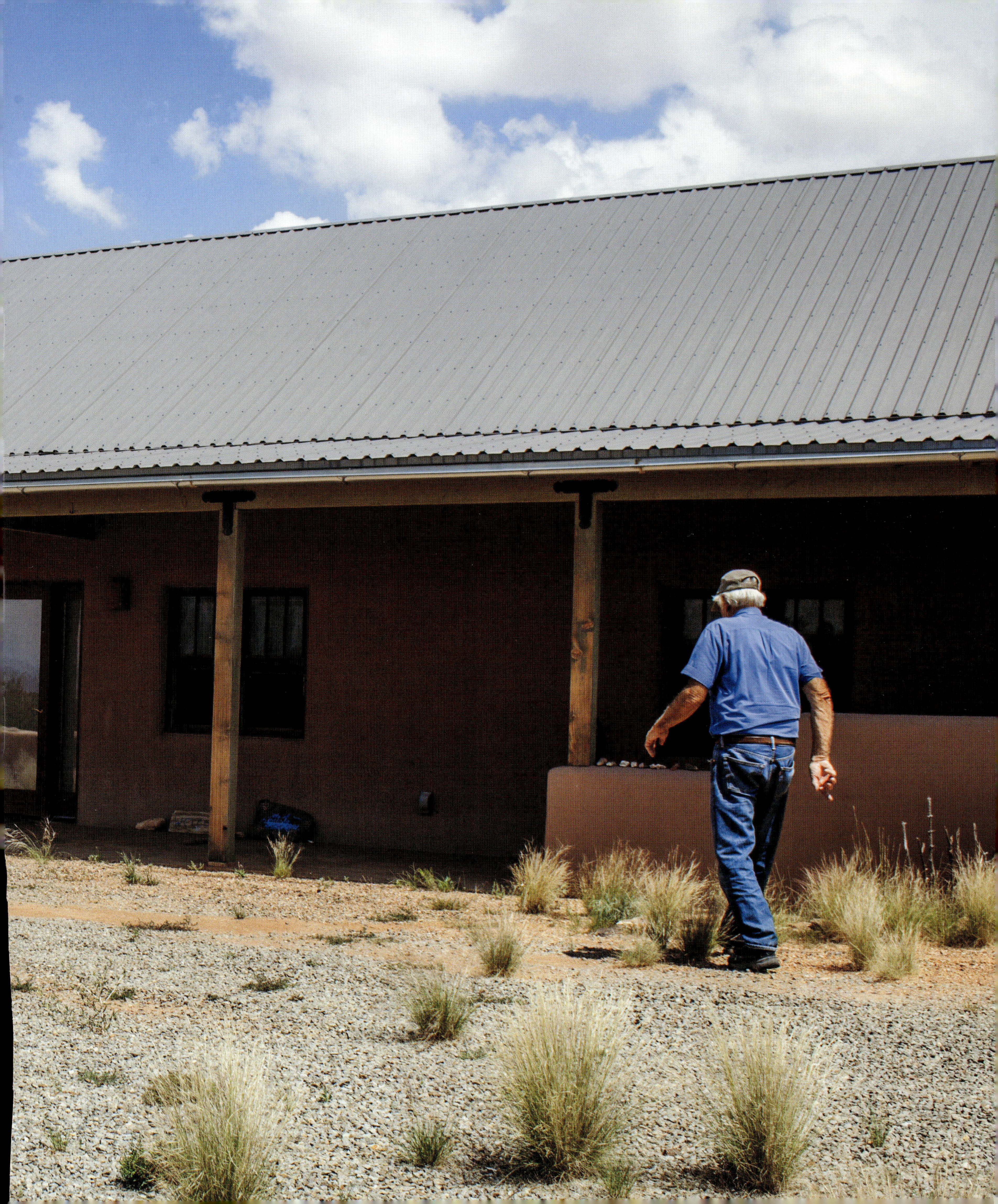

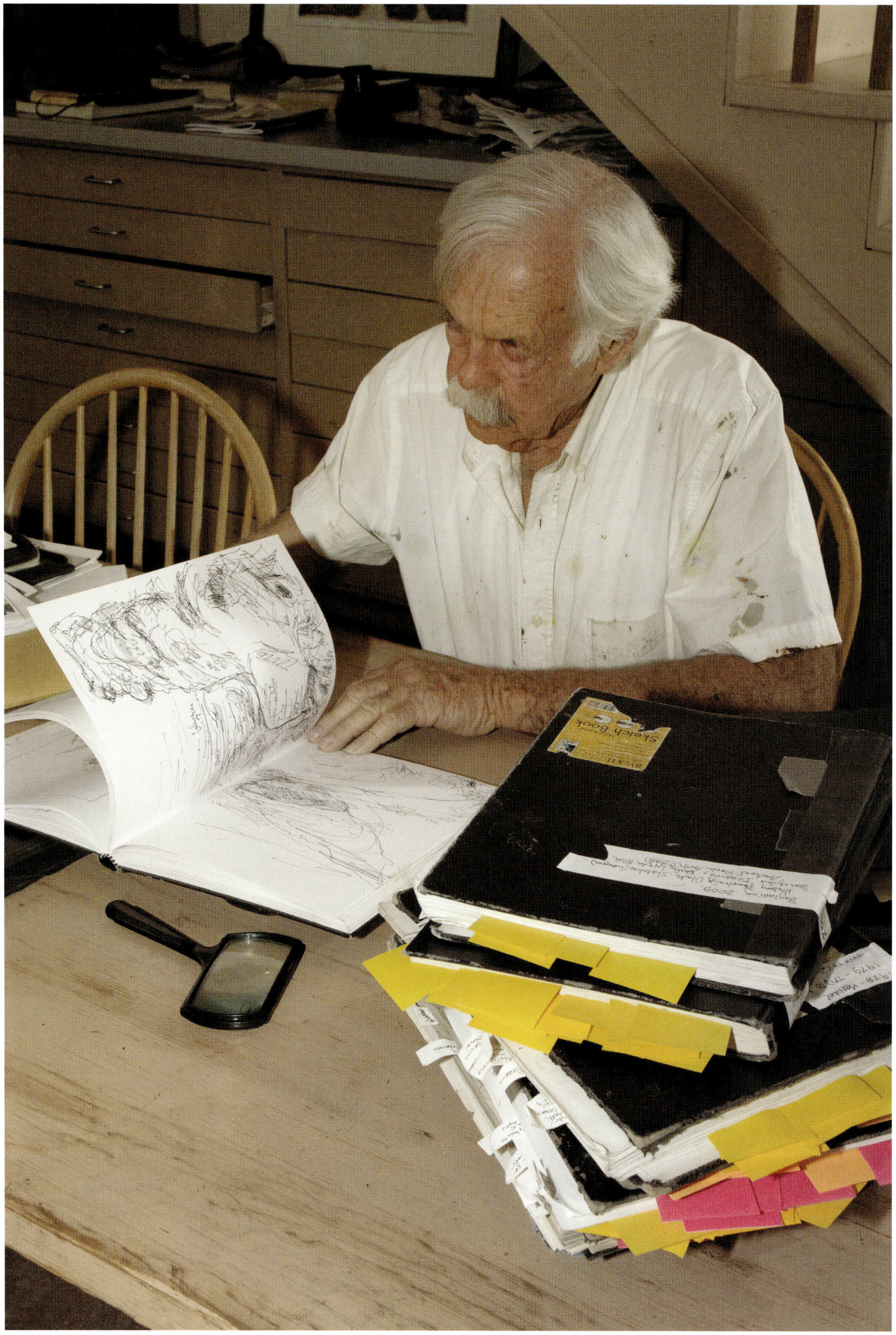

Acknowledgments

It's a very satisfying experience to see a selection of my images and glimpses of my memories and dreams presented in a book. What an honor, too, to have distinguished individuals Bernie Lopez, Dana Newmann, Rebecca Solnit, Joe Traugott, and MaLin Wilson-Powell contribute comments and essays about my life and work. Behind all my thoughts and efforts lie my caring, love, and deep gratitude for my family: my mother, Mildred; my father, Hal; my siblings John, Sarah, Archie, and Phillip; my first wife, Sharon Joyce, and our three children, Tamara, Valli, and Joe; and our three grandchildren, Ty, Aiden, and Clementine. In so many direct and indirect or subtle ways I acknowledge the strong influences of my various teachers, mentors, lovers and friends—past and present. They have all informed my physical and psychological pathway. A direct hug and huge thanks to Meridel Rubenstein for her love, support, and consistent belief in my vision. I am grateful for Ciel Bergman for curation of the exhibition called "Dust and Stars: An Alchemy of Memory." I want to also thank Ray Graham and Siegfried Halus for their support. And in this immediate book effort my many thanks to Mary Wachs, Editorial Director, David Skolkin, Art Director, and staff at the Museum of New Mexico Press; to Tamara, Valli, and Joe West, and Tara Gibbons for images, photos, and encouragement; and to Elizabeth Brooks West for editorial work. Thanks, too, to James Hart for constant support and documentation of my work, and to John Eddy for advice in composition, computer expertise, and photography. For me, the journey has been intense and rewarding.

¡Grácias a tódos!

Jerry West with sketchbooks, 2014. Photograph by John Eddy.

Project editor: Mary Wachs
Design and production: David Skolkin
Art file preparation and digital management: John Eddy and James Hart
Composition: Set in Sabon
Manufactured in Singapore
10 9 8 7 6 5 4 3 2 1

Library of Congress Cataloging-in-Publication Data
West, Jerry R., 1933-
[Works. Selections]
Jerry West : the alchemy of memory : a selective retrospective / by Jerry R. West ; With essays by Rebecca Solnit and MaLin Wilson-Powell.—Foreword / Joseph Traugott—Jerry West : the vernacular sublime / MaLin Wilson-Powell—A bird in the hand (and seventeen more in a Ponderosa pine) / Rebecca Solnit—Artist's statement.
pages cm
ISBN 978-0-89013-603-4 (clothbound : alk. paper) 1. West, Jerry R., 1933—Themes, motives. I. Solnit, Rebecca. A bird in the hand. II. Wilson-Powell, MaLin. Jerry West. III. Title.
N6537.W377A4 2015
759.13--dc23
2014037046

Museum of New Mexico Press
PO Box 2087
Santa Fe, New Mexico 87504
mnmpress.org

Credits: Page 2: detail (plate 20), 1981. Photographs by Meridel Rubenstein: 4–5: Jerry West, late 1980s; 6: Jerry West's studio, 2014; 32–33: Jerry West in his studio, 2014. 188–89: Jerry West at Sarah West Vattano and Frank Vattano's house, 2014.

Original endsheets by Jerry R. West
Front: *Red Grief, Exaltation and Joy of Imprinting*, Oil on linen, 40 X 24 in.
Back: *A Blue Gnawing Urge for a Homeostatic Prairie World*, Oil on linen, 40 X 24 in.

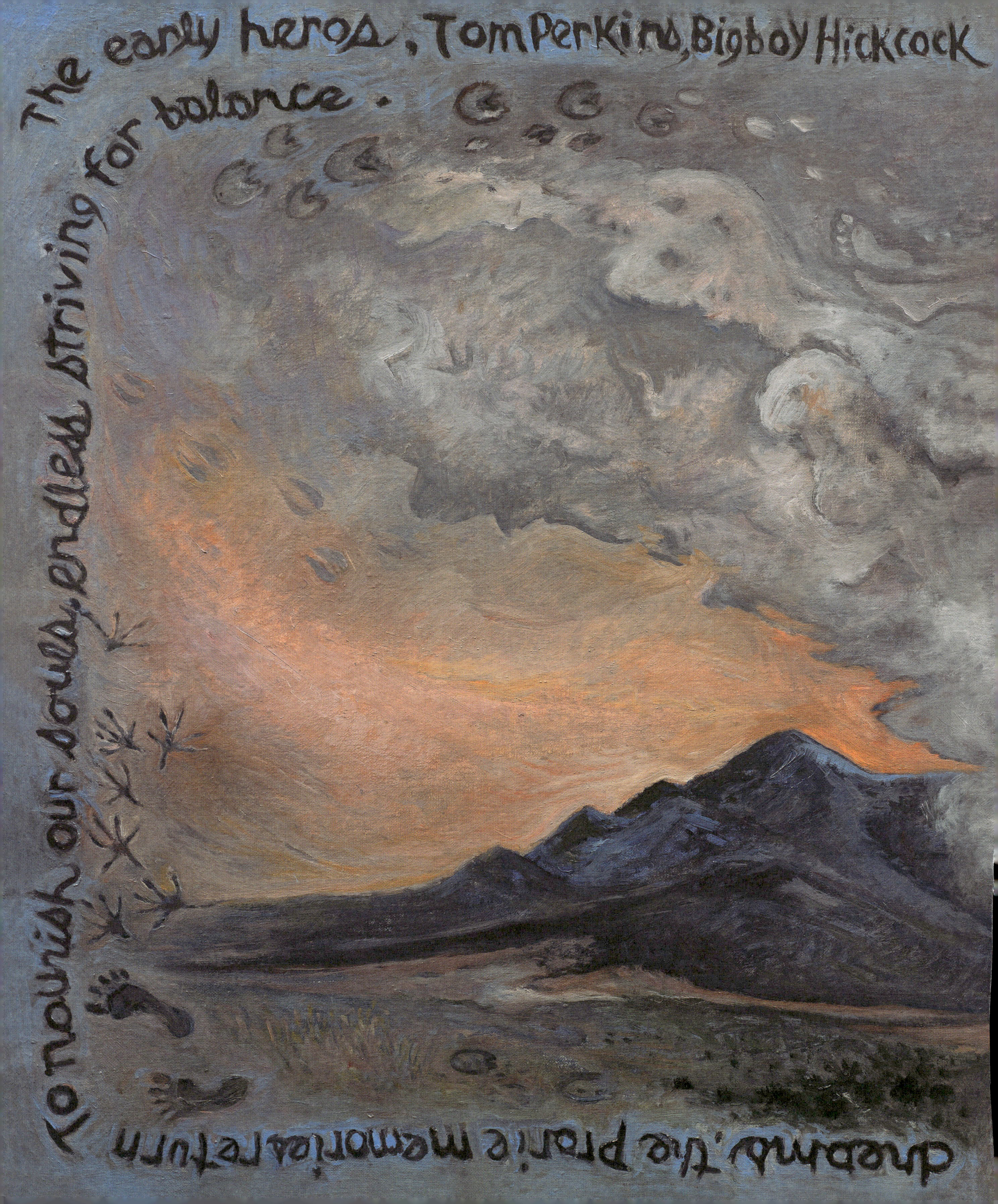
The early heros, Tom Perkins, Bigboy Hickcock
dreams, the prarie memories return
To nourish our souls, endless striving for balance.